OXFORD COGNITIVE SCIENCE SERIES

CONTEXT AND CONTENT

OXFORD COGNITIVE SCIENCE SERIES

General Editors
MARTIN DAVIES, JAMES HIGGINBOTHAM, JOHN O'KEEFE,
CHRISTOPHER PEACOCKE, KIM PLUNKETT

Forthcoming in the series

Mindreading
Stephen Stich and Shaun Nichols

Face and Mind: The Science of Face Perception
Andy Young

CONTEXT AND CONTENT

*Essays on Intentionality in
Speech and Thought*

ROBERT C. STALNAKER

OXFORD

UNIVERSITY PRESS

OXFORD

UNIVERSITY PRESS

Great Clarendon Street, Oxford OX2 6DP

Oxford University Press is a department of the University of Oxford
It furthers the University's objective of excellence in research, scholarship,
and education by publishing worldwide in

Oxford New York

Athens Auckland Bangkok Bogotá Buenos Aires Calcutta
Cape Town Chennai Dar es Salaam Delhi Florence Hong Kong Istanbul
Karachi Kuala Lumpur Madrid Melbourne Mexico City Mumbai
Nairobi Paris São Paulo Singapore Taipei Tokyo Toronto Warsaw

with associated companies in Berlin Ibadan

Oxford is a registered trade mark of Oxford University Press
in the UK and in certain other countries

Published in the United States
by Oxford University Press Inc., New York

British Library Cataloguing in Publication Data
Data available

Library of Congress Cataloging in Publication Data
Stalnaker, Robert.
Context and content: collected papers on intentionality in speech
and thought / Robert C. Stalnaker.
(Oxford cognitive science series)
Includes bibliographical references and index.
1. Pragmatics. 2. Intentionality (Philosophy) I. Title.
II. Series.
B831.5.S73 1999 121—dc21 98–49339
ISBN 0–19–823708–1
ISBN 0–19–823707–3 (Pbk.)

3 5 7 9 10 8 6 4 2

Typeset by Hope Services (Abingdon) Ltd.
Printed in Great Britain
on acid-free paper by
Biddles Ltd.,
Guildford and King's Lynn

For Tom and Joanna

ACKNOWLEDGEMENTS

All but one of the papers collected here were previously published. I thank the publishers and editors for their permission to reprint them. The dates and places of original publication are listed on p. x.

The papers are published in their original form, except for minor corrections (such as, at one point, changing "true" to "false" and at another "guilt" to "innocence"). Second thoughts and retrospective interpretation and elaboration are confined to the Introduction.

I want to thank Tony Gray for editorial assistance in preparing the manuscript—checking, updating and unifying the notes and references, and ferreting out errors and infelicities. Thanks also to Ulrich Meyer for editorial help at a later stage, including preparation of the index and to Robert Ritter, who managed the copy-editing.

Thanks to the series editors and to Peter Momtchiloff of the Oxford University Press for their support of this project, their wise editorial advice, and their patience when I took much longer than promised.

These papers were written over a period of more than twenty-five years, and I want to thank, but won't try to name, the many people whose comments, criticism, and advice over the years helped me to get a little clearer about the issues I discuss in them. Some but obviously not all are acknowledged in the notes to individual papers, and to the introduction.

This book is dedicated to my children, Tom and Joanna, who grew from infants to adults while these papers were being written. I thank them for both the distraction and stimulation that they provided, and more generally for enriching my life, as they continue to do.

R.S.

Cambridge, Mass.
September 1998

CONTENTS

DETAILS OF FIRST PUBLICATION

"Pragmatics," *Synthese* **22**, 1970. Also included in *The Semantics of Natural Language* (G. Harman and D. Davidson, eds.), Dordrecht: Reidel, 1972. Reprinted with kind permission from Kluwer Academic Publishers.

"Pragmatic Presuppositions," *Semantics and Philosophy* (Milton K. Munitz and Peter Unger, eds.), New York: New York University Press, 1974. Reprinted by permission of New York University Press.

"Indicative Conditionals," *Philosophia* **5**, 1975. Also included in *Language in Focus* (Asa Kasher, ed.), Dordrecht: Reidel, 1975. Reprinted with kind permission from Kluwer Academic Publishers.

"Assertion," *Syntax and Semantics* **9**. New York: Academic Press, 1978. Reprinted by permission of Harcourt Brace.

"On the Representation of Context," *Journal of Logic, Language, and Information*, **7**, 1998. Reprinted with kind permission from Kluwer Academic Publishers.

"Semantics for Belief," *Philosophical Topics* **15**, 1987. Reprinted with kind permission of the editor.

"Indexical Belief," *Synthese* **49**, 1981. Reprinted with kind permission from Kluwer Academic Publishers.

"Belief Attribution and Context," *Contents of Thought* (Robert Grimm and Daniel Merrill, eds.), Tucson: U. of Arizona Press, 1988. Reprinted by permission of the University of Arizona Press.

"On What's in the Head," *Philosophical Perspectives*, *3*: *Philosophy of Mind and Action Theory*, 1989. Reprinted with permission of the editor.

"Narrow Content," *Propositional Attitudes*: *The Role of Content in Logic, Language and Mind* (C. Anthony Anderson and Joseph Owens, eds.), Stanford: CSLI, 1990. Reprinted with permission from CSLI Publications.

"Twin Earth Revisited," *Proceedings of the Aristotelian Society*, 1993. Reprinted with the permission of the Aristotelian Society.

"Mental Content and Linguistic Form," *Philosophical Studies* **58**, 1990. Reprinted with kind permission from Kluwer Academic Publishers.

"The Problem of Logical Omniscience, I," *Synthese* **89**, 1991. Reprinted with kind permission from Kluwer Academic Publishers.

"The Problem of Logical Omniscience, II" is published here for the first time.

Introduction

This collection includes papers, published over a period of more than twenty-five years, on intentionality in speech and thought. My aim in this introduction is to sketch some common themes that recur in them and to point to some things in the individual papers that I think need to be emphasized, qualified, or interpreted from hindsight.

Michael Dummett has suggested in a number of places that it is a defining dogma of analytic philosophy that "the philosophy of thought can be approached only through the philosophy of language. That is to say, there can be no account of what thought is, independently of its means of expression." Some philosophers, Dummett remarks, have rejected the doctrine of the priority of language over thought, but "on the face of it, they are overturning the fundamental axiom of all analytic philosophy, and hence have ceased to be analytic philosophers."[1] I hadn't realized before I read this that the diverse strains of the analytic philosophical tradition were held together by such an explicit article of faith, but my discomfort in discovering that I was a heretic was tempered somewhat by recognition that I was in good company in my apostasy: not only Gareth Evans, who Dummett mentions in this context, but also such philosophers as Paul Grice, Roderick Chisholm, David Lewis and Daniel Dennett have strayed from the faith.

There is, of course, no very interesting issue about what defines orthodoxy in analytic philosophy, but Dummett also made a substantive point in the same context: that "in practice," this deviation from orthodoxy makes little difference since "although they challenge the traditional strategy of explanation in analytic philosophy, they accept and make use of the same general doctrines concerning the structure of thoughts and sentences; they differ only about what is to be explained in terms of the other."[2] On this point I have to register disagreement: I want not only to be a heretic, but also to insist that the heresy matters. I have argued, and continue to believe, that what I have called "the linguistic picture"—the family of doctrines, metaphors and strategies that assume, in one way or another, the priority of linguistic over mental representation—has had a

I want to thank Alex Byrne, Jim Higginbotham, Chris Peacocke, and Jason Stanley for very helpful comments on an earlier version of this introduction.

[1] Dummett (1991: 3–4).   [2] Ibid. 4.

profound influence on our conception of intentionality, a distorting influence that has impeded a clear understanding not only of thought, but also of speech. It matters what is explained in terms of what, and more generally how the philosophical problems about mental and linguistic representation are formulated, and the order in which they are addressed. It is intuitively natural to think of speech as the expression of thought, and to assume that the utterances and inscriptions produced in using language derive their content from beliefs and intentions of the speakers who produce them. I think these assumptions are not only intuitively natural, but also the best basis for a philosophical understanding of intentionality. So I would like to reverse Dummett's axiom: the philosophy of language can be approached only through the philosophy of thought.

I discussed the linguistic picture most explicitly in the book *Inquiry*, but the priority of thought over language is a theme throughout the papers collected here. My initial concern was with speech, and my approach was inspired and heavily influenced by the work of Paul Grice in which it was argued that we should see speech as action to be explained, like any other kind of action, in terms of the beliefs and purposes of the agent. Language is a device for achieving certain purposes, and we should separate, as best we can, questions about what language is used to do from questions about the means it provides for doing it. To put language and speech in context, we need a general account of rational activity, and of the cognitive and motivational states that explain it.

Rational activities such as deliberation, contemplation, inquiry, communication all essentially involve an agent who is distinguishing between possibilities. Speech is just one kind of activity in which we do this, but it is a useful one with which to begin. To understand what a speaker is doing when she says how things are, we need to understand how she is distinguishing between different ways that things might be. Here I am echoing Dummett, who says that "to grasp the content of an assertion, one needs to know only what possibilities it rules out, or positively expressed, under what conditions it is correct."[3]

But what is a possibility? As with other central philosophical concepts like truth and existence, it is difficult to give an answer to this question that is both general and substantive, but one should be able to say something general about the *kind* of thing we are talking about when we talk about possibilities, counterfactual situations, or possible worlds. Different philosophers will say different things about this, but my own answer is that a possible world is a kind of property that the world might have had. (So "possible *state* of the world" would be a less misleading, if also less

---

[3] Dummett (1991: 47).

picturesque, label than "possible world", since possibilities are ways the world might have been rather than worlds that are those ways.) To say that possible worlds are properties is to distinguish them, first, from parallel universes (possible worlds as David Lewis conceives of them),[4] and second from entities that are essentially linguistic or representational (State descriptions, or complete novels).[5]

Possibilities are what acts and states with content distinguish between, but can't one give some more substantive description of the possibilities? Do they have a structure (might they be identified, for example, with arrangements of individuals or properties in space-time, or with paths through some branching time structure)? Such more specific accounts of the nature of possibilities belong to substantive metaphysical theories and to other applications to which a conception of possibility might be put, and not to the abstract conception itself. One can say what the possibilities are only by distinguishing between them in some particular context.

The "possible worlds" analysis of propositional content (a proposition is a function from possible worlds to truth-values, or equivalently, a set of possible worlds) is just an attempt to provide a perspicuous representation of an old and familiar idea—the idea that the content of a statement or a belief should be explained in terms of its truth-conditions. The truth-conditions of a statement, on one way of understanding what this means, are the possible circumstances that, if realized, would make the statement true. This representation aims to provide a conception of truth-conditions that is conceptually independent of any particular means used, either by minds or by language, to represent those conditions.

The possible worlds analysis of content is controversial for a number of reasons that need to be distinguished. First, one might be skeptical about the very idea that content can be separated conceptually from form and means—from the vehicles of speech and thought. Explanations of the semantic properties of expressions in terms of translation relations between languages, or in terms of the conceptual roles or uses of expressions are examples of accounts that try to avoid contents as objects altogether. The attempt to do semantics without propositional content is motivated more by pessimism about the possibility of an adequate account of propositions than it is by optimism about the possibility of explaining the phenomena without them. But I think the pessimism is properly directed against the idea of absolute, context-independent propositional objects. If we think of propositions as functions from some given domain of relevant alternative possible situations to truth-values, we may be able to reconcile the conceptual distinction between form and content

---

[4] Lewis (1986).   [5] Carnap (1947: 9) and Jeffrey (1983: 208–9).

with the phenomena that motivate skepticism about propositions and possible worlds.

Second, one might accept the assumption of conceptual independence, but prefer a more fine-grained abstract object with a structure that is reflected in the vehicles of representation—propositional complexes that have objects and properties, or perhaps Fregean senses, as constituents. One might think that the fine-grained structure is essential to what is represented. But at least those with this second worry must admit that propositions, whatever they are, *have* truth-conditions, and that representation, whatever else it might be, distinguishes between possibilities. Even if there is some kind of fine-grained proposition that is essentially involved in representation, and that is useful for describing it, we can agree that anything with representational content has truth-conditional or informational content, and that we can begin by considering its role in the description and explanation of rational activities, including speech.

The specific concern of the first five of these papers is with the interaction of speech acts with the contexts in which they are performed. These papers seek to construct some descriptive apparatus to represent and clarify the abstract structure of discourse, and to use that apparatus to explain some particular linguistic phenomena concerning reference and descriptions, presuppositions, indicative conditionals, negative existential assertions and suppositions. I began with an attempt to characterize *pragmatics*—the study of the relation between linguistic expressions and their contexts of use. The aim was to represent the interaction of context and content. First, context influences content, since the expressions used to say something are often context-dependent: what they are used to say is a function, not only of the meanings of the expressions, but also of facts about the situations in which they are used. But second, the contents that are expressed influence the context: speech acts affect the situations in which they are performed. If speech and its interpretation both affect and are affected by context in regular ways, then the pattern of interaction may result in regularities in speech—systematic relations between the contents of successive speech acts. In such cases, regularities that appear on the surface to be semantic are explained pragmatically: by the way one speech act alters the context, which in turn constrains the interpretation of a subsequent speech act. To represent and explain this kind of phenomenon, we need a single concept of context that is both what determines the contents of context-dependent expressions, and also what speech acts act upon.

The focus of early formal work on what Richard Montague called "pragmatics" was exclusively on one side of this interaction: on the way that content is influenced by context. Montague's formal pragmatics began as a straightforward generalization of possible worlds semantics for modal logic. The central idea of modal semantics was that sentences had truth-values relative to a possible world. Montague suggested that the relativity of context-dependent expressions might be explained in a similar way. To interpret languages with tenses, personal pronouns, and other kinds of context-dependent expressions, he extended modal semantics by replacing the possible worlds with the more neutral and general notion of an *index*, which is a sequence of parameters on which truth-values and other extensions of expressions depend. So if the language in question had tenses and a first-person pronoun, the index would contain a speaker and a time as well as a possible world. A sentence such as "I love Mary" would be true relative to an index ⟨John, June 14, 1998, *w*⟩ just in case in world *w*, John loves Mary on June 14, 1998.

David Kaplan's theory of demonstratives[6] modified the general index theory in two related ways: first, he proposed that a pragmatic theory should distinguish two different ways in which truth-values and other extensions may be dependent on the circumstances in which expressions are used: the meaning of a sentence determines content, relative to a context, but content determines a truth-value only relative to a possible world. The facts that determine what is said need to be distinguished from the facts that determine whether what is said is true. So Kaplan's theory was a two-dimensional, or double-index theory: a context was represented by an index of the kind proposed in Montague's formal pragmatics, and sentences were interpreted relative to these indices. But it was contents, rather than truth-values, that were the values of the interpretation function, where contents were themselves represented by functions from possible worlds to truth-values.

The second modification Kaplan proposed was to constrain the indices so that they could appropriately represent contexts. In the abstract theory, an index is just a list of parameters (speaker or agent, time, place, possible world) that is supposed to include everything that needs to be specified to determine truth-values for the sentences of the language. Nothing is said about the relations between the different parameters, or about how they are determined by the facts about the situations in which the sentences are used. Implicit in Kaplan's constraints on indices is an attempt to connect the facts about the utterance event to the context for interpreting it. The constraints are the obvious ones: an index containing an agent, time, place and possible world can represent a context only if the agent is a person who is at the place at the time in the world.

The index theory's paradigms of context-dependent features are tense and personal pronouns, cases where it is easiest to specify the facts about

[6] Kaplan (1989).

an utterance that fix the components of the index. But context-dependence is pervasive: sentences containing quantifiers and modal auxiliaries must be interpreted relative to contextually determined domains of individuals and possible worlds; adjectives such as "large" and "warm" are interpreted relative to contextually determined comparison classes. When one looks beyond "I," "here" and "now," it is less clear how the facts about the situation in which the utterance takes place fix the relevant contextual parameters, and in the general case, the index theory, even in Kaplan's version, says nothing about this. The pragmatic framework that I was promoting aimed to give a general representation of the features of a situation that determine the elements listed in an index. My central assumption was that a context should be represented by a body of information that is presumed to be available to the participants in the speech situation. A context set is defined as the set of possible situations that are compatible with this information—with what the participants in the conversation take to be the common shared background. The contextual factors relevant to interpreting John's utterance of "I love Mary" will then be, not simply the index, but the fact that the relevant body of information includes the information that John is speaking and that the utterance is taking place on June 14, 1998.

It is a substantive claim that the information relevant to determining the content of context-dependent speech acts is presumed to be available to the participants of a conversation—that it is included in the presuppositions of the context—but it is a claim that is motivated by natural assumptions about the kind of action one performs in speaking. It is not unreasonable to suppose that speakers, in speaking, are normally aiming to communicate—at least to have the addressees understand what is being said. Succeeding in this aim requires that the information relevant to determining content be available to the addressee. The representation of context as a body of presupposed information is also appropriate to the other side of the interaction between context and content, since it is reasonable to suppose that a body of information is also what speech acts act on. If the goal of speech, or at least one central goal, is to exchange information, then it is natural to explain the force of speech acts as the attempt to add to or alter a body of information that is presumed to be shared by the participants in the conversation.

The outline of this pragmatic framework emerged gradually from the consideration of a variety of puzzles about specific linguistic phenomena: Keith Donnellan's distinction between referential and attributive descriptions, the so-called projection problem for presuppositions, a puzzle about reasoning with indicative conditionals, problems about negative existential statements and suppositions in the context of direct reference theories of proper names. In considering these problems, I did not see myself as proposing empirical hypotheses to explain linguistic phenomena, but as trying to find the resources for a perspicuous abstract representation of the phenomena so that it can be made clearer just what an empirical theory needs to explain. Let me say a little about how the general framework developed in response to some of the problems.

Debates between philosophers about theories of definite descriptions made use of a notion of *presupposition*, and for the most part it was assumed, first, that it was sentences or statements that had presuppositions, and second that the presupposition relation should be explained in terms of the semantic content—the truth-conditions—of the sentences or statements that had them. Roughly, the received view was that Q presupposes that P if the truth of P is required for either the truth or the falsity of Q. But in trying, in "Pragmatics," to get clear about Donnellan's account of referential definite descriptions, it seemed to me that the relevant notion of presupposition is one that should be characterized independently of the truth-conditions of what is said by speakers making presuppositions. Presupposition, as ordinarily understood, is a propositional attitude, and not a semantic relation. It is speakers who make presuppositions; what they presuppose are the things they take for granted when they speak—things they take to go without saying. If this is what presupposition is, then the falsity of something one presupposes will not necessarily be incompatible with the truth or falsity of what one says when making those presuppositions.

This conception of speaker presupposition seemed to me applicable to the wider range of phenomena that linguists used the notion of presupposition to describe. Linguists had tended to follow the philosophers in assuming that presupposition was a semantic relation, and I argued in "Pragmatic Presupposition," that this assumption was getting in the way of a clear account of the phenomena. But the phenomena in question (for example, that saying "Harry regrets ordering the mushroom cheesecake" presupposes that Harry ordered the mushroom cheesecake) were generalizations about the use of sentences, while the notion of presupposition I was promoting applies to an attitude of speakers in particular contexts. Presupposing, it seems, is like meaning, referring, expressing, implying—something that both speakers and the words they use can be said to do.

Is there a notion of pragmatic *sentence* presupposition that might be used to describe the phenomena? I suggested that one might define a notion of presupposition *requirement* in something like the following way: Sentence S presupposes that P if and only if the use of S would be inappropriate in a context in which the speaker was not presupposing that P. But I emphasized (and want to re-emphasize here) that such a notion of

Handwritten margin notes: ESSAY 1 ; ESSAY 2

presupposition requirement is, at best, a concept for describing surface phenomena, and not a theoretical concept that might be expected to play a role in the explanation of the phenomena. The reason for this is that the notion of *inappropriateness* is not a theoretical notion. An utterance may be odd, deviant, unacceptable or inappropriate for any number of reasons: it may be ungrammatical, semantically uninterpretable, neither true nor false, uninformative, gratuitously obscure, impolite. No part of linguistic theory will include, in its repertoire of explanatory concepts, the concept of inappropriateness or oddity, and one should not expect to find exceptionless generalizations couched in such terms. Rather, the overall theory will give an account of the grammatical devices and semantic and pragmatic rules that speakers and hearers use to accomplish their purposes in discourse. Such an account, if it is adequate, will yield explanations, for particular utterances that we find odd or deviant, of why they violate some rule, or are in some way ill-suited to serve the ends that (according to the theory) they are designed to serve.

The strategy I used to try to explain some of the rough generalizations about presupposition was the classic Gricean strategy: to try to use simple truisms about conversation or discourse to explain regularities that seemed complex and unmotivated when they are assumed to be facts about the semantics of the relevant expressions. But as Grice emphasized, to sustain this kind of explanation, one needs to make the simple truisms, and the explanations using them, explicit. In "Indicative Conditionals" and "Assertion" I tried to be a little more explicit about the way some speech acts change the context, and to use what I took to be intuitively natural assumptions to sketch explanations of some additional phenomena. The puzzle that sets the problem of the first of these two papers is an argument that seems to be compelling in virtue of its abstract form, but that cannot be assumed to be semantically valid without accepting some counterintuitive consequences. The proposed solution exploits the kind of interaction of context and content described above. The idea was to explain a systematic relation between the premise and conclusion of an abstract argument form, not directly in terms of generalizations about the semantic contents of the premise and conclusion, but indirectly in terms of the way the premise acts on the context, and the context in turn constrains the interpretation of the conclusion. The particular explanation I offer is quite schematic, and the assumptions it rests on are oversimplified. The main idea was to illustrate a pattern of explanation rather than to defend the particular semantic analysis and pragmatic assumptions required for the instance of the pattern that I exhibited. With hindsight, one can see in the pattern of argument I discussed an instance of what later came to be called nonmonotonic reasoning: inferences that are reasonable, but become unreasonable when the premises are strengthened. I think the kind of interaction of context and content I was trying to illustrate is relevant more generally to the phenomena that form the subject matter for the application of nonmonotonic logic.

In "Assertion," I look more closely at the way speech acts change the context. Once one has an account, however platitudinous, of what assertions are supposed to do, it becomes possible to explain facts about appropriateness conditions for utterances by showing that except under certain conditions, the utterance would be ill-suited to accomplish what it is supposed to accomplish. In order to state and apply one of the principles used in such explanations, I introduced a bit of descriptive apparatus borrowed from two-dimensional modal logic. This apparatus has achieved some notoriety, and I think it has sometimes been misinterpreted and misapplied, so I want to say something here about how I see its significance and limitations.

First, it is helpful to distinguish an account of a certain kind of abstract object from an account of the use to which that object is put. The object I borrowed from two-dimensional modal logic is a *propositional concept*—a function from a given set of possible worlds to a proposition, where a proposition is itself a function from possible worlds to truth-values. Equivalently, one can describe a propositional concept as a function from a pair of possible worlds to a truth-value.

One might use this kind of abstract object in various ways. One might, for example, construct a formal language and give it a semantics that takes these two-dimensional intensions to be the semantic values of the sentences. But the application I proposed was different; I introduced propositional concepts for the purpose of describing a certain kind of epistemic situation. Suppose that some person knows, believes, or presupposes that a particular utterance event is taking place. If we represent what a person knows, believes or presupposes by a set of possible worlds, then what we are supposing is that the utterance event in question takes place in each of the possible worlds compatible with what the person knows, believes or presupposes. Now we might be interested in what this person (who could be the speaker, an addressee, or a bystander) knows, believes or is presupposing about the *content* expressed in this utterance event. Even if she knows that the utterance occurred, she might still be ignorant or mistaken about what that utterance was being used to say. We can represent such a person's knowledge or ignorance, beliefs or doubts about the content of the utterance by saying what the content is in each of the possible situations compatible with her knowledge or beliefs, or with the presuppositions she is making. That is, we can use a propositional concept, defined on the relevant possible worlds, to represent the epistemic situation. Used in this way, the two-dimensional intension does not represent a kind of meaning with which a semantic theory interprets a language. It cannot be identified with the meaning of the utterance in question because the semantics for the language of the utterance is itself something that the person might be ignorant or mistaken about. If the content expressed in an utterance were itself a two-dimensional intension, then to represent a person's beliefs about the contents of utterances, we would need three-dimensional intensions—function from possible worlds to two-dimensional intensions.

As discussed above, the meanings in David Kaplan's semantics for context-dependent languages are a kind of two-dimensional intension—what he calls *character*, and distinguishes from *content*. The character of a sentence is a function from context to content, where content determines a function from possible worlds to truth-values. I have emphasized in a number of places that one should not confuse my use of the two-dimensional apparatus with Kaplan's. Characters are meanings associated with sentence types by a semantic theory. In contrast, propositional concepts, in the use to which I put them, are associated with particular utterance tokens, and are derivative from the semantic properties that those tokens have in the possible worlds in which they occur. There is no conflict between Kaplan's theory and the descriptive apparatus I use; these contrasting uses of the two-dimensional framework address different questions, and should both find a place in the explanation of phenomena involving languages with demonstrative and personal pronouns, and other context-dependent expressions.

The truism that I introduced propositional concepts to clarify was this: the speaker should presuppose that the addressees are able to understand what he is saying, which is to say that he should presuppose that they have whatever information is required to interpret what he is saying. This maxim (which is satisfied just in case the propositional concept for the utterance, defined on the set of possible worlds compatible with the context is constant) helps to makes the connection between the notion of context defined by the index theory (a list of parameters, or factors on which the content of context-dependent expressions depend) and the notion of context as the set of possible situations compatible with what is being presupposed. Since the relevant contextual parameters must be available, and presupposed to be available, they will be incorporated into the speaker's presuppositions, and so will be represented by the set of possible situations that constitutes the context set.

I suggested that an assertion should be understood as a proposal to change the context by adding the content to the information presupposed. This is an account of the *force* of an assertion, and it respects the traditional distinction between the content and the force of a speech act. Propositional content is represented by a (possibly partial) function from possible worlds to truth-values; assertive force is represented by the way in which any such function is used to change the context that the speaker shares with those to whom he is speaking. Meaning determines the content of an assertion as a function of context, and the assertion rule takes the prior context set to a posterior context set, which is the intersection of the prior set with that content. Some of the dynamic semantic theories subsequently developed by linguists have blurred the distinction between content and force by combining the two steps (meaning plus prior context to content, and prior context plus content to posterior context) into one. Irene Heim, for example, proposed to represent the meaning of a sentence as its *context-change potential*,[7] which is a function taking the prior context directly to the posterior context. I think this streamlined representation captures much of what is important about the dynamic process of speech, but what it leaves out is the possibility of evaluating the truth or falsity of what is said relative to possible situations that are not compatible with the prior context. Sometimes when a statement rests on false presuppositions, the question of the actual truth of the statement does not arise, but other times a speaker may succeed in making a claim that is actually true or false, even when taking for granted, in making the claim, something that is in fact false. In such cases, our semantic theory should tell us what is said, and not just how what is said changes the context. Sentences that say different things in some contexts may nevertheless change contexts in the same way.

Let me use a familiar example to illustrate the point, an example of what Keith Donnellan called the referential use of a definite description. Suppose I say "the man drinking a martini is a philosopher" in a context in which there is a particular man who is presupposed to be the unique man (in the relevant domain of people) who is drinking a martini. I am right, let us further suppose, that the man is a philosopher. But despite what I am presupposing, no one in the room is actually drinking a martini; the man in question is drinking Perrier. Different semantic accounts of definite descriptions will reach different conclusions about the content of my statement in this case. The Russellian concludes that what I said is false, while the Strawsonian claims that it is neither true nor false. Donnellan argued, against both of these accounts, that the statement is true (since it is about the man whom I presuppose to be drinking a martini). But despite their differences, all of these theorists would agree about the context-change potential of the statement, since all agree about how it should be evaluated relative to a possible world in which there is a unique man drinking a martini who is also the person to whom the speaker

---

[7] Heim (1982).

intended to refer. Possible worlds compatible with what is presupposed in the context all meet this condition, and only those worlds are relevant to the way my statement changed the context. The contrasts between the different semantic analyses of definite descriptions emerge only when we consider, not just how such statements affect the context, but also what was said in the context, and whether it was actually true.

Possible situations incompatible with a context may be important, since even if speakers and those to whom they are speaking ignore them, the theorists cannot if they want to give a clear description of a discourse from an external point. The interpretation of what is said, and our understanding of what is going on in a discourse, depend not only on what the participants think, but also on how they are actually situated in the world. For this reason, I would prefer to maintain the content/force distinction, factoring the context-change potential of a sentence into two conceptually distinguishable steps: first, the determination of content, as a function of context, and second the use of that content, by a general rule of assertion, to change the context.

"Assertion" concludes by applying the two-dimensional apparatus to some puzzles about proper names in statements and suppositions about identity and existence. Saul Kripke's causal account of names had put a spotlight on one way that semantic values of expressions might be a function of empirical facts that are external to the users of the expressions— facts about the causal history of the use of the name that linguistically competent speakers might be ignorant about. Propositional concepts provided the resources to give a schematic representation of the relations between the different ways in which the facts contribute to the truth of what is said, and for clarifying what is going on in some of the puzzle cases. Specifically, there is an operation on propositional concepts—an operation I called *diagonalization*—that yields a proposition that is relevant to describing situations in which speakers or addressees have only partial knowledge of facts relevant to determining what is said. Let me describe the operation in the abstract, and then consider its application.

Propositional concepts—functions from possible worlds to propositions, which are themselves functions from possible worlds to truth-values—can be pictured by a two-dimensional matrix such as the following:

	i	j	k
i	F	T	F
j	T	F	F
k	F	T	T

The rows of the matrix are the propositions that are the values of the function—call them the *horizontal propositions*. The *diagonal* proposition determined by the propositional concept, which may be different from any of the horizontal propositions, is the one that for each world x is true at x if and only if the horizontal proposition expressed at x is true at x. So in the matrix displayed above, the diagonal (read from top left to bottom right) is the proposition that is false in i and j, but true in k.

If a propositional concept is used to represent a person's epistemic situation with respect to an utterance token, then the diagonal proposition represents the information the person would receive if she came to know that the utterance token expressed a truth (without necessarily knowing what truth it was that was expressed). In a case where someone had only partial knowledge of facts relevant to the determination of the content of an utterance, the diagonal proposition would be a particular mix of information about semantic determinants for the utterance with information about the subject matter of the utterance. So, for example, suppose I get an undated postcard that I know was written in Barcelona saying "Rain yesterday, but it was sunny and warm today." Since I don't know when it was written, I don't know exactly what was said, but I do learn (assuming I trust the writer) that the postcard was written on a day that was sunny and warm in Barcelona—a piece of information that is partly about the subject matter of the statement and partly about the circumstances in which it was made.

In the above example, the information I gleaned from the postcard, was the diagonal proposition of the propositional concept determined (relative to my knowledge) by what the writer said. But the writer would instead have said what he in fact only conveyed if the message had been "Rain on the day before this postcard is being written, but it is sunny and warm on the day it is being written."

I suggested, in "Assertion," that in some cases (where a specific pragmatic rule was apparently violated) one should identify what was said with the diagonal proposition of the propositional concept determined by the context. The idea was to try to reconcile the semantic account of names that Kripke had defended with the phenomena that seemed to support the Fregean account that he argued against. On Kripke's account, "Hesperus is Phosphorus" is a necessary truth, but (assuming the Kripkean semantics) the diagonal proposition of the propositional concept determined by a context in which the statement might be made would be a contingent proposition, and one that is an intuitively plausible candidate for the information that speakers intend to convey in such contexts. According to this qualified defense of the Kripkean semantics, in these special cases, the horizontal propositions of the propositional concept do not themselves represent what is said: they represent what is said *according to the normal semantic rules* as they are in the relevant possible world. In such a case, the normal semantic rules are overridden, but they still play an essential role in determining what is said, since the diagonal is parasitic on the propositions determined, in the different possible worlds, according to those rules.

I should emphasize that the diagonal is not a distinctive kind of proposition, but just a distinctive way of representing or determining a proposition. The same proposition that is determined by diagonalizing on some propositional concept might also be expressed directly. In the case of "Hesperus is Phosphorus," the diagonal determined when we assume the Kripkean semantics is a proposition that would be directly determined if the sentence had a Fregean semantics, according to which "Hesperus" and "Phosphorus" each have a sense that determines a referent as a function of certain empirical facts about the use of the name.

I note in "Assertion" that the two-dimensional apparatus provides a way to represent what is going on in the striking examples Kripke had used to illustrate a contrast between the necessary/contingent distinction and the a priori/a posteriori distinction. The examples of necessary a posteriori truths, and contingent a priori truths could be represented by propositional concepts where the modal status of the diagonal diverged from that of the horizontal proposition expressed in the actual world. (For example, contingent a priori truths correspond to propositional concepts whose horizontal propositions are contingent, but whose diagonal is necessary.) I continue to think that this apparatus helps to clarify Kripke's examples, but I would emphasize now more than I did then what this abstract apparatus does not explain: one should not conclude that any account has been given of the nature of a priori truth or knowledge. It is straightforward to define an abstract property of propositional concepts—the necessity of the diagonal—but before drawing any conclusions about the epistemic status of an utterance associated with a propositional concept that has this property, one has to consider what set of possibilities the concept is defined on, and how the utterance is related to the propositional concept. One might conclude that *if* the relevant set of worlds included all those compatible with an agent's knowledge, then she would know that the utterance expressed a truth. But this knowledge would not deserve the label "a priori knowledge" unless the agent knew a priori that the actual world was among those in the relevant set, and the two-dimensional apparatus does not pretend to offer any account of that.

Let me use a familiar example[8] to illustrate the point. Gareth Evans introduced a name "Julius," using what Kripke had called a reference-

---

[8] Evans (1982: 31).

fixing definition: "Julius" is stipulated to be a proper name for the person (whoever he or she might be) who invented the zip. The name is to be a rigid designator—a term whose referent, in any possible world, is the person who invented the zip in the actual world. Now suppose i is the actual world, j is a counterfactual world in which Benjamin Franklin invented the zip, and k is a world in which Marie Curie was its inventor. For these worlds, the following matrix might seem appropriate for the utterance: "Julius invented the zip"[9] (at least if we make the plausible assumption that, in fact, neither Franklin nor Curie was the actual inventor of the zip):

	i	j	k
i	T	F	F
j	F	T	F
k	F	F	T

The statement is a contingent a priori truth, since the diagonal is necessary, while the horizontal propositions are contingent. But for this representation to be right, we must add that the stipulation in question was made in each of the worlds i, j and k. One who did not know about the stipulation, or did not understand it, would not know that the statement was true. To put the point in terms of the apparatus, suppose we added a possible world m to the set on which the matrix is defined. m is a world that is just like the actual world,[10] except for the fact that in that world, the name "Julius" is stipulated to be the inventor of bifocals instead of the zip. As the extended matrix for "Julius invented the zip" shows, the diagonal is no longer necessary, relative to the set of these four possible worlds.

	i	j	k	m
i	T	F	F	T
j	F	T	F	F
k	F	F	T	F
m	F	T	F	F

One might be tempted to protest that a possible world like m is not relevant to the a priori status of the actual statement. It is a familiar point that

[9] Strictly speaking, to have a more plausible candidate for an *a priori* truth, we should consider the more cautious statement, "If any one person invented the zip, then Julius did." But this detail will not affect the point I am making.

[10] In particular, m is like the actual world in that the inventor of bifocals was Benjamin Franklin.

the necessity and a prioricity of mathematical truths such as "7+5=12" is not compromised by the undisputed fact that it is only contingently true (and known only a posteriori) that we use arithmetical notation as we do. (So, for example, we might have used a base 8 arithmetical notion, with the same numerals for one through seven. If we had, "7+5=12" would have expressed a falsehood, but this of course does not imply that 7+5 would not have been 12.) But the two-dimensional apparatus was introduced for the purpose of representing (on the vertical dimension) variations in the propositions expressed. According to the way we are associating propositional concepts with particular utterances, the row we have added to the matrix is the right one for world *m*, since the horizontal proposition for that world is determined by the correct interpretation of the utterance *as it is used in world m*. If we are to represent a priori truth by the necessity of the diagonal, we must either find grounds for excluding worlds like *m*, or else find a different way of associating propositional concepts with utterance events.

The papers discussed so far were all written more than twenty years ago, and a lot has happened since in the study of semantics and pragmatics. Some sophisticated semantic theories (discourse representation theory, update semantics, dynamic predicate logic and dynamic Montague grammar, among others) have focussed on the dynamic processes of discourse and on the interconnection of semantics and pragmatics. The line—or more accurately a number of distinct lines—between semantics and pragmatics shift and blur. But I think there is one line that is worth continuing to draw and redraw: between an abstract account of the functions and purposes of discourse and a theory of the devices that particular languages and linguistic practices use to serve those functions and accomplish those purposes. The last of the papers in this first part, "On the Representation of Context"—written very recently—tries to shift attention back to some of the foundational questions about speech contexts and what goes on in them, and to the Gricean strategy of explaining some of the facts about what happens in conversations in terms of general assumptions about the purposes for which the participants engage in conversation. Even though semantic theories of the mechanisms of particular languages have increasingly had to bring context and discourse structures into their orbit, the Gricean strategy continues to be important, and can perhaps help to simplify the explanations of some of the phenomena that the dynamic semantic theories were developed to explain.

The remaining papers in this collection focus more on thought than on speech, though the first step is to consider speech about thought. The abstract semantics for the ascription of belief and some other propositional attitudes seems simple enough: to say something of the form "*x* believes that P" is to say that the person x stands in the belief relation to an object denoted by the expression "that P." If we continue to assume that the contents of thought are the same as the contents of speech acts, then we should be able to conclude that whatever kind of thing semantic theory provides as the contents of assertions will also serve as the referents of that-clauses. And one should expect that the complexities in the explanation of the relation between the meaning of a sentence and the content of a speech acts it is used to make will have parallels in complexities in the explanation of the relation between the meanings of sentential clauses and the propositions they are used to denote. The papers on attributing attitudes explore some of these parallels, and extend and apply the apparatus developed in the earlier papers to some familiar puzzles about belief. The extension brings out new problems and complexities—new dimensions of context-dependence—and it is important to emphasize the contrasts, as well as the parallels, between puzzles about simple assertions and puzzles about the attribution of attitudes. The new complexities arise from the fact that there are two agents involved in the attitude attributions—the speaker and the subject of the attribution—and two interacting contexts.

I will make three sets of remarks about what is going on in the paper on attitude attribution. The first is another cautionary comment about propositional concepts and diagonalization—this time about the use of the apparatus to describe cases of attitude attribution. The second expresses some reservations about the arguments in "Indexical Belief" and corrects what I think are some misleading suggestions that paper makes. The third is a comment on *de re* belief attribution and its relation to the general case of belief attribution.

Much of the discussion in the literature about the semantics for belief attribution has focussed on a family of examples involving errors or ignorance about identities. There was Quine's Ralph, who was acquainted with Bernard J. Ortcutt in two different situations, believing that he was two different men, one a spy and one not.[11] Later came Kripke's Pierre, who in his youth in France had read and come to believe that a city called "Londres," was pretty, and who subsequently moved to London (not realizing that this was the same city he had read about), learned English, and came to believe that London was not pretty.[12] And there were various amnesiacs whose identity confusions concerned themselves.[13] Frege, of course, had set the stage for all of this with his arguments for the sense/reference distinction, arguments that appealed to the differences in the cognitive status of different names for the same thing.

[11] Quine (1966).   [12] Kripke (1979).
[13] Castañeda (1966, 1967), and Perry (1977, 1979).

It is natural to look to the two-dimensional apparatus, which had been applied to the Fregean puzzles in the assertion context, to help to clarify what is going on in the puzzle cases about belief. If propositional concepts and diagonalization contribute to an account of what is said by one who asserts or denies that Hesperus is Phosphorus, it ought to provide a parallel account of the belief that is attributed when one says that O'Leary believes or doubts that Hesperus is Phosphorus. But as is noted in "Semantics for Belief" the extension of the apparatus for describing assertions to the description of belief is not straightforward. In the cases of speech, propositional concepts are used to describe an epistemic situation with respect to the possible worlds compatible with the context in which an assertion is made. We can safely assume that the speaker presupposes that he is speaking—that the utterance event is taking place. This means that the utterance will be made, not only in the actual world, but in all of the possible worlds compatible with the context. So a unique propositional concept, defined for those possibilities, is determined for the utterance. But when I am telling you about one of the beliefs of some third party, the relevant possible worlds for determining the content of that belief are those that might, for all that I am presupposing, be compatible with the beliefs of that person. In these possible worlds my utterance may not exist at all, since the believer we are talking about may be unaware of our conversation. If we want to use a propositional concept to describe the context for a belief ascription, we will need to do some work to construct one. I suggest in "Semantics for Belief" that to get a propositional concept on which one might diagonalize, one should consider what the speaker *would* be saying if he were speaking in the possible worlds that are compatible with the beliefs of the subject of the belief ascription. But this is rough and vague, and may need to be interpreted charitably to get a plausible account of how speakers use their own words to describe the world as someone else sees it. If I say that the Babylonians didn't believe that Hesperus is Phosphorus, it seems not unreasonable to think that I am saying that there are possible worlds compatible with the beliefs of the Babylonians in which astronomical bodies are differently arranged in a way that would result in the names "Hesperus" and "Phosphorus" as I am in fact using them, having different referents. (It is *my* use of those names, and not the Babylonians' use, that is relevant. We don't assume, in describing their beliefs, that they used those names at all.) But there is a problem: in one straightforward sense, if I had been using those names as I am actually using them, then I would have been referring to Venus with both of them, since that is what I am in fact using them to do. But the intended counterfactual supposition requires that the relevant notion of *same use* be compatible with the names having different referents. We have to assume that we can separate, in context, the use of the names from the causal facts that give the names their referents. I don't assume, and don't believe, that there is any general procedure for doing this—any general way of factoring out an internal component of the semantics for names, or other expressions. I think the two-dimensional apparatus is best seen as providing not a solution to a problem—a general semantic analysis for belief—but a representation of the problem that helps reveal some of the sources of puzzles about belief attribution—the problems speakers have when they try to use their own resources for describing the world (resources that presuppose their own conception of how things are) to describe the states of mind of others who they know do not share that conception. When I describe another person's state of mind, I do it by referring to things, properties and relations in the world, and then using those things to define a set of possibilities that is intended to represent the way the world is according to the person. But when one person's conception of the world is very different from that of another who is trying to describe it, it may not be clear how this is to be done. It may be unclear not only how to use our language to describe the world according to the Babylonians, or Kripke's Pierre, or Quine's Ortcutt, but also which possible worlds are the ones best suited for representing what those characters really think.[14]

"Indexical Belief," uses the two-dimensional framework to try to clarify some puzzles about a person's beliefs and thoughts about himself, cases where the content of thought seemed to be irreducibly first-person. I suggest in that paper that with the help of the magical diagonalization operation, we could reconcile cases of essentially indexical thought with what John Perry called the doctrine of propositions, which is roughly the doctrine that the objects of belief are all impersonal, timeless bearers of truth-value. It is argued that the ignorance of the amnesiac who has read about someone who is in fact himself, or of the shopper wondering who was making the mess that he himself was in fact making, or of the pair of seemingly omniscient gods who don't know which is which, was in relevant ways just like the ignorance of the Babylonians, Ortcutt and Pierre. They are all cases that involve some kind of identity confusion, and all should be explained in the same way. This now seems to me at best misleading, and wrong if it implies that there is not a distinctive problem about indexical belief, or that nothing is left out by the representation of a belief state by a set of timeless propositions, or a set of possible worlds.

---

[14] Some of my former students—in particular, Joe Lau and Josep Macià—have helped me to see more clearly some of the problems with diagonalization in the belief attribution case. Lau (1994) raises some challenging problems for it.

The reason I thought, and continue to think, that it is important to represent the contents of indexical beliefs as impersonal propositions is that we want our notion of content to help explain persistence and change of belief, agreement and disagreement between different believers, and the communication of beliefs. When, for example, I tell the amnesiac who he is, he learns something that I already knew, so there had better be a proposition that represents what I knew, and he learned. I took the problem posed by the examples to be the problem of saying what the relevant propositions were in those cases—to identify the proposition that the amnesiac or the shopper was ignorant or wrong about. To do this, I followed my usual strategy, asking what the world was like according to the believer. Just as in the world according to Pierre, there are two cities, a pretty one called "Londres" (in French) and an ugly one called "London" (in English), so in some of the worlds compatible with the beliefs that the amnesiac Lingens has as he wonders who and where he is, there are two men, one named "Lingens" who he has read about and a different one who is doing the wondering.

I still think this is roughly the right way to go about answering *this* question, and I think it helps to reconcile the phenomena with the assumption that propositions are the objects of belief. But even if this strategy succeeds, I don't think it gives us reason to deny that there is, in some sense, an irreducible indexical element to belief—that the believer and the time of belief play a special role of some kind in determining the contents of belief. In discussing David Lewis's proposal that the objects of belief should be sets of *centered* possible worlds (a possible world, plus a designated time and person), I conceded that "the possible situations in terms of which intentional states and processes are defined are normally, perhaps essentially, centered in the sense that they all contain a representation of the mental state or process itself." But this remark misstates what must be conceded. It is not enough to say that the possible worlds compatible with someone's beliefs will all contain a person who has those beliefs, or who is thinking a certain thought—that is not a sense in which those possible worlds are centered. The believer must identify himself with the person in the possible worlds compatible with her beliefs, or must identify the thought as *this* thought. I don't want to claim that this identification can be reduced to, or explained as, a belief in some proposition. The knowledge that I am now thinking *this* thought is not any kind of cognitive achievement.

The distinctive problem of indexical belief is best brought out by considering, not just cases (such as David Lewis's case of the two omniscient gods, or Hector Castañeda and John Perry's cases of amnesiacs) of indexical ignorance—ignorance of who one is—but also cases of different believers who know the ways that they are differently situated, but who, in one sense, do not differ in what they believe. Suppose O'Leary knows he is in the basement, and that Daniels is in the kitchen. Daniels also knows this—that he is in the kitchen and that O'Leary is in the basement. Each knows who and where he himself is, and who and where the other is. The possible worlds compatible with the two men's beliefs are the same—they don't disagree about anything, and there is nothing relevant that one believes and the other is ignorant about. Yet there is obviously a significant difference between their doxastic situations: O'Leary identifies himself as the one in the basement, while Daniels identifies himself as the one in the kitchen. This difference between the belief states of the two men is not reflected in a representation of a belief state by a set of possible worlds.

We need to account for this difference, but I still want to resist the temptation to represent the belief states in the way Lewis suggests—by self-ascribed properties, or equivalently by sets of centered possible worlds. The problem is that this would be to treat a difference in perspective in the same way as a disagreement. Despite the fact that Daniels and O'Leary agree in their beliefs, the sets of *centered* worlds that Lewis would use to represent the beliefs of the two men are disjoint, as they would be if they disagreed. And it is not clear that one could recapture the way in which they agree simply by saying that two belief states are in agreement when the corresponding sets of uncentered worlds are the same. For consider the case (discussed by Lewis and Perry) of mad Heimson who believes that he is Hume. All his impersonal beliefs about Hume are correct, let us assume, or better, let us assume that they are the same as Hume's beliefs about Hume. Still, it would not be right to say that Hume and Heimson don't disagree about anything.

In general, two questions need to distinguished: (1) what is the content of belief? (2) what is the nature of the relation between the believer and the content that constitutes its being the content of his or her belief? I think one should locate the essential indexical element in the answer to the second question. The objects of belief are propositions (sets of possible situations), but identifying some such set as x's beliefs at time t requires designating x and t in those possible situations—'calibrating" the situations compatible with belief with the believer and time of belief.

These last remarks suggest that my response to the problem of indexical belief (as I now see it) is in a way close to that of John Perry, who distinguishes belief contents from belief states. But Perry has a different conception of content, and I argue, in the last part of the paper, that it does not adequately represent the informational content of belief.[15]

[15] Discussion and correspondence with Cara Spencer and Philip Robbins have helped me to better appreciate some of the problems about indexical belief. Both are completing dissertations that have interesting things to say about the issues.

The paper "Belief Attribution and Context" develops some of the parallels between the way the content of an assertion is determined as a function of a context and the way the content of an embedded clause determines a content as a function of what I called a *derived context*, and considers some of the ways that the two contexts interact in the interpretation of belief ascriptions. The paper concludes by considering *de re* belief ascriptions. This is an important issue, since I think the different ways of analyzing *de re* belief ascriptions reflect and help to bring out contrasting ways of thinking about the nature of belief in general, and about the relation between belief and the way we describe it.

In a *de re* belief ascription, the speaker refers to an individual and describes the content of a belief as a function of that individual. When I say that Ralph believes Ortcutt to be a spy, I am referring to Ortcutt, and using *him* to say something about the content of Ralph's beliefs. As Quine noted in the classic paper that first focussed attention on this phenomenon, the most decisive cases in which what we are saying about Ralph's beliefs is a function of the *person* Ortcutt, and not his name or some concept of him, are cases of quantification into belief contexts: there is someone (namely Ortcutt) who is believed by Ralph to be a spy.

So much is common ground, but there are very different accounts of just what we are saying, in a *de re* belief ascription, about Ralph's beliefs. One idea is that in such cases we are ascribing belief in a proposition of a particular kind—a proposition that involves the individual as a constituent, or at least that can be determined as a function of the individual. To say that Ralph believes Ortcutt to be a spy is to ascribe to Ralph belief in the proposition that Ortcutt *himself* is a spy—the proposition that is true in the possible worlds in which *he* is a spy. A contrasting idea, implicit in Quine's account, is that the *de re* ascription does not ascribe a particular belief to Ralph, but only makes a general claim about his beliefs: it picks out a *set* of belief contents, and says that Ralph has one of these beliefs. The details will depend on what is assumed about what belief contents are; suppose our theorist takes the object of belief to be a Fregean intension that has a structure paralleling the semantic structure of a sentence, with senses as primitive constituents. Then she might interpret "Ralph believes Ortcutt to be a spy" to say that Ralph believes some proposition or other of the form "α is a spy" where the constituent α is a singular-term-sense whose corresponding referent is Ortcutt. That is, the pattern of analysis is something like this: x believes$_R$ F of y iff $(\exists \alpha)$ (x believes$_N$ $\langle F\alpha \rangle$ and α denotes y).[16]

---

[16] This pattern of analysis is implicit in Quine (1966), and is made explicit in Kaplan (1969). Quine, of course, wanted ultimately to avoid talk of propositions and other intensions, but he was willing to talk of such things at a shallow level of analysis, to get at the

One can see in these contrasting strategies the way that questions about the nature of belief and about the logical form of belief ascription interact. The first account is simpler and more straightforward, but it requires a conception of the objects of belief that recognizes something like singular propositions—a conception that some theorists will find unacceptable. And it requires that one be able to explain what it is to believe a singular proposition—a task that is made more acute by the problems posed by the familiar puzzle cases. The second strategy gives a more complex account of the semantics of *de re* belief ascription, but it permits one to reconcile the fact that we can quantify into belief contexts, and describe belief contents as a function of individuals, with the assumption that all belief contents are essentially mediated by conceptual or linguistic objects.

The two strategies for analyzing *de re* belief can each be generalized in ways that are motivated by the contrasting underlying pictures of belief. It is not only individuals that we use to describe the contents of beliefs—we describe them as a function of kinds, properties and relations, events and situations as well. When I say that O'Leary believes there is water in the bathtub, or that he has arthritis in his shoulder, I am referring to water, or to arthritis, and describing O'Leary's state of mind—the way O'Leary takes the world to be—in terms of that kind of stuff, or that disease. One who thinks of the contents of belief as some kind of essentially conceptual or quasi-linguistic objects might be tempted to respond to the way belief attribution seems to make reference to features of the believer's environment by extending the Quinean strategy of analysis. One might suggest that the lesson we should draw from the anti-individualist thought experiments of Tyler Burge and others is that belief ascriptions in general (wide content belief ascriptions) are only indirect and indefinite ways of describing underlying facts which are more directly and specifically described by giving the *narrow* content of the beliefs. I think most talk about narrow content is obscure and confused,[17] but one way to make sense of it is to

relevant structure. Ultimately, Quine wanted to use the pattern to analyze a sentential attitude, believes-true, where the quantifier ranges over names, and the brackets, "⟨,⟩" are quasi-quotation marks. In Kaplan's development of the pattern, he uses the metaphor of mental names and sentences. He also proposes that more constraints—psychological as well as semantic constraints—should be added to the denotation relation.

[17] What the Putnam–Burge thought experiments purport to show is that predicates like "believes that there is water in the bathtub" express relational rather than intrinsic properties. This is what is shown by an example of a possible situation in which a person lacks the property even though he is intrinsically exactly like someone who has it. It is the belief *properties* that are "wide," in this sense, not the content. Some theorists talk as if a belief might have both a wide and a narrow content—that O'Leary's belief—the one that has the wide content *that there is water in the bathtub*—might have another kind of content as well. But what does this mean—what is a belief? O'Leary has the property of believing that there is water in the bathtub, but what object are we talking about when we refer to the belief that he has—the particular belief that there is water in the bathtub? Perhaps sometimes we are

suppose that underlying the ordinary belief relation is a more basic narrow belief relation, and that the former should be analyzed in terms of the latter, together with a relation that connects wide contents with corresponding narrow contents. The abstract pattern, paralleling the Quinean paradigm, might go like this: x believes that P iff $(\exists Q)$ (x believes$_N$ Q, and $C(Q$, that $P)$, where "believes$_N$" now means narrow belief, rather than notional belief. The quantifier ranges over narrow contents, and the C relation relates narrow contents to their wide counterparts. The task set for the narrow content theorist who wants to turn this abstract schema into a theory is to say what narrow contents are, what the narrow belief relation is, and how narrow contents, together with their environment, determine corresponding wide contents.[18]

The Quinean project was to explain one particular kind of belief attribution in terms of ordinary belief attribution, to explain what appeared to be beliefs about particular individuals in terms of general beliefs. The generalization responds to the fact that some—perhaps almost all—general beliefs have some of the same problematic features that motivated an analysis that avoids any commitment to singular proposition as objects of belief. But the project changes its character when the problem—what needs to be reduced away—is the general case. One might better think of *de re* belief ascriptions, not as indirect and indefinite descriptions of

talking about the fact that he believes this. Other times we may be talking about what O'Leary believes—the content itself (as when we say that my belief about the matter is the same as O'Leary's). But I don't think there is an object appropriately called "the belief" that has a content that it might not have had. (A referent for the term "that belief" that could make it true to say "O'Leary might have had that belief—the belief that there was water in the bathtub—even if he didn't believe that there was water in the bathtub.")

One can make sense of the idea that when O'Leary believes that there is water in the bathtub, there is an underlying property that is the intrinsic component (what Dennett (1982) calls "the organismic contribution") of the belief property, in the way that one might take the mass of an object to be the intrinsic component of the object's weight. And one might hypothesize that this intrinsic component was itself an intentional property of some kind—a property that could be defined in terms of a relation some kind of propositional object (a narrow content). But it is not clear, even assuming this hypothesis, that one should locate the narrow/wide distinction in the content. One might use the very same abstract objects—propositions, whatever they are taken to be—to pick out both relational intentional properties and (if there are any) intrinsic intentional properties. One does not distinguish mass properties from weight properties by using narrow rather than wide numbers to measure them.

[18] The abstract pattern for the generalization of the Quinean analysis of relational belief follows a pattern of analysis suggested some time ago in Field (1978: 12). In Field's analysis, it was not narrow contents, but purely syntactic objects—mental sentences—that the quantifier ranged over, and the analogue of "believes$_N$" was "believes*"—an internal functional relation between a person and a mental sentence. The idea was to factor the intentional-psychological relation of belief into a psychological but nonintentional relation and a semantic but non-psychological relation—the relation between a sentence and the proposition it expressed.

underlying beliefs, but simply as examples that reveal in a particularly stark way a feature that is essential to intentional states themselves. I think one should understand the description of intentional states generally in the following way: what we are doing when we ascribe content—what it is to ascribe content—is to refer to some of the things, kinds, properties and relations that we find in the world, and to use those materials to characterize the world as someone else sees it (or as someone wishes it to be, or imagines it to be). It is not that this is an approximate or indirect way of describing the real underlying content of someone's conception of the world—it is as direct a way as there is of getting at what that content is.[19] Perhaps there is a sense in which there is something indirect about describing a person's state of mind by relating it to some possible ways that things might have been—by describing the world according to the person. If so, then intentionality generally is a kind of indirect description. The more direct way might be to describe the arrangements of neurons and the electrical activity in the person's brain, or the internal functional organization of that brain. I doubt that there is any notion of intentional content that will play a role in these more direct descriptions.[20]

The three papers in the part labeled "Externalism" are all attempts to defend the kind of perspective I have just been sketching. "On What's in the Head" argues that the lessons of the anti-individualist thought experiments are less paradoxical, and also more difficult to avoid, than some have supposed. Twin Earth thought experiments are well designed to make their point, but they may mislead one into thinking that it is easy to identify a notion of narrow content—the narrow content of our beliefs is the content we have in common with our Twin Earth twins. But we have too much in common with our twins—*all* intrinsic properties, and in most of the stories, a lot else as well.

In "Narrow Content" the ubiquitous two-dimensional framework makes another appearance, this time to help describe some puzzles about belief that Brian Loar discusses, and some theoretical ideas that he

---

[19] One might argue that the externalist picture—the idea that to attribute content is to refer to things and properties of things in the world, and use them to describe other people's states of mind—supports a Russellian conception of proposition (as a complex consisting of objects and properties) rather than the possible worlds conception. I have no quarrel with Russellian propositions, but I take them to represent recipes for determining informational contents. Consider a propositional complex, $\langle F, a \rangle$, where F is a property and a an individual. To understand this as a proposition, one must understand it as something that says that a has the property F, which is to say, to understand it as something that is true in all and only possible situations in which a has property F.

[20] That's not quite right. One might expect an internal functional theory of a brain to make use of a notion of information and information transfer, but the information would be information about the internal properties of the system. I don't think the contents of such informational states are what anyone has in mind by narrow content.

develops in response to the puzzles. I suggest that something like diag-onalization gives a representation of what Loar calls "realization condi-tions," and contrasts with ordinary truth-conditions. My main point in this paper is to argue that while this apparatus lends support to some of Loar's explanations of the cases, it does not yield a notion of narrow con-tent. What Loar calls psychological content, I argue, is just ordinary con-tent, and the mental states described in terms of this kind of content are relational, and not intrinsic properties—properties that depend on how the people who have them are situated in the world. Once again, it is the limitations of the two-dimensional framework that need to be empha-sized. It provides no simple formula for reading narrow content out of the facts. In considering whether a two-dimensional intension might be a nar-row content, we have to consider not just the properties of the abstract object, but what the facts are in virtue of which that abstract object is the content of some person's mental state. As I apply the apparatus, the propositional concept associated with some person's state of mind is deriv-ative from the ordinary propositional content of the person's mental states in the different possible worlds. As discussed above, one can use the ap-paratus in different ways: one might assume that some psychosemantic theory for a mental language assigned two-dimensional intensions to our mental sentences. But unless the facts in virtue of which the psychosemantics is correct are intrinsic facts about the person, the two-dimensional intensions won't be any "narrower" than the ordinary contents.

An information-theoretic story about intentionality—the idea that the content of intentional states should be explained, in part, in terms of the information that those states are disposed to carry—plays a role in all these papers, but it is in "Twin Earth Revisited" that it is argued most explicitly that the externalist story about intentional states is supported not only by compelling examples, but by a theoretical account of inten-tionality. This paper argues that the theoretical account also helps to bring out what is paradoxical about the anti-individualist's stories, to sharpen some puzzles about intentionality, and to show why attributions of con-tent are essentially context-dependent.

One constant throughout all the papers collected here has been my use and defense of the possible worlds conception of informational content—the assumption that the content of speech acts and intentional mental states should be identified with their truth-conditions, represented by a set of possible situations. My tenacity (some would say stubbornness) in defending an account of content that has few other defenders, and that faces daunting problems has even earned me an entry in the Philosophical Lexicon—a dictionary of words made from philosophers' names. (A stalnaker is "an *idée fixe* that brings a theory or a theorist to a halt.")[21] I address some of the most serious difficulties that the commitment to this coarse-grained conception of content saddles me with in the three papers in the last part.

Actually, I'm open-minded, and ready to grant that there are other objects around that might be plausibly labeled "propositions," or "contents," that might play a role in the description of semantic properties and intentional mental acts and states, and that might even sometimes be the referents of that-clauses. For example, the structures exemplified in structured meanings, or in Russellian propositional complexes, seem unproblematic, and if it is made clear what the ultimate constituents of such things are, then it will be clear enough what they themselves are. But the challenge is to explain the role of such structured objects in the description and explanation of intentional states. One needs an account of what states of belief, desire and intention *are* that explains how the fine-grained structure of some notion of proposition contributes to distinguishing between different states of belief, desire or intention. In "Mental Content and Linguistic Form" I spell out this challenge, and consider some contrasting ways in which the quasi-linguistic structures in structured propositions might be involved in intentional mental states.

The problem of logical omniscience—the topic of the last two papers—is the most daunting problem facing the kind of account of intentionality that I defend. I don't propose a solution to the problem—the aim is just to get clearer about what the problem is, and to argue that it is a deep problem—one we all face—and not a problem that can be solved or avoided simply by opting for some fine-grained conception of propositional content. The first of the two papers argues that while a language-of-thought "belief-box" conception of belief might provide a basis for a distinction between explicit and implicit beliefs, it would not be the distinction that needs to be explained, which is the distinction between beliefs that are accessible or available to be expressed and used, and information that is merely implicit in what we believe. The second paper on logical omniscience considers the problem as it arises in the context of some models of knowledge developed and applied by theoretical computer scientists to understand distributed systems. Again, no solution is proposed, but I hope that the consideration of some failed strategies for solving it helps to bring out some different dimensions of the problem. Since the problem is at best only identified, and not solved, in these two papers, perhaps there should be a "Logical Omniscience III." There are some positive things that might be said and I think the distributed systems models I discuss will

---

[21] Dennett (1987: 17).

be relevant to a more constructive project of distinguishing knowledge or belief that is available from information that is merely implicit. The distributed systems theory gives a representation of a community of interacting knowers, and it is the individual knowers who are (as represented in the theory) logically omniscient. But an individual knower could itself be represented as a distributed system, and some of the knowledge of the system as a whole might be unavailable (for some purpose) because it is distributed, or not integrated. The individual components—the subpersonal knowers—would themselves, if unanalyzed, be represented as logically omniscient, but if our component "knowers" are simple enough this won't be implausible. As Dan Dennett remarked a long time ago in defending explanations of artificial intelligence that appeal to homunculi: "If one can get a team or a committee of *relatively* ignorant, narrow-minded, blind homunculi to produce the intelligent behavior of the whole, this is progress."[22] This strategy can help explain the limitations, as well as the capacities, of intelligent being. Progress on the problem of logical omniscience will be made if we represent a knower as a community of relatively ignorant, narrow-minded, specialized knowers, since the less a knower knows, the easier it is for it to be logically omniscient. But all this is just undeveloped speculation—grist for the mill of further work.

[22] Dennett (1978: 123).

PART I

Representing Contexts

1

Pragmatics

Until recently, pragmatics—the study of language in relation to the users of language—has been the neglected member of the traditional three-part division of the study of signs: syntax, semantics, pragmatics. The problems of pragmatics have been treated informally by philosophers in the ordinary language tradition, and by some linguists, but logicians and philosophers of a formalistic frame of mind have generally ignored pragmatic problems, or else pushed them into semantics and syntax. My project in this paper is to carve out a subject matter that might plausibly be called pragmatics and which is in the tradition of recent work in formal semantics. The discussion will be programmatic. My aim is not to solve the problems I shall touch on, but to persuade you that the theory I sketch has promise. Although this paper gives an informal presentation, the subject can be developed in a relatively straightforward way as a *formal pragmatics* no less rigorous than present-day logical syntax and semantics. The subject is worth developing, I think, first to provide a framework for treating some philosophical problems that cannot be adequately handled within traditional formal semantics, and second to clarify the relation between logic and formal semantics and the study of natural language.

I shall begin with the second member of the triad, semantics. The boundaries of this subject are not so clear as is sometimes supposed, and since pragmatics borders on semantics, these boundaries will determine where our subject begins. After staking out a claim for pragmatics, I shall describe some of the tasks that fall within its range and try to defend a crucial distinction on which the division between semantics and pragmatics is based.

I. Semantics

If we look at the general characterizations of semantics offered by Morris and Carnap, it will seem an elusive subject. Semantics, according to them,

The research for and preparation of this paper was supported by the National Science Foundation, grant number GS–2574. I would like to thank Professors David Shwayder and Richmond Thomason for their helpful comments on a draft of this paper.

concerns the relationship between signs and their *designata*. The *designatum* of a sign, Morris writes, is what is "taken account of in virtue of the presence of the sign." He also says "a *designatum* is not a thing, but a kind of object, or a class of objects."[1] Carnap is equally vague in giving a general characterization. The designatum of an expression, he says, is what he who uses it intends to refer to by it, "e.g., to an object or a property or a state of affairs. . . . (For the moment, no exact definition for 'designatum' is intended; this word is merely to serve as a convenient common term for different cases—object, properties, etc., whose fundamental differences in other respects are not hereby denied.)"[2]

Though a clear general definition is hard to come by, the historical development of formal semantics is well delineated. The central problems in semantics have concerned the definition of truth, or truth-conditions, for the sentences of certain languages. Formal semantics abstracts the problem of giving truth-conditions for sentences away from problems concerning the purposes for which those sentences are uttered. People do many things with language, one of which is to express *propositions* for one reason or another, propositions being abstract objects representing truth-conditions. Semantics has studied that aspect of language use in isolation from others. Hence I shall consider semantics to be the study of propositions.

The explication of *proposition* given in formal semantics is based on a very homely intuition: when a statement is made, two things go into determining whether it is true or false. First, what did the statement say: what proposition was asserted? Second, what is the world like; does what was said correspond to it? What, we may ask, must a proposition be in order that this simple account be correct? It must be a rule, or a function, taking us from the way the world is into a truth-value. But since our ideas about how the world is change, and since we may wish to consider the statement relative to hypothetical and imaginary situations, we want a function taking not just the actual state of the world, but various possible states of the world into truth-values. Since there are two truth-values, a proposition will be a way—any way—of dividing a set of possible states of the world into two parts: the ones that are ruled out by the truth of the proposition, and the ones that are not.[3]

Those who find the notion of a *possible world* obscure may feel that this explication of proposition is unhelpful, since formal semantics generally takes that notion, like the notion of an individual, as primitive.[4] Some

---

[1] Morris (1938: 4–5).   [2] Carnap (1939: 4).   [3] See Scott (1970).
[4] This is not an inevitable strategy. Instead of taking individuals and possible worlds as primitive, defining properties and relations are functions from one to the other, one might take individuals, properties and relations as primitive and define possible worlds in terms of these.

explanation is perhaps needed, but I am not sure what kind. Even without explanation, the notion has, I think, enough intuitive content to make it fruitful in semantics. I shall say only that one requirement for identifying a possible world is to specify a domain of individuals said to exist in that world.[5]

If we explain propositions as functions from possible worlds into truth-values, they will have the properties that have traditionally been ascribed to them. Propositions are things that may be considered in abstraction on the one hand from particular languages and linguistic formulations (the sentences that express them), and on the other hand from the kinds of linguistic acts in which they figure (for example the assertions and commands in which a proposition is asserted or commanded). Thus once the homely intuition mentioned above has done its work, we may forget about assertions and consider propositions themselves, along with similar things such as functions taking individuals into propositions, and functions taking propositions into propositions.

Generally, the study of formal semantics has proceeded by first setting up a language, and then laying down rules for matching up the sentences of that language with propositions or truth-values. But the languages are set up usually for no other purpose than to represent the propositions, or at least this is how formalized languages have been used by philosophers. Regimentation or formalization is simply a way to make clearer what the truth-conditions are—what proposition is expressed by what is regimented or formalized. But with an adequate theory of propositions themselves, such philosophical analyses can proceed without the mediation of a regimented or formalized object language. Rather than translate a problematic locution into an object language in which it is clear what propositions are expressed by the sentences, one can simply state what proposition is expressed by that locution. The effect is the same. Unless one is concerned with proof theory, he may drop the language out altogether with no loss.

According to this characterization of semantics, then, the subject has no essential connection with languages at all, either natural or artificial. (Of course semantical theories are expressed *in* language, but so are theories about rocks.) This is not to deny the possibility of a *causal* relation between language and our conception of a proposition. It may be, for

[5] A theory of possible worlds and propositions defined in terms of them is not committed to any absolute notion of synonymy or analyticity. Since propositions are functions taking possible worlds as arguments, a domain of possible worlds must be specified as the domain of the function. But the domain need not be *all* possible worlds in any absolute or metaphysical sense. We may leave open the possibility that the domain may be extended as our imaginations develop, or as discoveries are made, or as our interests change. Propositional identity is, of course, relative to the specification of a domain of possible worlds.

example, that the fact that we think of a possible world as a domain of individuals together with the ascription of properties to them is a result of the fact that our language has a subject-predicate structure. It is also not to deny that the study of the grammar of natural language may be a rich source of insight into the nature of propositions and a source of evidence for distinctions among propositions. If we find in grammar a device for marking a distinction of content, we may presume that there is a distinction of content to be marked. But whatever the causal or evidential story, we may still abstract the study of propositions from the study of language. By doing so, I think we get a clearer conception of the relation between them.

Though one may study propositions apart from language, accounting for the relation between language and propositions still falls partly within the domain of semantics. One of the jobs of natural language is to express propositions, and it is a semantical problem to specify the rules for matching up sentences of a natural language with the propositions that they express. In most cases, however, the rules will not match sentences directly with propositions, but will match sentences with propositions relative to features of the context in which the sentence is used. These contextual features are a part of the subject matter of pragmatics, to which I shall now turn.

II. Pragmatics

Syntax studies sentences, semantics studies propositions. Pragmatics is the study of linguistic acts and the contexts in which they are performed. There are two major types of problems to be solved within pragmatics: first, to define interesting types of speech acts and speech products; second, to characterize the features of the speech content which help determine which proposition is expressed by a given sentence. The analysis of illocutionary acts is an example of a problem of the first kind; the study of indexical expressions is an example of the second. My primary concern will be with problems of the second kind, but I shall say a few general things about the first before I go on to that.

Assertions, commands, counterfactuals, claims, conjectures and refutations, requests, rebuttals, predictions, promises, pleas, speculations, explanations, insults, inferences, guesses, generalizations, answers and lies are all kinds of linguistic acts. The problem of analysis in each case is to find necessary and sufficient conditions for the successful (or perhaps in some cases normal) performance of the act. The problem is a pragmatic one since these necessary and sufficient conditions will ordinarily involve the presence or absence of various properties of the context in which the act is performed,[6] for example, the intentions of the speaker, the knowledge, beliefs, expectations or interests of the speaker and his audience, other speech acts that have been performed in the same context, the time of utterance, the effects of the utterance, the truth-value of the proposition expressed, the semantic relations between the proposition expressed and some others involved in some way.

Almost all of the speech act types mentioned above involve the expression of a proposition, and in the first type of pragmatic problem, the identity of that proposition is taken to be unproblematic. In most cases, however, the context of utterance affects not only the force with which the proposition is expressed, but also the proposition itself. It may be that the semantical rules determine the proposition expressed by a sentence or clause only relative to some feature of the situation in which the sentence is used.

Consider a statement "everybody is having a good time." I assume that you understand the *sentence* well enough. Now assume also that you are omniscient with respect to people have a good time: you know for each person that ever lived and for each time up to now whether or not that person was having a good time at that time. Under these conditions, you may still be in doubt about the truth of the statement for at least two reasons: first, you do not know when it was made; second, you do not know what class of people it was made about. It is unlikely that the speaker meant everybody in the universe. He may have meant everybody at some party, or everyone listening to some philosophical lecture, and if so, then we have to know what party, or what lecture before we know even what was said, much less whether what was said is true.

Statements involving personal pronouns and demonstratives furnish the most striking examples of this kind. When you say "We shall overcome," I need to know who you are, and for whom you are speaking. If you say "that is a great painting," I need to know what you are looking at, or pointing to, or perhaps what you referred to in your previous utterance. Modal terms also are notoriously dependent on context for their interpretation. For a sentence using *can, may, might, must* or *ought*, to determine a proposition unambiguously, a domain of "all possible worlds" must be specified or intended. It need not be *all* conceivable worlds in any absolute sense, if there is such a sense. Sentences involving modals are usually to be

___

[6] This is not necessarily so, however. Since speech act types can be *any* way of picking out a class of particular speech acts, one might define one in such a way that the context was irrelevant, and the problem of analysis reduced to a problem of syntax or semantics, as for example the speech act of uttering a grammatical sentence of English, or the speech act of expressing the proposition X.

construed relative to all possible worlds consistent with the speaker's knowledge, or with some set of presuppositions, or with what is morally right, or legally right, or normal, or what is within someone's power. Unless the relevant domain of possible worlds is clear in the context, the proposition expressed is undetermined.

The formal *semantic* analysis of such concepts as universality and necessity isolates the relevant contextual or pragmatic parameters of an interpretation (as, for example, a domain of discourse in classical first order logic, a set of possible worlds and a relation of relative possibility on them in Kripke's semantics for modal logic), and defines truth conditions relative to these parameters. The second kind of pragmatic problem is to explicate the relation of these parameters to each other, and to more readily identifiable features of linguistic contexts.

The scheme I am proposing looks roughly like this: The syntactical and semantical rules for a language determine an interpreted sentence or clause; this, together with some features of the context of use of the sentence or clause determines a proposition; this in turn, together with a possible world, determines a truth-value. An interpreted sentence, then, corresponds to a function from contexts into propositions, and a proposition is a function from possible worlds into truth-values.

According to this scheme, both contexts and possible worlds are partial determinants of the truth-value of what is expressed by a given sentence. One might merge them together, considering a proposition to be a function from context-possible worlds (call them points of reference) into truth-values. Pragmatics-semantics could then be treated as the study of the way in which, not propositions, but truth-values are dependent on context, and part of the context would be the possible world in which the sentence is uttered. This is, I think, the kind of analysis of pragmatics proposed and developed by Richard Montague.[7] It is a simpler analysis than the one I am sketching; I need some argument for the necessity or desirability of the extra step on the road from sentences to truth-values. The step is justified only if the middlemen—the propositions—are of some independent interest, and only if there is some functional difference between contexts and possible worlds.

The independent interest in propositions comes from the fact that they are the objects of illocutionary acts and propositional attitudes. A proposition is supposed to be the common content of statements, judgments, promises, wishes and wants, questions and answers, things that are possible or probable. The meanings of sentences, or rules determining truth-values directly from contexts, cannot plausibly represent these objects.

[7] Montague (1974). Montague uses the phrase "point of reference" as does Dana Scott in (1970).

If O'Leary says "Are you going to the party?" and you answer, "Yes, I'm going," your answer is appropriate because the proposition you affirm is the one expressed in his question. On the simpler analysis, there is nothing to be the common content of question and answer except a truth-value. The propositions are expressed from different points of reference, and according to the simpler analysis, they are different propositions. A truth-value, of course, is not enough to be the common content. If O'Leary asks "Are you going to the party?" it would be inappropriate for you to answer, "Yes, snow is white."

When O'Leary says at the party, "I didn't have to be here you know," he means something like this: it was not necessary that O'Leary be at that party. The words *I* and *here* contribute to the determination of a proposition, and this proposition is what O'Leary declares to be not necessary. Provided he was under no obligation or compulsion to be there, what he says is correct. But if the proposition declared to be not necessary were something like the meaning of the sentence, then O'Leary would be mistaken since the sentence "I am here" is true from all points of reference, and hence necessarily true on the simpler analysis.

Suppose you say "He is a fool" looking in the direction of Daniels and O'Leary. Suppose it is clear to me that O'Leary is a fool and that Daniels is not, but I am not sure who you are talking about. Compare this with a situation in which you say "He is a fool" pointing unambiguously at O'Leary, but I am in doubt about whether he is one or not. In both cases, I am unsure about the truth of what you say, but the source of the uncertainty seems radically different. In the first example, the doubt is about what proposition was expressed, while in the second there is an uncertainty about the facts.

These examples do not provide any criteria for distinguishing the determinants of truth which are part of the context from those which are part of the possible world, but they do support the claims that there is a point to the distinction, and that we have intuitions about the matter. I certainly do not want to suggest that the distinction is unproblematic, or that it is not sometimes difficult or arbitrary to characterize certain truth determinants as semantic or pragmatic.[8] I want to suggest only that there are clear cases on which to rest the distinction between the context and the possible world, and differences in language use which depend on how it is made. To lend more detailed support to the suggestion, I shall first discuss a concept

---

[8] Tenses and times, for example, are an interesting case. Does a tensed sentence determine a proposition which is sometimes true, sometimes false, or does it express different timeless propositions at different times? I doubt that a single general answer can be given, but I suspect that one's philosophical views about time may be colored by a tendency to think in one of these ways or the other.

of *pragmatic presupposition* which is central to the characterization of contexts, as opposed to possible worlds, and second describe a kind of *pragmatic ambiguity* which depends on the distinction.

III. Presuppositions

The notion of presupposition that I shall try to explicate is a pragmatic concept, and must be distinguished from the semantic notion of presupposition analyzed by van Fraassen.[9] According to the *semantic* concept, a proposition P presupposes a proposition Q if and only if Q is necessitated both by P and by *not-P*. That is, in every model in which P is either true or false, Q is true. According to the *pragmatic* conception, presupposition is a propositional attitude, not a semantic relation. People, rather than sentences or propositions are said to have, or make, presuppositions in this sense. More generally, any participant in a linguistic context (a person, a group, an institution, perhaps a machine) may be the subject of a presupposition. Any proposition may be the object, or content of one.

There is no conflict between the semantic and pragmatic concepts of presupposition: they are explications of related but different ideas. In general, any semantic presupposition of a proposition expressed in a given context will be a pragmatic presupposition of the people in that context, but the converse clearly does not hold.

To presuppose a proposition in the pragmatic sense is to take its truth for granted, and to assume that others involved in the context do the same. This does not imply that the person need have any particular mental attitude toward the proposition, or that he need assume anything about the mental attitudes of others in the context. Presuppositions are probably best viewed as complex dispositions which are manifested in linguistic behavior. One has presuppositions in virtue of the statements he makes, the questions he asks, the commands he issues. Presuppositions are propositions implicitly *supposed* before the relevant linguistic business is transacted.

The set of all the presuppositions made by a person in a given context determines a class of possible worlds, the ones consistent with all the presuppositions. This class sets the boundaries of the linguistic situation. Thus, for example, if the situation is an inquiry, the question will be, which of the possible worlds consistent with the presuppositions is the actual world? If it is a deliberation, then the question is, which of *those* worlds shall we make actual? If it is a lecture, then the point is to inform the audi-

---

[9] van Fraassen (1968b, 1968a).

ence more specifically about the location of the actual world within that class of possible worlds. Commands and promises are expected to be obeyed and kept within the bounds of the presuppositions. Since the presuppositions play such a large part in determining what is going on in a linguistic situation, it is important that the participants in a single context have the same set of presuppositions if misunderstanding is to be avoided. This is why presupposition involves not only taking the truth of something for granted, but also assuming that others do the same.

The boundaries determined by presuppositions have two sides. One cannot normally assert, command, promise, or even conjecture what is inconsistent with what is presupposed. Neither can one assert, command, promise or conjecture what is itself presupposed. There is no point in expressing a proposition unless it distinguishes among the possible worlds which are considered live options in the context.

Presuppositions, of course, need not be true. Where they turn out false, sometimes the whole point of the inquiry, deliberation, lecture, debate, command or promise is destroyed, but at other times it does not matter much at all. Suppose, for example, we are discussing whether we ought to vote for Daniels or O'Leary for President, presupposing that they are the Democratic and Republican candidates, respectively. If our real interest is in coming to a decision about who to vote for in the Presidential election, then the debate will seem a waste of time when we discover that in reality, the candidates are Nixon and Muskie. However, if our real concern was with the relative merits of the character and executive ability of Daniels and O'Leary, then our false presupposition makes little difference. Minor revisions might bring our debate in line with new presuppositions. The same contrast applies to a scientific experiment performed against the background of a presupposed theoretical framework. It may lose its point when the old theory is rejected, or it may easily be accommodated to the new theory. Sometimes, in fact, puzzlement is resolved and anomalies are explained by the discovery that a presupposition is false, or that a falsehood was presupposed. An experimental result may be more easily accommodated to the new presuppositions than to the old ones.

Normally, presuppositions are at least *believed* to be true. That is one reason that we can often infer more about a person's beliefs from his assertions than he says in them. But in some cases, presuppositions may be things we are unsure about, or even propositions believed or known to be untrue. This may happen in cases of deception: the speaker presupposes things that his audience believes but that he knows to be false in order to get them to believe further false things. More innocently, a speaker may presuppose what is untrue to facilitate communication, as when an anthropologist adopts the presuppositions of his informant in questioning him. Most innocent of all are cases of fiction and pretending: speaker and audience may conspire together in presupposing things untrue, as when the author of a novel presupposes some of what was narrated in earlier chapters. In some contexts, the truth is beside the point. The actual world is, after all, only one possible world among many.

The shared presuppositions of the participants in a linguistic situation are perhaps the most important constituent of a context. The concept of pragmatic presupposition should play a role, both in the definition of various speech acts such as assertion, prediction, or counterfactual statement, and also in specifying semantical rules relating sentences to propositions relative to contexts.

IV. Pragmatic Ambiguity

The best example of the kind of ambiguity that I shall describe is given in Keith Donnellan's distinction between referential and attributive uses of definite descriptions.[10] After sketching an account of his distinction within the theory of pragmatics, I shall give some examples of other pragmatic ambiguities which have similar explanations.

Consider the following three statements, together with parenthetical comments on the contexts in which they were made:

(1) Charles Daniels is bald (said about a philosopher named Charles Daniels by one of his friends).
(2) I am bald (said by Charles Daniels, the man mentioned above).
(3) The man in the purple turtleneck shirt is bald (said by someone in a room containing one and only one man in a purple turtleneck shirt, that man being Charles Daniels).

The question is, what proposition was expressed in each of these three cases? In the first case, since "Charles Daniels" is a proper name, and since the speaker knows the intended referent well, there is no problem: the proposition is the one that says that *that* man has the property of being bald. In possible worlds in which that same man, Charles Daniels, is bald, the statement is true; in possible worlds in which he is not bald, the statement is false. What is the truth-value in possible worlds where he does not exist? Perhaps the function is undefined for those arguments. We need not worry about it though, since the existence of Charles Daniels will be presupposed in any context in which that proposition is expressed.

[10] Donnellan (1966).

The second statement expresses exactly the same proposition as the first since it is true in possible worlds where the referent of the pronoun, *I*, Charles Daniels, is bald, and false when he is not. To believe what is expressed in the one statement is to believe what is expressed in the other; the second might be made as a report of what was said in the first. To interpret the second *sentence*, one needs to know different things about the context than one needs to know to interpret the first, but once both statements are understood, there is no important difference between them.

In both cases, there is a pragmatic problem of determining from the context which individual is denoted by the singular term. The answer to this question fixes the proposition—the content of what is said. In case (1), a relatively unsystematic convention, the convention matching proper names to individuals, is involved. In case (2), there is a systematic rule matching a feature of the context (the speaker) with the singular term *I*. Different rules applied to different sentences in different contexts determine the same proposition.

What about the third case? Here there are two ways to analyze the situation corresponding to the referential and attributive uses of definite descriptions distinguished by Donnellan. We might say that the relation between the singular term "the man in the purple turtleneck shirt" and the referent, Charles Daniels, is determined by the context, and so the proposition expressed is the same as that expressed by statements (1) and (2). As with the term *I*, there are relatively systematic rules for matching up definite descriptions with their denotations in a context: the referent is the one and only one member of the appropriate domain who is *presupposed* to have the property expressed in the description. The rule cannot always be applied, but in the case described, it can be.

Alternatively, we might understand the rule picking out the denotation of the singular term to be itself a part of the proposition. This means that the relation between the definite description and its denotation is a function, not of the context, but of the possible world. In different possible worlds the truth-value of the proposition may depend on different individuals. It also means that we may understand the proposition—the content of the statement—without knowing who the man in the purple turtleneck shirt is, although we may have to know who he is in order to know that it is true.

The simpler account of pragmatics which merges possible worlds with contexts cannot account for Donnellan's distinction. If one goes directly from sentence (together with context) to truth-value, one misses the ambiguity, since the truth-conditions for the sentence in a fixed context (in normal cases at least) coincide for the two readings. If one goes from sentence together with context to proposition, and proposition together with possible world to truth-value, however, the ambiguity comes out in the intermediate step. There are at least three important differences between the referential and attributive uses of descriptions. These differences provide further argument for a theory which allows the distinction to be made and which gives some account of it.

First, in modal contexts and contexts involving propositional attitudes, the distinction makes a difference even for the *truth-value* of statements in which descriptions occur. Compare

(4) The man in the purple turtleneck shirt might have been someone else.

(5) The man in the purple turtleneck shirt might have worn white tie and tails.

Both statements say approximately that a certain proposition was possibly true. But in each case there are two propositions that can be intended, and which one is chosen may make a different in the truth-value of the ascription of possibility to the proposition. If the first means, roughly, that Daniels might have been someone else, it is false, perhaps contradictory. On the other hand, if it means that someone else might have been the one wearing the turtleneck shirt (perhaps he almost lent it to me), then it may be true. The second statement can mean either that Daniels might have worn white tie and tails, or that it might have been the case that whoever was the one wearing a purple turtleneck shirt was *also* wearing white tie and tails. Clearly, the truth-conditions are different for these two readings.

In a formal language containing modal or epistemic operators and descriptions, the distinction can be interpreted as a *syntactical* distinction. That is, statements (4) and (5) could each be formalized in two syntactically different ways with the description falling inside of the scope of the modal operator in one and outside the scope in the other.[11] But this procedure has two limitations: (*a*) it would be highly implausible to suggest that the *English* sentences (4) and (5) are syntactically ambiguous. There are no natural syntactical transformations of (4) and (5) which remove the ambiguity. (*b*) modal and propositional attitude concepts may be involved, not only as parts of statements, but as comments on them and attitudes toward them. The content of statement (3) above, which cannot be treated as syntactically ambiguous even in a formalized language, may be doubted, affirmed, believed or lamented. What one is doing in taking these attitudes or actions depends on which of the two readings is given to the statement.

---

[11] See Thomason and Stalnaker (1968b, 1968a).

Second, as Donnellan noted, the distinction makes a difference for the presuppositions required by the context in which the statement is made. In general, we may say that when a simple subject-predicate statement is made, the existence of the subject is normally presupposed. When you say "the man in the purple turtleneck shirt is bald," you presuppose that the man in the purple turtleneck shirt exists. But of course the same ambiguity infects that statement of presupposition; how it is to be taken depends on what reading is given to the original statement. If the statement is given the referential reading, then so must be the presupposition. What is presupposed is that Daniels exists. If the statement is given the attributive reading, then the presupposition is that there is one and only one man (in the appropriate domain) wearing a purple turtleneck shirt. This is exactly the presupposition difference pointed out by Donnellan. Within the framework I am using, the different presuppositions can be seen to be instances of a single principle.

Third, the distinction is important if one considers what happens when the description fails to apply uniquely in the context. In *both* referential and attributive uses of descriptions, it is a presupposition of the context that the description applies uniquely, but if this presupposition is false, the consequences are different. In the case of referential uses, Donnellan has noted, the fact that the presupposition fails may have little effect on the statement. The speaker may still have successfully referred to someone, and successfully said something about him. When the presupposition fails in the attributive sense, however, that normally means that nothing true or false has been said at all. This difference has a natural explanation within our framework.

Where the rules determining the denotation of the singular term are considered as part of the context, what is relevant is not what is true, but what is presupposed. The definite description in statement (3) above, on the referential reading, denotes the person who is *presupposed* to be the one and only one man in a purple turtleneck shirt (in the relevant domain). If there is no one person who is presupposed to fit the description, then reference fails (even if some person does *in fact* fit the description uniquely). But if there is one, then it makes no difference whether that presupposition is true or false. The presupposition helps to determine the proposition expressed, but once that proposition is determined, it can stand alone. The fact that Daniels is bald in no way depends on the color of his shirt.

On the attributive reading, however, the rule determining the denotation of the description is a part of the proposition, so it is what is true that counts, not what is presupposed. The proposition is about whoever uniquely fits the description, so if no one does, no truth-value is determined.

The points made in distinguishing these two uses of definite descriptions can be generalized to apply to other singular terms. Proper names, for example, are normally used to refer, but can be used in a way resembling the attributive use of definite descriptions. When you ask, "Which one is Daniels?" you are not *referring* to Daniels, since you do not presuppose of any one person that he is Daniels. When I answer "Daniels is the bald one" I am using "the bald one" referentially, and the name Daniels attributively. I am telling you not that Daniels is bald, but that he is Daniels. Using this distinction, we can explain how identity statements can be informative, even when two proper names flank the identity sign.

It has been emphasized by many philosophers that referring is something done by people with terms, and not by terms themselves. That is why reference is a problem of pragmatics, and it is why the role of a singular term depends less on the syntactic or semantic category of the term itself (proper name, definite description, pronoun) than it does on the speaker, the context, and the presuppositions of the speaker in that context.

The notion of pragmatic ambiguity can be extended to apply to other kinds of cases. In general, a sentence has the potential for pragmatic ambiguity if some rule involved in the interpretation of that sentence may be applied either to the context or to the possible world. Applied to the context, the rule will either contribute to the determination of the proposition (as in the case of the referential use of definite descriptions) or it will contribute to the force with which the proposition is expressed. Applied to the possible world, the rule is incorporated into the proposition itself, contributing to the determination of a truth-value. Conditional sentences, sentences containing certain modal terms, and sentences containing what have been called parenthetical verbs are other examples of sentences which have this potential.

If a person says something of the form "If A then B", this may be interpreted either as the categorical assertion of a conditional proposition or as the assertion of the consequent made conditionally on the truth of the antecedent. In the former case, a proposition is determined on the level of semantics as a function of the propositions expressed by antecedent and consequent. In the latter case, the antecedent is an additional presupposition made temporarily, either because the speaker wishes to commit himself to the consequent only should the antecedent be true, or because the assertion of the consequent would not be relevant unless the antecedent is true (as in, for example, "there are cookies in the cupboard if you want some").[12]

---

[12] See Stalnaker (1968) for a semantical theory of conditional propositions. Nuel Belnap in (1979) has developed a theory of conditional assertion.

A sentence of the form "It may be that *P*" can be interpreted as expressing a modal proposition, that proposition being a function of *P*, or it may be interpreted as making explicit that the negation of *P* is not presupposed in the context. In the latter case, *P* is the only *proposition* involved. The modal word indicates the force with which it is expressed.

A sentence of the form "I suppose that *P*" may be meant as a report about a supposition of the speaker, or as a rather tentative assertion of *P*. To read it the second way is to treat *I suppose* as a *parenthetical verb*, since on this reading, the sentence is synonomous with "*P*, I suppose." The differences between these two readings are explored in Urmson's famous article on parenthetical verbs.[13]

Each of these examples has its own special features and problems. I do not want to suggest that they are instances of a common form. But the ambiguity, in each case, rests on the distinction between context and possible world.

V. Conclusion

Let me summarize the main points that I have tried to make. In section I I claimed that semantics is best viewed as the study of propositions, and argued that propositions may be studied independently of language. In section II I defined pragmatics as the study of linguistic acts and the contexts in which they are performed. Two kinds of pragmatic problems were considered; first, the definition of speech acts—the problem of giving necessary and sufficient conditions, not for the truth of a proposition expressed in the act, but for the act being performed; second, the study of the ways in which the linguistic context determines the proposition expressed by a given sentence in that context. The formulation of problems of the second kind depends on a basic distinction between contextual determinants of propositions and propositional determinants of truth. I argued that the distinction has an intuitive basis, and is useful in analyzing linguistic situations. In the final two sections, I tried to support this distinction, first by characterizing a pragmatic notion of presupposition that is a central feature of contexts as opposed to possible worlds, and second by describing a kind of pragmatic ambiguity which rests on the distinction.

In this sketch of a theory of pragmatics, I have relied on some undefined and problematic concepts, for example, possible worlds, contexts, and presuppositions. I have given some heuristic account of these concepts, or

---

[13] Urmson (1952).

relied on the heuristic accounts of others, but I have made no attempt to reduce them to each other, or to anything else. It may be charged that these concepts are too unclear to be the basic concepts of a theory, but I think that this objection mistakes the role of basic concepts. It is not assumed that these notions are clear. In fact, one of the points of the theory is to clarify them. So long as certain concepts all have *some* intuitive content, then we can help to explicate them all by relating them to each other. The success of the theory should depend not on whether the concepts can be defined, but on whether or not it provides the machinery to define linguistic acts that seem interesting and to make conceptual distinctions that seem important. With philosophical as well as scientific theories, one may explain one's theoretical concepts, not by defining them, but by using them to account for the phenomena.

2

Pragmatic Presuppositions

There is a familiar intuitive distinction between what is *asserted* and what is *presupposed* in the making of a statement. If I say that the Queen of England is bald, I presuppose that England has a unique queen, and assert that she is bald. If I say that Sam regrets that he voted for Nixon, I presuppose that Sam voted for Nixon, and assert that he feels bad about it. If I say that Ted Kennedy is the only person who could have defeated Nixon in 1972, I presuppose that Ted Kennedy could have defeated Nixon in 1972, and assert that no one else could have done so. Philosophers have discussed this distinction mainly in the context of problems of reference. Linguists have discussed it in many other contexts as well. They have argued that the phenomenon of presupposition is a pervasive feature of the use of natural language, one that must play a role in the semantic analysis of many words and phrases.

The principle criterion that has been used to identify presuppositions can be stated in the following way: Q is presupposed by an assertion that P just in case under normal conditions one can reasonably infer that a speaker believes that Q from either his assertion or his denial that P. One who denies the example statements listed above—who says that the Queen of England is *not* bald, that Sam does *not* regret that he voted for Nixon, or that Ted Kennedy is *not* the only person who could have defeated Nixon in 1972, normally makes the same presuppositions as the person who makes the affirmative statements. Linguists have used this criterion to identify many examples of the phenomenon. The criterion, and many of the examples, are relatively clear and uncontroversial; it is clear that there is a phenomenon to be explained. But it is much less clear what kind of explanation of it should be given. Granted that either the statement that the Queen of England is bald, or the speaker who makes it, presupposes that England has a unique queen. But what is it about the statement, or

This paper was read at the University of Texas conference on performatives, conversational implicature, and presupposition in March, 1973, as well as at New York University. I, and I hope the paper, benefited from stimulating comments by linguists and philosophers at both places.

the speaker, which constitutes this fact? There are two very different kinds of answers to this question.

The first answer is that presupposition is a semantic relation holding between sentences or propositions. This kind of account draws the distinction between presupposition and assertion in terms of the content or truth-conditions of the sentence uttered or the proposition expressed. Here is an example of such a definition: a proposition that P presupposes that Q if and only if Q must be true in order that P have a truth-value at all. The presuppositions of a proposition, according to this definition, are necessitated by the truth, and by the falsity, of the proposition. When any presupposition is false, the assertion lacks a truth-value.

The second answer is that presupposition should be given a pragmatic analysis. The distinction between presupposition and assertion should be drawn, not in terms of the content of the propositions expressed, but in terms of the situations in which the statement is made—the attitudes and intentions of the speaker and his audience. Presuppositions, on this account, are something like the background beliefs of the speaker—propositions whose truth he takes for granted, or seems to take for granted, in making his statement.

The pragmatic account is closer to the ordinary notion of presupposition, but it has frequently been assumed that the semantic account is the one that is relevant to giving a rigorous theoretical explanation of the linguistic phenomena. I want to argue that this assumption is wrong. I will suggest that it is important for correctly understanding the phenomena identified by linguists to give the second kind of analysis rather than the first. In terms of the pragmatic account, one can give intuitively natural explanations of some facts that seem puzzling when presupposition is viewed as a semantic relation. The pragmatic account makes it possible to explain some particular facts about presuppositions in terms of general maxims of rational communication rather than in terms of complicated and *ad hoc* hypotheses about the semantics of particular words and particular kinds of constructions. To argue this, I will sketch an account of the kind I want to defend, and then discuss some of the facts identified by linguists in terms of it.

Let me begin by rehearsing some truisms about communication. Communication, whether linguistic or not, normally takes place against a background of beliefs or assumptions which are shared by the speaker and his audience, and which are recognized by them to be so shared. When I discuss politics with my barber, we each take the elementary facts of the current political situation for granted, and we each assume that the other does. We assume that Richard Nixon is the President, that he recently defeated George McGovern by a large margin, that the United States has recently been involved in a war in Vietnam, which is a small country in Southeast Asia, and so forth. That we can reasonably take these facts for granted obviously makes our communication more efficient. The more common ground we can take for granted, the more efficient our communication will be. And unless we could reasonably treat *some* facts in this way, we probably could not communicate at all.

Which facts or opinions we can reasonably take for granted in this way, as much as what further information either of us wants to convey, will guide the direction of our conversation—will determine what is said. I will not say things that are already taken for granted, since that would be redundant. Nor will I assert things incompatible with the common background, since that would be self-defeating. My aim in making assertions is to distinguish among the possible situations which are compatible with all the beliefs or assumptions that I assume that we share. Or it could be put the other way around: the common background is defined by the possible situations which I intend to distinguish among with my assertions, and other speech acts. Propositions true in all of them are propositions whose truth is taken for granted.

Although it is normally inappropriate because unnecessary for me to assert something that each of us assumes the other already believes, my assertions will of course always have consequences which are part of the common background. For example, in a context where we both know that my neighbor is an adult male, I say "My neighbor is a bachelor," which, let us suppose, entails that he is adult and male. I might just as well have said "my neighbor is unmarried." The same information would have been conveyed (although the nuances might not have been exactly the same). That is, the *increment of information*, or of content, conveyed by the first statement is the same as that conveyed by the second. If the asserted proposition were accepted, and added to the common background, the resulting situation would be the same as if the second assertion were accepted and added to the background.

This notion of common background belief is the first approximation to the notion of pragmatic presupposition that I want to use. A proposition *P* is a pragmatic presupposition of a speaker in a given context just in case the speaker assumes or believes that *P*, assumes or believes that his addressee assumes or believes that *P*, and assumes or believes that his addressee recognizes that he is making these assumptions, or has these beliefs.

I do not propose this as a definition or analysis, first since it is far from clear what it is to believe or assume something, in the relevant way and second since even assuming these notions to be clear, the definition would need further qualification. My aim is not to give an analysis but rather to point to a familiar feature of linguistic contexts which, I shall argue, is the feature in terms of which a certain range of linguistic phenomena should be explained. The notion has, I think, enough intuitive content to enable us to identify a lot of particular cases, and the general outlines of the definition are clear enough to justify some generalizations about presuppositions which help to explain the facts. Before defending this claim by discussing some of the facts, I will make two remarks about the general notion.

First, note that it is persons rather than sentences, propositions or speech acts that have or make presuppositions. This goes against the prevailing technical use of the term, according to which presuppositions, whether semantic or pragmatic, are normally taken to relate two linguistic things. One might define such a relation in terms of the pragmatic notion in something like one of the following ways: (a) One might say that a sentence x presupposes that Q just in case the use of x to make a statement is appropriate (or normal, or conversationally acceptable) only in contexts where Q is presupposed by the speaker; or (b) one might say that the statement that P (made in a given context) presupposes that Q just in case one can reasonably infer that the speaker is presupposing that Q from the fact that the statement was made; or (c) one might say that the statement that P (made in a given context) presupposes that Q just in case it is necessary to assume that the speaker is presupposing that Q in order to understand or interpret correctly the statement. As stated, these suggested definitions are vague, and each is different from the others. But I do not think it would be fruitful to refine them, or to choose one over the others. It is true that the linguistic facts to be explained by a theory of presupposition are for the most part relations between linguistic items, or between a linguistic expression and a proposition. They are, as I interpret them, facts about the constraints, of one kind or another, imposed by what is said on what is appropriately presupposed by the speaker, according to various different standards of appropriateness. But I think all the facts can be stated and explained directly in terms of the underlying notion of speaker presupposition, and without introducing an intermediate notion of presupposition as a relation holding between sentences (or statements) and propositions.

This last point is a strategic recommendation, and not a substantive claim. As I said, one *could* define such a notion in various ways; I just doubt the theoretical utility of doing so. My purely strategic motive for emphasizing this point is that I want to avoid what I think would be a fruitless debate over which of various explications of the notion of pragmatic sentence presupposition best accords with the use of the term "presupposition" by linguists. I do not want to deny that, in an adequate theory of conversation, one will need a notion or notions of conversational acceptability, and that once one has such a notion one has all the material for a definition of pragmatic sentence presupposition. A rough definition of "conversational acceptability" might be something like this: a speech act is conversationally acceptable in the relevant sense just in case it can reasonably be expected to accomplish its purpose in the normal way in which the normal purposes of such speech acts are accomplished. But such a notion would get its content from an account of the mechanisms by which the normal purposes of speech acts are accomplished, and the notion of speaker presupposition is intended to be one theoretical concept useful for giving such an account. It is in this way that it is a more basic concept than the concept of conversational acceptability.

Second, let me suggest one way that the definition given above needs to be qualified. In normal, straightforward serious conversational contexts where the overriding purpose of the conversation is to exchange information, or conduct a rational argument, what is presupposed by the speaker, in the sense intended, is relatively unproblematic. The presuppositions coincide with the shared beliefs, or the presumed common knowledge. The difficulties in applying the notion come with contexts in which other interests besides communication are being served by the conversation. If one is talking for some other purpose than to exchange information, or if one must be polite, discreet, diplomatic, kind, or entertaining as well as informative, then one may have reason to act as if the common background were different than one in fact knows it to be. For example, when I talk to my barber, neither of us expects to learn anything; we are talking just to be civil, and to pass the time. If we haven't much to say, we may act as if the background of common knowledge is smaller than it really is. "Cold today, isn't it?" "Sure is, windy too." "Well, spring will be here before long." Although there is little actual communication going on here, it is clear that what is going on is to be understood in terms of genuine communication. We are pretending to communicate, and our pretense can be explained in terms of the same categories as a serious exchange of information.

In other cases, a speaker may act as if certain propositions are part of the common background when he knows that they are not. He may want to communicate a proposition indirectly, and do this by presupposing it in such a way that the auditor will be able to infer that it is presupposed. In such a case, a speaker tells his auditor something in part by pretending that his auditor already knows it. The pretense need not be an attempt at deception. It might be tacitly recognized by everyone concerned that this is what is going on, and recognized that everyone else recognizes it. In some cases, it is just that it would be indiscreet, or insulting, or tedious, or

unnecessarily blunt, or rhetorically less effective to assert openly a proposition that one wants to communicate.[1]

Where a conversation involves this kind of pretense, the speaker's presuppositions, in the sense of the term I shall use, will not fit the definition
sketched above. That is why the definition is only an approximation. I shall
say that one actually does make the presuppositions that one seems to
make even when one is only pretending to have the beliefs that one normally has when one makes presuppositions. Presupposing is thus not a
mental attitude like believing, but is rather a linguistic disposition—a disposition to behave in one's use of language as if one had certain beliefs, or
were making certain assumptions.[2]

[1] This is a special case of what Grice has called *exploitation*, since the speaker exploits
the rules governing normal conversation in order to communicate something which is not
exactly said. See Grice (1989).

[2] It was suggested by Jerry Sadock (personal communication) that the definition should
be modified in another way to account for examples of the following kind: I am asked by
someone who I have just met, "Are you going to lunch?" I reply, "No, I've got to pick up
my sister." Here I seem to *presuppose* that I have a sister, even though I do not assume that
the addressee knows this. Yet the statement is clearly acceptable, and it does not seem right
to explain this in terms of pretense, or exploitation. To meet this problem, Sadock suggests
replacing the clause in the definition, "speaker assumes or believes that the addressee
assumes or believes that *P*" with the clause, "speaker assumes or believes that the addressee
has no reason to doubt that *P*."

The reason that I resist this suggestion, even though I recognize the force of the example,
is that some basic generalizations about speaker presuppositions would fail if it were
adopted. For example, one important generalization, alluded to above, is that it is unnecessary, in fact inappropriate, to assert what is presupposed. But consider a routine lecture
or briefing by an acknowledged expert. It may be that everything he says is something that
the audience has no reason to doubt, but this does not make it inappropriate for him to
speak. The problem is that the modification would work only for cases where the addressee
could infer what was being presupposed from the overt speech act. But this is not the only
case where speaker presuppositions are important.

Two alternative responses to the example are possible: (a) one can explain it in terms of
exploitation; (b) one can deny that there is a presupposition made at all in this kind of
example.

To respond in the first way is, I admit, to stretch the notion of exploitation, first because
the example lacks the flavor of innuendo or diplomatic indirection which characterizes the
clearest cases of communication by pretense, and second because in the best cases of
exploitation, it is the main point of the speech act to communicate what is only implied,
whereas in this example, the indirectly communicated material is at best only a minor piece
of required background information. Nevertheless, the explanation of how communication
takes place in this example may be thought to be similar in form to explanations of how it
takes place in the more familiar cases: the addressee infers that the speaker accepts that Q
from the fact that he says that P because normally one says that P only when it is common
background knowledge that Q.

To take the second option is to deny the generalization that the speaker *always* presupposes the existence of a unique referent (in the relevant domain of discourse) fitting any definite description (like "my sister") which he uses. To make this plausible, one would have
to give an explanation of why one is *usually* expected to presuppose the existence of a
unique referent when one uses a definite description—an explanation which also explains
the exceptions to the rule.

The presumed background information—the set of presuppositions which in part defines a linguistic context—naturally imposes constraints on what can reasonably or appropriately be said in that context. Where the constraints relate to a particular kind of grammatical construction, or to a particular expression or category of expressions, one has a linguistic fact to be explained. This is the case with the sample sentences with which I began. One of the facts could be stated like this: it is inappropriate to say "The Queen of England is bald" (or to say "the Queen of England is not bald") except in a context in which it is part of the presumed background information that England has a queen. Compare this with a description that interprets the phenomena in terms of a semantic concept of presupposition: the proposition expressed by "the Queen of England is bald" has a truth-value only if England has a unique queen. The first description, in contrast to the second, makes no claim at all about the content of the statement—about the truth-conditions of what is said. The description in terms of the pragmatic notion does not rule out a semantic *explanation* for the fact that a certain presupposition is required when a certain statement is made, but neither does it demand such an explanation. That is, one *might* explain why it is appropriate for a speaker to say "the Queen of England is bald" only if he presupposes that England has a queen in terms of the following two assumptions: first, that the statement lacks a truth-value unless England has a queen, and second, that one normally presupposes that one's statements have a truth-value. But one also might explain the fact in a different way. The *facts* about presuppositions, I am suggesting, can be separated from a particular kind of semantic explanation of those facts. This separation of the account of presupposition from the account of the content of what is said will allow for more diversity among presupposition phenomena than would be possible if they all had to be forced into the semantic mold. Let me suggest, more specifically, four of the advantages of making this move.

First, if presupposition is defined independently of truth-conditions, then it is possible for the constraints on presuppositions to vary from context to context, or with changes in stress or shifts in word order, without those changes requiring variation in the semantic interpretation of what is said. This should make possible a simpler semantic theory; at the very least, it should allow for more flexibility in the construction of semantic theories. For example, D. T. Langendoen points out in a paper on presupposition and assertion that normally, if one said "my cousin isn't a boy anymore" he would be asserting that his cousin had grown up, presupposing that he is male. But one might, in a less common context, use the same sentence to assert that one's cousin had changed sexes, presupposing that she is young.[3] If a semantic account of presupposition is given of this case, then one must say that the sentence is therefore ambiguous. On the pragmatic account, one just points to two different kinds of situations in which a univocal sentence could be used.

Second, if presupposition is defined independently of truth-conditions, then one can separate the question of entailment relations from the question of presupposition. On the semantic account, presupposition and entailment are parallel and incompatible semantic relations. *A* presupposes that *B* if and only if *B* is necessitated by *both A* and its denial. *A* entails *B* if and only if *B* is necessitated by *A* but *not* by its denial. Thus the claim that the sentence, "Sam realizes that *P*" *entails* that *P* conflicts with the claim that that sentence presupposes, in the semantic sense, that *P*. But using the pragmatic account, one may say that sometimes when a presupposition is required by the making of a statement, what is presupposed is also entailed, and sometimes it is not. One can say that "Sam realizes that *P*" entails that *P*—the claim is false unless *P* is true. "Sam does not realize that *P*," however, does not entail that *P*. That proposition may be true even when *P* is false. All this is compatible with the claim that one is required to presuppose that *P* whenever one asserts or denies that Sam realizes it.

Third, the constraints imposed by a statement on what is presupposed seem to be a matter of degree, and this is hard to explain on the semantic account. Sometimes no sense at all can be made of a statement unless one assumes that the speaker is making a certain presupposition. In other cases, it is mildly suggested by a speech act that the speaker is taking a certain assumption for granted, but the suggestion is easily defeated by countervailing evidence. If a speaker says to me, "Sam was surprised that Nixon lost the election," then I have no choice but to assume that he takes it for granted that Nixon lost. But if he says, "If Eagleton hadn't been dropped from the Democratic ticket, Nixon would have won the election" (without an "even" before the "if" or a "still" after the "Nixon"), there is a suggestion that the speaker presupposes that Nixon in fact did not win, but if the statement is made in the right context, or with the right intonation, the suggestion is overruled. This difference in degree, and variation with context is to be expected on the pragmatic account, since it is a matter of the strength of an inductive inference from the fact that a statement was made to the existence of a background assumption or belief.

Fourth, and perhaps most important, the pragmatic analysis of presupposition, because it relates the phenomena to the general communication situation, may make it possible to explain some of the facts in terms of

---

[3] Langendoen (1971).

general assumptions about rational strategy in situations where people exchange information or conduct argument. One way to explain the fact that a particular assertion requires or suggests a certain presupposition is to hypothesize that it is simply a fact about some word or construction used in making the assertion. In such a case, the fact about the presupposition requirement must be written into the dictionary, or into the semantics. But since we have an account of the *function* of presuppositions in conversations, we may sometimes be able to explain facts about them without such hypotheses. The propositions that P and that Q may be related to each other, and to common beliefs and intentions, in such a way that it is hard to think of a reason that anyone would raise the question whether P, or care about its answer, unless he already believed that Q. More generally, it might be that one can make sense of a conversation as a sequence of rational actions only on the assumption that the speaker and his audience share certain presuppositions. If this kind of explanation can be given for the fact that a certain statement tends to require a certain presupposition, then there will be no need to complicate the semantics or the lexicon.

For example, consider the word "know." It is clear that "x knows that P" entails that P. It is also clear that in most cases when anyone asserts or denies that x knows that P, he presupposes that P. Can this latter fact be explained without building it into the semantics of the word? I think it can. Suppose a speaker were to assert that x knows that P in a context where the truth of P is in doubt or dispute. He would be saying in one breath something that could be challenged in two different ways. He would be leaving unclear whether his main point was to make a claim about the truth of P, or to make a claim about the epistemic situation of x (the knower), and thus leaving unclear what direction he intended or expected the conversation to take. Thus, given what "x knows that P" means, and given that people normally want to communicate in an orderly way, and normally have some purpose in mind, it would be unreasonable to assert that x knows that P in such a context. One could communicate more efficiently by saying something else. For similar reasons, it would normally be inappropriate to say that x does not know that P in a context where the truth of P was in question. If the speaker's reason for believing his assertion were that he thought that P was false, or that he thought that x didn't believe that P, or didn't have reason to believe that P, then his statement would be gratuitously weak. And it would be unusual for a speaker to be in a position to know that one of these situations obtained, without knowing which.

This is a tentative and incomplete sketch of an explanation. Much more would have to be said to make it convincing. My point is to make it plausible that, in some cases at least, such explanations might be given, and to argue that where they can be given, there is no reason to build specific rules about presuppositions into the semantics.

I want now to illustrate these advantages of the pragmatic account by looking at some linguistic facts in terms of it. The two sets of facts I will consider are taken from two recent papers by Lauri Karttunen.[4]

First, on a distinction between two kinds of factive verbs. It is well known that among verbs that take a nominalized sentence complement (for example *believe, know, intend, see*) one can distinguish a subclass known as factive verbs (*know, regret, discover, see*, as contrasted with *believe, intend, assert, claim*). A number of syntactic and semantic criteria are used to draw the distinction, but the distinguishing mark that is relevant here is the following: if *V* is a factive verb, then *x V's that P* presupposes (and, I would say, entails as well) that *P*. If I assert or deny that Jones regrets, realizes, or discovers that Nixon won the election, then I presuppose that Nixon did in fact win. Karttunen has drawn a further distinction among two kinds of factive verbs which, he argues, requires a distinction between two kinds of presupposition relations. One kind of factive verb (labeled the *full factives*) includes *regret, forget* and *resent*. The basis for the distinction is as follows: with full factives, it is not only an assertion or denial of the proposition *x V's that P* that requires the presupposition that *P*, but also the *supposition* that *x V's* that *P* in the antecedent of a conditional, or the claim that the proposition *might* be true. With semi-factives, it is only the assertion or denial that require the presupposition. For example, consider the two statements

Sam may regret that he voted for Nixon.
If Sam regrets that he voted for Nixon, then he is a fool.

Because these two statements clearly require the presupposition that Sam voted for Nixon, *regret* is seen to be a full factive.

The following is Karttunen's example to illustrate the contrast between full factives and semi-factives. Compare

If I $\left\{\begin{array}{l}\text{regret} \\ \text{realize} \\ \text{discover}\end{array}\right.$ later that I have not told the truth,
I will confess it to everyone.

In the first statement, the speaker clearly presupposes that he has not told the truth. In the other two cases, he clearly does not presuppose this. Thus *realize* and *discover* are seen to be semi-factives.

To explain the difference, Karttunen postulates a distinction between a strong and a weak kind of semantic presupposition. If *P* is necessitated by

⁴ Karttunen (1971, 1973).

Possibly Q, and by *Possibly not-Q*, then *Q* strongly presupposes that *P*. Weak semantic presuppositions are defined in the usual way.

In discussing this example, I want to dispute both the data, and the theoretical account of them. I agree that there is a sharp contrast in the particular example given, but the matter is less clear if one looks at other examples. Consider:

> If Harry discovers that his wife is playing around, he will be upset.
> If Harry had discovered that his wife was playing around, he would have been upset.
> If Harry had realized that his wife was playing around, he would have been upset.
> Harry may realize that his wife has been playing around.
> Harry may never discover that his wife has been playing around.

There is, I think, in all these cases a presumption that the speaker presupposes that Harry's wife is, or has been, playing around. The presumption is stronger in some of the examples than in others, but it seems to me that in some of them it is as strong as with *regret*. Further, if we assume that with the so-called semi-factives like *discover* and *realize*, there is *always* a presumption that the speaker presupposes the truth of the proposition expressed in the complement, we can still explain why the presumption is defeated in Karttunen's particular example. The explanation goes like this: if a speaker explicitly supposes something, he thereby indicates that he is not *pre*supposing it, or taking it for granted. So when the speaker says "if I realize later that *P*," he indicates that he is not presupposing that he will realize later that *P*. But if it is an open question for a speaker whether or not he will at some future time have come to realize that *P*, he can't be assuming that he already knows that *P*. And if he is not assuming that he himself knows that *P*, he can't be assuming that *P*. Hence *P* cannot be presupposed. A roughly parallel explanation will work for *discover*, but not for *regret*.

One can explain another of Karttunen's examples in a similar way. Consider the three questions:

$$\text{Did you} \left\{ \begin{array}{l} \text{regret} \\ \text{realize} \\ \text{discover} \end{array} \right. \text{that you had not told the truth?}$$

Here *realize* seems to go with *regret* and not with *discover*. The first two questions seem to require that the speaker presuppose that the auditor did not tell the truth, while the third does not. Again, we can explain the difference, even while assuming that there is a presumption that the presupposition is made in all three cases. The reason that the presumption is defeated in the third case is that the speaker could not make that presupposition without assuming an affirmative answer to the question he is asking. But in general, by asking a question, one indicates that one is not presupposing a particular answer to it. This explanation depends on the particular semantic properties of *discover*, and will not work for *realize* or *regret*.[5] It also depends on the fact that the subject of the verb is the second-person pronoun. Hence if the explanation is right, one would expect the presupposition to reappear in the analogous third-person question, "Did Sam discover that he hadn't told the truth?" It seems that it does.

Since on the pragmatic account, the constraints on presuppositions can vary without the truth-conditions changing, we can allow presupposition differences between first- or second-person statements and questions and the corresponding third-person statements and questions without postulating separate semantic accounts of propositions expressed from different points of view. So, while we have noted differences in the presuppositions required or suggested by the following two statements,

If Harry discovers that his wife has been playing around, he will be upset.

If I discover that my wife has been playing around, I will be upset (said by Harry).

This difference does not prevent us from saying that the two statements both have the same semantic content—that the same proposition is expressed in both cases. It would not be possible to say this on a semantic account of presupposition.

If the explanations I have sketched are on the right track, then we can account for at least some of the differences between factive and semi-factive verbs without distinguishing between two different kinds of presupposition relations. We can also account for some differences among semi-factives, and differences between first- and third-person statements without complicating the semantics. The explanation depends on just two things: first, some simple and very general facts about the relation between pragmatic presuppositions and assertions, questions, and suppositions;

---

[5] The relevant difference between *realize* and *discover* is this: because *realize* is a stative verb, a past tense statement of the form *x didn't realize that P* must be about some particular time in the past (determined by the context), and not about *all* times in the past. This means that *x didn't realize that P* may be true, even though *x now* knows that *P*. In contrast, because *discover* is an inchoative verb, *x didn't discover that P* may be about *all* times in the past. For this reason, normally, *x didn't discover that P* implies that *x* has not *yet* discovered that *P*, and so does not know that *P*. Therefore, if a speaker presupposes that *P*, he assumes that *x has* discovered that *P*, and so assumes a particular answer to the question he is asking.

second, on the ordinary semantic properties of the particular verbs involved.[6]

The second set of facts that I will discuss concerns the presuppositions of compound sentences: How do the presuppositions required by a conditional or conjunctive statement relate to the presuppositions that would be required by the component parts, stated alone? In general, what is the relation between the presuppositions required by an assertion that A and the assertion that B on the one hand, and by an assertion that A *and* B or that *if* A, *then* B on the other? Karttunen defends the following answer to the question: let S be a sentence of the form A *and* B or *If* A, *then* B. S presupposes that C if and only if either A presupposes that C, *or* B presupposes that C and A does not semantically entail that C. In other words, the presuppositions of a conjunction are the presuppositions required by either of the conjuncts, *minus any required by the second conjunct which are entailed by the first*. The presuppositions of a conditional are the presuppositions of either antecedent or consequent minus those required by the consequent and entailed by the antecedent. So if I say "Harry is married, and Harry's wife is a great cook," I assert, and do not presuppose, that Harry is married. But the second conjunct, stated alone (*Harry's wife is a great cook*), would require the presupposition that Harry is married. The sentence with conjuncts in reverse order would be unacceptable in any normal context (*Harry's wife is a great cook, and Harry is married*).

Now if we regard Karttunen's generalization as a generalization about *semantic* presuppositions, then we will interpret it as a hypothesis about the way the truth-value (or lack of it) of a conjunction or conditional relates to the truth-values of the parts. The hypothesis has the consequence that the conjunction *and* is not truth-functional, since the truth-value of a conjunctive statement will in some cases depend on entailment relation between the conjuncts. It has the consequence that *and* is not symmetric. A *and* B may be false while B *and* A lacks a truth-value. Finally, it has the consequence that the simple conjunction *and* is governed by mysteriously complicated rules.

---

[6] Two disclaimers: First, I do not want to leave the impression that I think I have explained very much here. I have not made any attempt to explain the source of the presumption that the complements of both factive and semi-factive verbs are presupposed. I have tried to explain only how the presupposition is cancelled in certain cases. Also, the presumption is clearly harder to defeat in some cases than in others: harder with *realize* than with *discover*, and harder with full factives than with semi-factives. I have said nothing that would explain this. My hope, however, is that such explanations can be given using the general strategy which I am recommending. Second, I do not want to deny that there are systematic differences between factives and semi-factives. One difference is that full factives all require not only the presupposition that the proposition expressed in the complement is true, but also the presupposition that the subject of the verb knows or knew that it is. None of the semi-factives requires or suggests this second presupposition; in fact, they rule it out.

On the other hand, if we regard Karttunen's generalization as a generalization about *pragmatic* presuppositions, then we can reconcile it with the standard truth-functional account of *and*, and we can explain the generalization without postulating any *ad hoc* semantic or pragmatic rules. The explanation goes like this: first, once a proposition has been asserted in a conversation, then (unless or until it is challenged) the speaker can reasonably take it for granted for the rest of the conversation. In particular, when a speaker says something of the form *A and B*, he may take it for granted that *A* (or at least that his audience recognizes that *he* accepts that *A*) after he has said it. The proposition that *A* will be added to the background of common assumptions before the speaker asserts that *B*. Now suppose that *B* expresses a proposition that would, for some reason, be inappropriate to assert except in a context where *A*, or something entailed by *A*, is presupposed. Even if *A* is *not* presupposed initially, one may still assert *A and B* since by the time one gets to saying that *B*, the context has shifted, and it is by then presupposed that *A*.[7]

As with the explanation sketched in the earlier discussion, this explanation rests on just two things: first, a simple pragmatic assumption about the way presuppositions shift in the course of a conversation—an assumption that says, roughly, that a speaker may build on what has already been said; second, an uncontroversial assumption about the semantic properties of the word *and*—in particular, that when one asserts a conjunction, he asserts both conjuncts. If we interpret presupposition to mean *pragmatic* presupposition, then we can deduce Karttunen's generalization from these two almost trivial assumptions.

The analogous generalization about conditional statements is explainable on equally simple assumptions. Here we need first the assumption that what is explicitly *supposed* becomes (temporarily) a part of the background of common assumptions in subsequent conversation, and second that an *if* clause is an explicit supposition. Again, Karttunen's generalization can be derived from these obvious assumptions.

I have been arguing in this paper for the fruitfulness of separating semantic from pragmatic features of linguistic expressions and situations, and of explaining a certain range of phenomena in terms of pragmatic rather than semantic principles. This goes against the trend of the work of generative semanticists such as George Lakoff and John Ross, who have emphasized the difficulty of separating syntactic, semantic, and pragmatic problems, and who have sometimes suggested that such distinctions as

---

[7] In a paper at the Texas conference on performatives, conversational implicature and presuppositions, Karttunen put forward an explanation of his generalization which is very similar to this. Our accounts were developed independently.

between syntactic and semantic deviance or semantic and pragmatic regularities are of more use for avoiding problems than for solving them. Partly to respond to this concern, I will conclude with some general remarks about the distinction between semantics and pragmatics, and about what I am *not* recommending when I suggest that the distinction be taken seriously.

First remark: semantics, as contrasted with pragmatics, can mean either the study of *meaning* or the study of *content*. The contrast between semantic and pragmatic claims can be either of two things, depending on which notion of semantics one has in mind. First, it can be a contrast between claims about the particular conventional meaning of some word or phrase on the one hand, and claims about the general structure or strategy of conversation on the other. Grice's distinction between conventional implicatures and conversational implicatures is an instance of this contrast. Second, it can be a contrast between claims about the truth-conditions or *content* of what is said—the proposition expressed—on the one hand, and claims about the *context* in which a statement is made—the attitudes and interests of speaker and audience—on the other. It is the second contrast that I am using when I argue for a pragmatic rather than a semantic account of presuppositions. That is, my claim is that constraints on presuppositions are constraints on the contexts in which statements can be made, and not constraints on the truth-conditions of propositions expressed in making the statements. I also made use of the other contrast in arguing for this claim. I conjectured that one can explain many presupposition constraints in terms of general conversational rules without building anything about presuppositions into the meanings of particular words or constructions. But I make no general claim here. In some cases, one may just have to write presupposition constraints into the dictionary entry for a particular word. This would make certain presupposition requirements a matter of *meaning*, but it would not thereby make them a matter of *content*. There may be facts about the meaning of a word which play no role at all in determining the truth-conditions of propositions expressed using the word.

Second remark: in recommending a separation of content and context I as not suggesting that there is no interaction between them. Far from it. The semantic rules which determine the content of a sentence may do so only relative to the context in which it is uttered. This is obviously the case with sentences using personal pronouns, demonstratives, quantifiers, definite descriptions, or proper names. I suspect it happens in less obvious cases as well. But this interaction does not prevent us from studying the features which define a linguistic context (such as a set of pragmatic presuppositions) in abstraction from the propositions expressed in such contexts, or from studying the relationships among propositions in abstraction from the contexts in which they might be expressed.

A final remark: in some cases, distinctions such as that between semantic and pragmatic features may be used as a way to set problems aside. Some linguists have accused other linguists of using the distinction between syntax and semantics in this way. Deviant sentences which seem to conflict with syntactic generalizations are not treated as counter-examples, but instead are thrown into a "semantic wastebasket" to be explained away by some future semantic theory. In the same way, some may be suspicious that I am setting up a pragmatic wastebasket, and recommending that all the interesting problems be thrown away.

I do not think that this is always a bad procedure, but it is not what I am suggesting here. I am recommending instead the development and application of a pragmatic theory in which detailed explanations of phenomena relating to linguistic contexts can be given. It is true that traditionally the more well-developed and the more rigorous linguistic theories have focussed on questions of grammar and content, while the discussions which emphasized the role of conversational context have been more informal and less theoretical. But there is no necessity in this. Potentially at least, a theory of pragmatics, and the notion of pragmatic presupposition can be as precise as any of the concepts in syntax and semantics. Although the explanations I have sketched in this paper are informal and incomplete, I think they suggest a strategy for giving explanations of linguistic phenomena relating to contexts which are both rigorous and intuitively natural.[8]

---

[8] I have been accused, partly on the basis of this concluding paragraph, of being overly optimistic about the possibility of a formal theory of pragmatics which is both rigorous and sufficiently detailed to provide substantive explanations of linguistic phenomena. This accusation may be just, but my main point here is independent of this. However easy or difficult it proves to be to develop an adequate theory of conversation, one cannot simplify the task by building conversational rules into a semantic theory of the content of what is said.

3

Indicative Conditionals

"Either the butler or the gardener did it. Therefore, if the butler didn't do it, the gardener did." This piece of reasoning—call it the *direct argument*—may seem tedious, but it is surely compelling. Yet if it is a valid inference, then the indicative conditional conclusion must be logically equivalent to the truth-functional material conditional,[1] and *this* conclusion has consequences that are notoriously paradoxical. The problem is that if one accepts the validity of the intuitively reasonable direct argument from the material conditional to the ordinary indicative conditional, then one must accept as well the validity of many arguments that are intuitively absurd. Consider, for example, "the butler did it; therefore, if he didn't, the gardener did." The premise of this argument entails the premise of the direct argument, and their conclusions are the same. Therefore, if the direct argument is valid, so is this one. But this argument has no trace of intuitive plausibility. Or consider what may be inferred from the *denial* of a conditional. Surely I may deny that if the butler didn't do it, the gardener did without affirming the butler's innocence. Yet if the conditional is material, its negation entails the truth of its antecedent. It is easy to multiply paradoxes of the material conditional in this way—paradoxes that must be explained away by anyone who wants to defend the thesis that the direct argument is valid. Yet anyone who denies the validity of that argument must explain how an invalid argument can be as compelling as this one seems to be.

There are thus two strategies that one may adopt to respond to this puzzle: defend the material conditional analysis and explain away the paradoxes of material implication, or reject the material conditional analysis and explain away the force of the direct argument.[2] H. P. Grice, in his

The ideas in this paper were developed over a number of years. During part of this time my research was supported by the National Science Foundation, grant number GS–2574; more recently it was supported by the John Simon Guggenheim Memorial Foundation.

[1] The argument in the opposite direction—from the indicative conditional to the material conditional—is uncontroversially valid.

[2] This does not exhaust the options. Three other possible strategies might be mentioned. (1) Defend the direct argument, not by accepting the truth-functional analysis of the conditional, but by rejecting the truth-functional analysis of the disjunction. (2) Give a

William James lectures,[3] pursued the first of these strategies, using principles of conversation to explain facts about the use of conditionals that
seem to conflict with the truth-functional analysis of the ordinary indicative conditional. I will follow the second strategy, defending an alternative
semantic analysis of conditionals according to which the conditional
entails, but is not entailed by, the corresponding material conditional. I
will argue that, although the premise of the direct argument does not
semantically entail its conclusion, the inference is nevertheless a *reasonable
inference*. My main task will be to define and explain a concept of reasonable inference which diverges from semantic entailment, and which justifies this claim.

Grice's strategy and mine have this in common: both locate the source
of the problem in the mistaken attempt to explain the facts about assertion
and inference solely in terms of the semantic content, or truth-conditions,
of the propositions asserted and inferred. Both attempt to explain the
facts partly in terms of the semantic analysis of the relevant notions, but
partly in terms of pragmatic principles governing discourse. Both recognize that since assertion aims at more than truth, and inference at more
than preserving truth, it is a mistake to reason too quickly from facts
about assertion and inference to conclusions about semantic content and
semantic entailment.

My plan will be this: first, I will try to explain, in general terms, the
concept of reasonable inference and to show intuitively how there can be
reasonable inferences which are not entailments. Second, I will describe a
formal framework in which semantic concepts like content and entailment
as well as pragmatic concepts like assertion and inference can be made
precise. Third, within this framework, I will sketch the specific semantic
analysis of conditionals, and state and defend some principles relating
conditional sentences to the contexts in which they are used. Fourth, I will
show that, according to these analyses, the direct argument is a reasonable
inference. Finally, I will look at another puzzling argument involving reasoning with conditionals—an argument for fatalism—from the point of
view of this framework.

three-valued interpretation of the indicative conditional, assigning the neutral value when
the antecedent is false. (3) Interpret the indicative conditional as a conditional assertion
rather than the assertion of a conditional proposition. Alternative (1) might disarm this
particular puzzle, but it seems *ad hoc* and would not help with other persuasive arguments
for the material conditional analysis. Alternative (2) would conflict with some basic and
otherwise plausible pragmatic generalizations such as that one should not make an assertion unless one has good reason to think that it is true. Alternative (3) seems to me the most
promising and plausible alternative to the account I will develop, but to make it precise, I
think one needs much of the framework of a pragmatic theory that I shall use in my
account.

[3] Grice (1989).

I

Reasonable inference, as I shall define it, is a pragmatic relation: it relates speech acts rather than the propositions which are the contents of speech acts. Thus it contrasts with entailment which is a purely semantic relation. Here are rough informal definitions of the two notions: first, reasonable inference: an inference from a sequence of assertions or suppositions (the premises) to an assertion or hypothetical assertion (the conclusion) is *reasonable* just in case, in every context in which the premises could appropriately be asserted or supposed, it is impossible for anyone to accept the premises without committing himself to the conclusion; second, entailment: a set of propositions (the premises) *entails* a proposition (the conclusion) just in case it is impossible for the premises to be true without the conclusion being true as well. The two relations are obviously different since they relate different things, but one might expect them to be equivalent in the sense that an inference would be reasonable if and only if the set of propositions expressed in the premises entailed the proposition expressed in the conclusion. If this equivalence held, then the pragmatic concept of inference would of course have no interest. I shall argue that, and try to show why, the equivalence does not hold. Before discussing the specific framework in which this will be shown, let me try to explain in general terms how it is possible for an inference to be reasonable, in the sense defined, even when the premises do not entail the conclusion.

The basic idea is this: many sentences are context-dependent; that is, their semantic content depends not just on the meanings of the words in them, but also on the situations in which they are uttered. Examples are familiar: quantified sentences are interpreted in terms of a domain of discourse, and the domain of discourse depends on the context; the referents of first and second person pronouns depend on who is speaking, and to whom; the content of a tensed sentence depends on when it is uttered. Thus context constrains content in systematic ways. But also, the fact that a certain sentence is uttered, and a certain proposition expressed, may in turn constrain or alter the context. There are two ways this may happen: first, since particular utterances are appropriate only in certain contexts, one can infer something about a context from the fact that a particular utterance is made (together with the assumption that the utterance is appropriate); second, the expression of a proposition alters the context, at the very least by changing it into a context in which that proposition has just been expressed. At any given time in a conversation, the context will depend in part on what utterances have been made, and what propositions expressed, previously in the conversation. There is thus a two-way interaction between contexts of utterance and the contents of utterances. If there are general rules governing this interaction, these rules may give rise to systematic relations between propositions expressed at different points in a conversation, relations which are mediated by the context. Such relations may become lost if one ignores the context and considers propositions in abstraction from their place in a discourse. It is because entailment relates propositions independently of their being asserted, supposed or accepted, while reasonable inference concerns propositions which are expressed and accepted, that the two relations may diverge.

These general remarks are not an attempt to show that the notions of entailment and reasonable inference do in fact diverge, but only an attempt to point to the source of the divergence that will be shown. To show the divergence, I must say what contexts are, or how they are to be represented formally. I must say, for some specific construction (here, conditionals) how semantic content is a function of context. And I must state and defend some rules which relate contexts to the propositions expressed in them.

II

The framework I will use begins with, and takes for granted, the concept of a possible world. While model theory based on possible worlds is generally agreed to be a powerful and mathematically elegant tool, its intuitive content and explanatory power are disputed. It is argued that a theory committed to the existence of such implausible entities as possible worlds must be false. Or at least the theory cannot do any philosophical work unless it can provide some kind of substantive answer to the question, what is a possible world? Possible worlds are certainly in need of philosophical explanation and defense, but for the present I will make just a brief remark which will perhaps indicate how I understand this basic notion.[4]

It is a common and essential feature of such activities as inquiring, deliberating, exchanging information, predicting the future, giving advice, debating, negotiating, explaining and justifying behavior, that the participants in the activities seek to distinguish, in one way or another, among alternative situations that may arise, or might have arisen. Possible worlds theory, as an explanatory theory of rational activity, begins with the notion of an alternative way that things may be or might have been (which is all that a possible world is) not because it takes this notion to be unproblematic, but because it takes it to be fundamental to the different activities that

---

[4] See Lewis (1973: 84–91) for a defense of realism about possible worlds.

a theory of rationality seeks to characterize and relate to each other. The notion will get its content, not from any direct answer to the question, what is a possible world? or from any reduction of that notion to something more basic or familiar, but from its role in the explanations of such a theory. Thus it may be that the best philosophical defense that one can give for possible worlds is to use them in the development of substantive theory.

Taking possible worlds for granted, we can define a *proposition* as a function from possible worlds into truth-values.[5] Since there are two truth-values, this means that a proposition is any way of dividing a set of possible worlds into two parts—those for which the function yields the value true, and those for which it yields the value false. The motivation for this representation of propositions is that, as mentioned above, it is an essential part of various rational activities to distinguish among alternative possible situations, and it is by expressing and adopting attitudes toward propositions that such distinctions are made.

How should a context be defined? This depends on what elements of the situations in which discourse takes place are relevant to determining what propositions are expressed by context-dependent sentences and to explaining the effects of various kinds of speech acts. The most important element of a context, I suggest, is the common knowledge, or presumed common knowledge and common assumption of the participants in the discourse.[6] A speaker inevitably takes certain information for granted when he speaks as the common ground of the participants in the conversation. It is this information which he can use as a resource for the communication of further information, and against which he will expect his speech acts to be understood. The presumed common ground in the sense intended—the *presuppositions* of the speaker—need not be the beliefs which are really common to the speaker and his audience; in fact, they need not be beliefs at all. The presuppositions will include whatever the speaker finds it convenient to take for granted, or to pretend to take for granted, to facilitate his communication. What is essential is not that the propositions presupposed in this sense be believed by the speaker, but rather that the speaker believe that the presuppositions are common to himself and his audience. This is essential since they provide the context in which the speaker intends his statements to be received.

In the possible worlds framework, we can represent this background information by a set of possible worlds—the possible worlds not ruled out by the presupposed background information. I will call this set of possible

---

[5] See Cresswell (1973): 23–4, and my "Pragmatics," reprinted in Ch. 1 of the present volume, for brief discussions of the intuitive motivation of this definition of proposition.

[6] For a fuller discussion and defense of this concept, see Stalnaker (1977).

worlds the *context set*.[7] Possible worlds within the set are situations among which the speaker intends his speech acts to distinguish. I will sometimes talk of propositions being *compatible with* or *entailed by* a context. This means, in the first case, that the proposition is true in some of the worlds in the context set, and in the second case that the proposition is true in all of the worlds in the context set. Intuitively, it means, in the first case, that it is at least an open question in the context whether or not the proposition is true, and in the second case, that the proposition is presupposed, or accepted, in the context.

Propositions, then, are ways of distinguishing among any set of possible worlds, while context sets are the sets of possible worlds among which a speaker means to distinguish when he expresses a proposition.

III

The semantic analysis of conditionals that I will summarize here is developed and defended more fully elsewhere.[8] The analysis was constructed primarily to account for counterfactual conditions—conditionals whose antecedents are assumed by the speaker to be false—but the analysis was intended to fit conditional sentences generally, without regard to the attitudes taken by the speaker to antecedent or consequent or his purpose in uttering them, and without regard to the grammatical mood in which the conditional is expressed.

The idea of the analysis is this: a conditional statement, *if A, then B*, is an assertion that the consequent is true, not necessarily in the world as it is, but in the world as it would be if the antecedent were true. To express this idea formally in a semantic rule for the conditional, we need a function which takes a proposition (the antecedent) and a possible world (the world as it is) into a possible world (the world as it would be if the antecedent were true). Intuitively, the *value* of the function should be that world in which the antecedent is true which is most similar, in relevant respects, to the actual world (the world which is one of the *arguments* of the function). In terms of such a function—call it "f"—the semantic rule for the conditional may be stated as follows: a conditional *if A, then B*, is true in a possible world i just in case B is true in possible world $f(A, i)$.[9]

---

[7] Elsewhere, I have called this set the *presupposition set*, but this terminology proved misleading since it suggested a set of presuppositions—propositions presupposed—rather than a set of possible worlds. The terminology adopted here was suggested by Lauri Karttunen.

[8] Stalnaker (1968) and Stalnaker and Thomason (1970). See also Lewis (1973). The formal differences between Lewis's theory and mine are irrelevant to the present issue.

[9] If A is the impossible proposition—the one true in *no* possible world—then there will be no possible world which can be the value of the function, $f(A, i)$, and so the function is left undefined for this case. To take care of this special case, the theory stipulates that all conditionals with impossible antecedents are true.

It may seem that little has been accomplished by this analysis, since it just exchanges the problem of analyzing the conditional for the problem of analyzing a semantic function which is equally problematic, if not more so. In one sense this is correct: the analysis is not intended as a reduction of the conditional to something more familiar or less problematic, and it should not satisfy one who comes to the problem of analyzing conditionals with the epistemological scruples of a Hume or a Goodman. The aim of the analysis is to give a perspicuous representation of the formal structure of conditionals—to give the *form* of their truth-conditions. Even if nothing substantive is said about how antecedents select counterfactual possible world, the analysis still has non-trivial, and in some cases surprising, consequences for the logic of conditionals.

But what more can be said about this selection function? If it is to be based on *similarity* in some respect or other, then it must have certain formal properties. It must be a function that determines a coherent ordering of the possible worlds that are selected. And, since whatever the respects of similarity are that are relevant, it will always be true that something is more similar to itself than to anything else, the selection function must be one that selects the actual world whenever possible, which means whenever the antecedent is true in the actual world. Can anything more substantive be said about the relevant respects of similarity on which the selection is based? Not, I think, in the *semantic* theory of conditionals. Relevant respects of similarity are determined by the context, and the semantics abstracts away from the context by taking it as an unexplained given. But we can, I think, say something in a pragmatic theory of conditional statements about how the context constrains the truth-conditions for conditionals, at least for indicative conditionals.

I cannot *define* the selection function in terms of the context set, but the following constraint imposed by the context on the selection function seems plausible: if the conditional is being evaluated at a world in the context set, then the world selected must, if possible, be within the context set as well (where C is the context set, if $i \in C$, then $f(A, i) \in C$). In other words, all worlds within the context set are closer to each other than any worlds outside it. The idea is that when a speaker says "If A," then everything he is presupposing to hold in the actual situation is presupposed to hold in the hypothetical situation in which A is true. Suppose it is an open question whether the butler did it or not, but it is established and accepted that whoever did it, he or she did it with an ice pick. Then it may be taken as accepted and established that if the butler did it, he did it with an ice pick.

The motivation for the principle is this: normally a speaker is concerned only with possible worlds within the context set, since this set is defined as the set of possible worlds among which the speaker wishes to distinguish.

So it is at least a normal expectation that the selection function should turn first to these worlds before considering *counterfactual* worlds—those presupposed to be non-actual. Conditional statements can be directly relevant to their primary uses—deliberation, contingency planning, making hedged predictions—only if they conform to this principle.

Nevertheless, this principle is only a defeasible presumption and not a universal generalization. For some special purposes a speaker may want to make use of a selection function which reaches outside of the context set, which is to say he may want to suspend temporarily some of the presuppositions made in that context. He may do so provided that he indicates in some way that his selection function is an exception to the presumption. Semantic determinants like domains and selection functions are a function of the speaker's intentions; that is why we must allow for exceptions to such pragmatic generalizations. But they are a function of the speaker's intention *to communicate* something, and that is why it is essential that it be conveyed to the audience that an exception is being made.

I take it that the subjunctive mood in English and some other languages is a conventional device for indicating that presuppositions are being suspended, which means in the case of subjunctive *conditional* statements, that the selection function is one that may reach outside of the context set. Given this conventional device, I would expect that the pragmatic principle stated above should hold without exception for indicative conditionals.

In what kinds of cases would a speaker want to use a selection function that might reach outside of the context set? The most obvious case would be one where the antecedent of the conditional statement was counterfactual, or incompatible with the presuppositions of the context. In that case one is forced to go outside the context set, since there are no possible worlds in it which are eligible to be selected. But there are non-counterfactual cases as well.[10] Consider the argument, "The murderer used an ice pick. But if the butler had done it, he wouldn't have used an ice pick. So the murderer must have been someone else."[11] The subjunctive conditional premise in this *modus tollens* argument cannot be counterfactual since if it were the speaker would be blatantly begging the question by presupposing, in giving his argument, that his conclusion was true. But that premise does not conform to the constraint on selection functions, since the consequent denies the first premise of the argument, which presumably is accepted when the second premise is given.

---

[10] I was slow to see this despite the existence of clear examples in the literature. Comments by John Watling in a discussion of an earlier version of this paper helped me to see the point.

[11] This is Watling's example.

Notice that if the argument is restated with the conditional premise in the indicative mood, it is anomalous.

My second example of a subjunctive non-counterfactual conditional which violates the constraint is adapted from an example given by Alan Anderson many years ago.[12] "If the butler had done it, we would have found just the clues which we in fact found." Here a conditional is presented as evidence for the truth of its antecedent. The conditional cannot be counterfactual, since it would be self-defeating to presuppose false what one is trying to show true. And it cannot conform to the constraint on selection functions since if it did, it would be trivially true, and so no evidence for the truth of the antecedent. Notice, again that when recast into the indicative mood, the conditional seems trivial, and does not look like evidence for anything.

The generalization that all indicative conditionals conform to the pragmatic constraint on selection functions has the following consequence about appropriateness conditions for indicative conditionals: *It is appropriate to make an indicative conditional statement or supposition only in a context which is compatible with the antecedent.* In effect, this says that *counterfactual* conditionals must be expressed in the subjunctive. This follows since indicative conditionals are those which must conform to the constraint, while counterfactuals are, by definition, those which cannot.

I need just one more assumption in order to show that the direct argument is a reasonable inference—an assumption about conditions of appropriateness for making assertions. The generalization that I will state is a quite specific one concerning disjunctive statements. I am sure it is derivable from more general conversational principles of the kind that Grice has discussed, but since I am not sure exactly what form such general principles should take, I will confine myself here to a generalization which has narrow application, but which can be clearly stated and easily defended. The generalization is this: *a disjunctive statement is appropriately made only in a context which allows either disjunct to be true without the other.* That is, one may say *A or B* only in a situation in which both *A and not-B* and *B and not-A* are open possibilities. The point is that each disjunct must be making some contribution to determining what is said. If the context did not satisfy this condition, then the assertion of the disjunction would be equivalent to the assertion of one of the disjuncts alone. So the disjunctive assertion would be pointless, hence misleading, and therefore inappropriate.[13]

---

[12] Anderson (1951).

[13] As with the pragmatic constraint on selection functions, there may be exceptions to this generalization. One exception is a statement of the form *A or B or both*. (I assume that the meaning of "or" is given by the truth table for inclusive disjunction.) But statements

IV

All of the ingredients of the solution to the puzzle are now assembled and ready to put together. It may seem that this is a rather elaborate apparatus for such a simple puzzle, but each of the elements—propositions and contexts, the semantic analysis of conditionals, the pragmatic constraint on conditionals, and the generalization about appropriateness—is independently motivated. It is not that this apparatus has been assembled just to solve the little puzzle; it is rather than the puzzle is being used to illustrate, in a small way, the explanatory capacity of the apparatus.

The argument we began with has the form *A or B, therefore, if not-A, then B*. This inference form is a reasonable inference form just in case every context in which a premise of that form could appropriately be asserted or explicitly supposed, and in which it is accepted, is a context which entails the proposition expressed by the corresponding conclusion. Now suppose the premise, *A or B*, is assertable and accepted. By the constraint on the appropriateness of disjunctive statements, it follows that the context is compatible with the conjunction of *not-A* with *B*. Hence the antecedent of the conditional conclusion, *not-A*, is compatible with the context. Now it follows from the pragmatic constraint on selection functions that if a proposition *P* is *compatible* with the context, and another proposition *Q* is *accepted* in it, or *entailed* by it, then the conditional, *if P, then Q*, is entailed by it as well. So, since *not-A* is compatible with the context, and the premise *A or B* is accepted, the conditional *if not-A, then A or B*, must be accepted as well. But this conditional proposition entails the conclusion of the argument, *if not-A, then B*. So the inference is a reasonable one.

Since the argument works the other way as well, it follows that the indicative conditional and the material conditional are equivalent in the following sense: in any context where either might appropriately be asserted, the one is accepted, or entailed by the context, if and only if the other is accepted, or entailed by the context. This equivalence explains the plausibility of the truth-functional analysis of indicative conditionals, but

which conflict with the principle must satisfy two conditions if they are to be appropriate. First, the statement must wear on its face that it is an exception so that it cannot be misleading. Second, there must be some explanation available of the purpose of violating the generalization, so that it will not be pointless. In the case of the statement *A or B or both*, it is clear from the logical relation between the last disjunct and the others that it must be an exception, so it satisfies the first condition. The explanation of the point of adding the redundant third disjunct is this: the disjunctive statement, *A or B*, requires that *A and not-B* and *B and not-A* be compatible with the context, but leaves open whether *A and B* is compatible with the context. The addition of the third disjunct, while adding nothing to the *assertive content* of the statement, does change the appropriateness conditions of the statement, and thus serves to indicate something about the context, or about the presuppositions of the speaker.

it does not justify that analysis since the two propositions coincide only in their assertion and acceptance conditions, and not in their truth-conditions. The difference between the truth-conditions of the two propositions will show itself if one looks at acts and attitudes other than assertion and acceptance. To take the simplest case, it may be reasonable to deny a conditional, even when not denying the corresponding material conditional. For example, I know *I* didn't do it, so I know that it is false that if the butler didn't do it, I did. But since I don't know whether the butler did it or not, I am in no position to deny the material conditional, which is equivalent to the disjunction, either the butler did it or I did. I may even think that that disjunction is very probably true.

There are two other familiar inference forms involving conditionals which are judged to be reasonable, although invalid, by this analysis: contraposition and the hypothetical syllogism. It was one of the surprising consequences of the *semantic* analysis sketched above that these inferences are, in general, invalid. Nevertheless, these consequences count in favor of the semantic analysis rather than against it since there are clear counterexamples to both inference forms. But all the counterexamples involve subjunctive conditionals which are counterfactual conditionals whose antecedents are presupposed to be false. Now we can explain why there are no purely indicative counterexamples, and also why the arguments have the appearance of validity which they have. Both argument forms can be shown to be reasonable inferences, given that all conditionals involved are indicative, and given the assumption that indicative conditionals always conform to the pragmatic constraint on selection functions.[14]

V

I want to conclude by looking at a notorious argument involving indicative conditionals. The argument for fatalism is, I will argue, unreasonable as well as invalid. But it gains its appearance of force from the fact that it is an artful sequence of steps, each one of which has the form of a reasonable or of a valid inference. The trick of the argument, according to the diagnosis I will give, is that it exploits the changing context in an illegitimate way. Subordinate conclusions, legitimately drawn within their own subordinate contexts, are illegitimately detached from those contexts and combined outside of them. To make clear what I mean, let me sketch the argument. The specific form it takes, and the example used to present it,

---

[14] Strictly, the inference to the contrapositive is reasonable only relative to the further assumption that the indicative *conclusion* is not inappropriate.

are taken from Michael Dummett's discussion of fatalism in his paper, "Bringing about the Past."[15] The setting of the example is wartime Britain during an air raid. I reason as follows: "Either I will be killed in this raid or I will not be killed. Suppose that I will. Then even if I take precautions I will be killed, so any precautions I take will be ineffective. But suppose I am not going to be killed. Then I won't be killed even if I neglect all precautions; so, on this assumption, no precautions are necessary to avoid being killed. Either way, any precautions I take will be either ineffective or unnecessary, and so pointless."

To give an abstract representation of the argument, I will let K mean "I will be killed," P mean "I take precautions," Q mean "precautions are ineffective," and R mean "precautions are unnecessary." The argument, reduced to essentials, is this:

1. K or not-K
2. | K
3. | If P, K
4. | Q
5. | not-K
6. | if not-P, not-K
7. | R
8. Q or R

Now I take it that the main problem posed by this argument is not to say what is wrong with it, but rather to explain its illusion of force. That is, it is not enough to say that step x is invalid and leave it at that, even if that claim is correct. One must explain why anyone should have thought that it was valid. Judged by this criterion, Dummett's analysis of the argument does not solve the problem, even though, I think, what he says about the argument is roughly correct. Dummett argues that any sense of the conditional which will validate the inference from 2 to 3 (and 5 to 6) must be too weak to validate the inference from 3 to 4 (and 6 to 7). Hence, however the conditional is analyzed, the argument as a whole cannot be valid. Dummett's argument to this conclusion is convincing, but it would be a full solution to the problem only if he supplemented it by showing that there *are* in our language distinct senses of the conditional that validate each of those steps. This I do not think he can do, since I do not think the force of the argument rests on an equivocation between two senses of the conditional.

According to the semantic and pragmatic analyses sketched above, there is *one* sense of the conditional according to which the inference from

[15] Dummett (1964).

2 to 3 is a *reasonable inference*,[16] and which is also strong enough to justify the inference from 3 to 4. The fallacy, according to the diagnosis, is thus in neither of the steps that Dummett questions. Both of the subarguments are good arguments in the sense that anyone who was in a position to accept the premise, while it remained an open question whether or not the antecedent of the conditional was true, would be in a position to accept the conclusion. That is, if I were in a position to accept that I were going to be killed even though I hadn't yet decided whether or not to take precautions, then I would surely be reasonable to conclude that taking precautions would be pointless. Likewise if I knew or had reason to accept that I would not be killed.

The problem with the argument is in the final step, an inference which seems to be an instance of an unproblematically valid form—constructive dilemma—which has nothing essential to do with conditionals. The argument form that justifies step 8 is this: *A or B*; *C* follows from *A*; *D* follows from *B*; therefore, *C or D*. It is correct that the conclusion follows *validly* from the premise provided that the subarguments are *valid*. But it is not correct that the conclusion is a *reasonable inference* from the premise, provided that the subarguments are *reasonable inferences*. In the fatalism argument, the subarguments are reasonable, but not valid, and this is why the argument fails. So it is a confusion of validity with reasonable inference on which the force of the argument rests.

VI

One final remark: my specific motivation for developing this account of indicative conditionals is of course to solve a puzzle, and to defend a particular semantic analysis of conditionals. But I have a broader motivation which is perhaps more important. That is to defend, by example, the claim that the concepts of pragmatics (the study of linguistic contexts) can be made as mathematically precise as any of the concepts of syntax and formal semantics; to show that one can recognize and incorporate into abstract theory the extreme context-dependence which is obviously present in natural language without any sacrifice of standards of rigor.[17] I am

---

[16] As with contraposition, the inference from 2 to 3 is reasonable only relative to the further assumption that the conclusion of the inference is appropriate, which means in this case, only relative to the assumption that *P*, the antecedent of the conditional, is compatible with the content. This assumption is obviously satisfied since the setting of the argument is a deliberation about whether or not to make *P* true.

[17] I recognize, of course, that the definitions and generalizations presented here are nothing like a rigorous formal theory. But some parts of the apparatus (in particular, the semantics for conditionals) have been more carefully developed elsewhere, and I believe it is a

anxious to put this claim across because it is my impression that semantic theorists have tended to ignore or abstract away from context-dependence at the cost of some distortion of the phenomena, and that this practice is motivated not by ignorance or misperception of the phenomenon of context-dependence, but rather by the belief that the phenomenon is not appropriately treated in a formal theory. I hope that the analysis of indicative conditionals that I have given, even if not correct in its details, will help to show that this belief is not true.

APPENDIX

Entailment and reasonable inference relate propositions and speech acts, respectively, but in both cases, given an appropriate language, one can define corresponding logical notions—notions of entailment and reasonable inference which relate formulas, or sentences independently of their specific interpretations.

Let **L** be a language which contains sentences. A *semantic interpretation* of the language will consist of a set of possible worlds and a function which assigns *propositions* (functions from possible worlds into truth-values) to the sentences, relative to *contexts*. The formal semantics for the language will define the class of legitimate interpretations by saying, in the usual way, how the interpretation of complex expressions relates to the interpretation of their parts. A *context* is an n-tuple, the first term of which is a *context set* (a set of possible worlds). The other terms are whatever else, if anything, is necessary to determine the propositions expressed by the sentences.

Notation: I will use P, P_1, P_2, etc. as meta-variables for sentences, ϕ, ϕ_1, ϕ_2, etc. as meta-variables for propositions (for convenience, I will identify a proposition with the set of possible worlds for which it takes the value true); k, k_1, k_2, etc. will be variables ranging over contexts. $S(k)$ will denote the context set of the context k. $\|P\|_k$ will denote the proposition expressed by P in context k under the interpretation in question. (Reference to the interpretation is suppressed in the notation.)

Entailment. One may define several notions of entailment. The basic notion is a language-independent relation between propositions: ϕ_1 entails ϕ_2 if and only if ϕ_2 includes ϕ_1. The *logical* concept of entailment, entailment-in-**L**, is a relation between *sentences* of **L**: P_1 entails P_2 if and only if for all interpretations and all contexts k, $\|P_1\|_k$ entails $\|P_2\|_k$. Logical entailment is entailment in virtue of the logical structure of the sentences. Similarly, the logical concept of reasonable inference will identify the inferences which are reasonable in virtue of the logical structure of the sentences.

---

relatively routine matter to state most of the definitions and generalizations which are new in precise model-theoretic terms. Just to show how it might go, I will give in an appendix a very abstract definition of a logical concept of reasonable inference.

Pragmatic interpretations. To define the logical notion of reasonable inference, we need to expand the concept of an interpretation. A *pragmatic interpretation* of **L** will consist of a semantic interpretation, an *appropriateness relation*, and a *change function.* The appropriateness relation A is a two place relation whose arguments are a sentence of **L** and a context. $A(P, k)$ says that the assertive utterance of P in context k is appropriate. The change function g is a two place function taking a sentence of **L** and a context into a context. Intuitively, $g(P, k)$ denotes the context that results from the assertive utterance of P in context k.

Since **L** is unspecified here, I leave these notions almost completely unconstrained, but it is easy to see how the generalizations about disjunctive and conditional statements would be stated as postulates which give some substance to these notions as applied to a language containing these kinds of statements. Just as the semantics for a specific language will include semantic rules specifying the elements of the context and placing constraints on the allowable semantic interpretations, so the pragmatic theory for a specific language will include rules constraining the two distinctively pragmatic elements of a pragmatic interpretation, as well as the relations among the elements of the context.

I will give here just two constraints which will apply to any language intended to model a practice of assertion.

1. $A(P, k)$ only if $\|P\|_k \cap S(k) \neq 0$.

One cannot appropriately assert a proposition in a context incompatible with it.

2. $S(g(P, k)) = S(k) \cap \|P\|_k$.

Any assertion changes the context by becoming an additional presupposition of subsequent conversation. (In a more careful formulation the second of these would be qualified, since assertions can be rejected or contradicted. But in the absence of rejection, I think it is reasonable to impose this constraint.)

Both the appropriateness relation and the change function can be generalized to apply to finite sequences of sentences in the following way: Let σ be a finite sequence of sentences of **L**, $P_1, P_2, \ldots P_n$. Let $k_1, k_2, \ldots k_n$ be a sequence of contexts defined in terms of σ and a context k as follows: $k_1 = k$; $k_{i+1} = g(k_i, P_i)$. Then $A(\sigma, k)$ if and only if, for all i from 1 to n, $A(P_i, k_i)$. $g(\sigma, k) =_{df} k_n$.

Reasonable inference. The inference from a sequence of sentences of **L**, σ, to a sentence of **L**, P is *reasonable-in-***L** if and only if for all interpretations and all contexts k such that $A(\sigma, k)$, $S(g(\sigma, k))$ entails $\|P\|_{g(\sigma, k)}$.

Note that there is no language-independent concept of reasonable inference analogous to the language-independent notion of entailment. The reason is that, while we have in the theory a notion of proposition that can be characterized independently of any language in which propositions are expressed, we have no corresponding non-linguistic concept of statement, or assertion. One could perhaps be defined, but it would not be a simple matter to do so, since the identity conditions for assertion types will be finer than those for propositions. The reason for this is that different sentences may have different appropriateness conditions even when they express the same proposition.

4

Assertion

Let me begin with some truisms about assertions. First, assertions have content; an act of assertion is, among other things, the expression of a proposition—something that represents the world as being a certain way. Second, assertions are made in a context—a situation that includes a speaker with certain beliefs and intentions, and some people with their own beliefs and intentions to whom the assertion is addressed. Third, sometimes the content of the assertion is dependent on the context in which it is made, for example, on who is speaking or when the act of assertion takes place. Fourth, acts of assertion affect, and are intended to affect, the context, in particular the attitudes of the participants in the situation; how the assertion affects the context will depend on its content.

My aim in this paper is to sketch some theoretical concepts with which to develop these truisms, and to show how these concepts can be used to explain some linguistic phenomena. I want to suggest how content and context might be represented in a theory of speech, and how the interaction of content and context to which the above-mentioned truisms point might be described. I will not propose an analysis of assertion, but I will make some modest claims about the way assertions act on the contexts in which they are made, and the way contexts constrain the interpretation of assertions. In conclusion, I will look briefly at an example of a phenomenon which I think these modest claims help to explain.

Three notions will play a central role in the theory I will sketch: the notion of a PROPOSITION, the notion of a PROPOSITIONAL CONCEPT, and the notion of SPEAKER PRESUPPOSITION. Each of these three notions will be defined or explained in terms of the notion of a POSSIBLE WORLD, or a possible state of the world, so one might think it important to begin with the question, what is a possible world? This is a good question, but I will not try to answer it here, and I am not sure that an abstract theory of speech

The development of the ideas in this paper was stimulated by David Kaplan's lectures, some years ago, on the logic of demonstratives. The influence of Paul Grice's ideas about logic and conversation will also be evident. I have benefited from discussions of earlier versions of this paper with both of these philosophers and many others, including David Lewis, Zeno Vendler and Edmund Gettier. I am indebted to the John Simon Guggenheim Memorial Foundation for research support.

should say very much in answer to it. In particular inquiries, deliberations, and conversations, alternative states of the subject matter in question are conceived in various different ways depending on the interests and attitudes of the participants in those activities. But one thing that is common to all such activities, and essential to them, is that the participants do seek to distinguish among alternative ways that things might be, or might have been. It may be that the best way to bring out the formal structure of such activities is to focus on what is done with a given relevant set of alternative states of the world, setting aside questions about the nature of the alternatives themselves. The decision to treat possible worlds, or possible situations, as PRIMITIVE elements in a theory of propositions and propositional attitudes does not require an ontological commitment to possible worlds as basic entities of the universe. Rather, it is a decision to theorize at a certain level of abstraction.[1]

The analysis of proposition in terms of possible worlds was first proposed in the context of intuitive semantics for modal logic.[2] The analysis is this: A proposition is a function from possible worlds into truth-values (true or false). More roughly and intuitively, a proposition is a rule for determining a truth-value as a function of the facts—of the way the world is. Or, a proposition is a way—any way—of picking out a set of possible states of affairs—all those for which the proposition takes the value true.

The intuitive motivation for this analysis is something like the following. A proposition—the content of an assertion or belief—is a representation of the world as being a certain way. But for any given representation of the world as being a certain way, there will be a set of all the possible states of the world which accord with the representation—which **are** that way. So any proposition determines a set of possible worlds. And, for any given set of possible worlds, to locate the actual world in that set is to represent the world as being a certain way. So every set of possible worlds determines a proposition. Furthermore, any two assertions or beliefs will represent the world as being the SAME way if and only if they are true in all the same possible worlds. If we assume, as seems reasonable, that representations which represent the world as being the same way have the same content (express the same proposition), then we can conclude that there is a one-one correspondence between sets of possible worlds and propositions. Given this correspondence, it seems reasonable to use sets of possible worlds, or (equivalently) functions from possible worlds into truth-values, to play the role of propositions in our theory. The analysis

---

[1] I argued in Stalnaker (1976a) that one can take possible worlds seriously without accepting an implausible metaphysics.

[2] The possible worlds analysis of propositions was suggested originally by Saul Kripke in the early 1960s.

defines propositions in terms of their essential function—to represent the world.[3]

Supposing for convenience of exposition that there is just a small finite number of possible states of the world, we might represent a proposition by enumerating the truth-values that it has in the different possible worlds, as in the following matrix:

$$A \qquad i \quad j \quad k$$

T	F	T

i, j and k are the possible worlds—the different possible sets of facts that determine the truth-value of the proposition.

But there is also a second way that the facts enter into the determination of the truth-value of what is expressed in an utterance: It is a matter of fact that an utterance has the content that it has. What one says—the proposition he expresses—is itself something that might have been different if the facts had been different; and if one is mistaken about the truth-value of an utterance, this is sometimes to be explained as a misunderstanding of what was said rather than as a mistake about the truth-value of what was actually said. The difference between the two ways that truth-values depend on facts is exploited in the familiar riddle, *If you call a horse's tail a leg how many legs does a horse have*? The answer, of course, is four, since calling a tail a leg does not make it one, but one can see a different way to take the question.

Let me give a simple example: I said *You are a fool* to O'Leary. O'Leary is a fool, so what I said was true, although O'Leary does not think so. Now Daniels, who is no fool and who knows it, was standing near by, and he thought I was talking to him. So both O'Leary and Daniels thought I said something false: O'Leary understood what I said, but disagrees with me about the facts; Daniels, on the other hand, agrees with me about the fact (he knows that O'Leary is a fool), but misunderstood what I said. Just to fill out the example, let me add that O'Leary believes falsely that Daniels is a fool. Now compare the possible worlds i, j and k. i is the world as it is, the world we are in; j is the world that O'Leary thinks we are in; and k is the world Daniels thinks we are in. If we ignore possible worlds other than i, j and k, we can use matrix A to represent the proposition I actually expressed. But the following TWO-DIMENSIONAL matrix also represents the second way that the truth-value of my utterance is a function of the facts:

---

[3] I recognize that I am skating quickly over large problems here. In particular, the identity conditions which the analysis assigns to propositions have some extremely paradoxical consequences (such as that there is only one necessary proposition) which seem to make the analysis particularly unsuited for an account of the objects of propositional attitudes. I discuss some of these problems, inconclusively, in Stalnaker (1976a).

B	i	j	k
i	T	F	T
j	T	F	T
k	F	T	F

The vertical axis represents possible worlds in their role as context—as what determines what is said. The horizontal axis represents possible worlds in their role as the arguments of the functions which are the propositions expressed. Thus the different horizontal lines represent WHAT IS SAID in the utterance in various different possible contexts. Notice that the horizontal line following i is the same as the one following j. This represents the fact that O'Leary and I agree about what was said. Notice also that the vertical column under i is the same as the one under k. This represents the fact that Daniels and I agree about the truth-values of both the proposition I in fact expressed and the one Daniels thought I expressed.

In a sense, I said something true at i and false at j and k, even though in none of these worlds did I express the proposition that is true in i and false in j and k. Although not expressed in any of the contexts, this proposition is represented in the matrix. I will call it the DIAGONAL PROPOSITION since it is the function from possible worlds into truth-values whose values are read along the diagonal of the matrix from upper left to lower right. In general, this is the proposition that is true at i for any i if and only if what is expressed in the utterance at i is true at i. I shall say more about diagonal propositions later.

I will call what a matrix like B represents a PROPOSITIONAL CONCEPT. A propositional concept is a function from possible worlds into propositions, or, equivalently, a function from an ordered pair of possible worlds into a truth-value. Each concrete utterance token can be associated with the propositional concept it determines, and, I will suggest below, some of the principles constraining the interpretation and evaluation of assertions are constraints on propositional concepts determined by assertive utterances rather than simply on the propositions expressed. This is my motivation for introducing propositional concepts, but one can study this kind of structure from an abstract point of view, independently of utterances or contexts of utterance. The abstract theory of what I am calling propositional concepts has received some attention from logicians recently under the name TWO-DIMENSIONAL MODAL LOGIC.[4] The theory focusses on the notion of a two-dimensional modal operator.

[4] The most general discussion of two-dimensional modal logic I know of is in Segerberg (1973). See also Aqvist (1973) and Kamp (1971). The earliest investigations of two-dimensional operators were, I believe, carried out in the context of tense logic by Frank Vlach and Hans Kamp at UCLA.

A two-dimensional modal operator is an operator which takes a propositional concept into a propositional concept. If o is such an operator, then the meaning of o will be a rule that gives you the propositional concept expressed by oP in terms of the one expressed by P, for any P. I will describe one such operator, and contrast it with more traditional extensional and intensional sentence operators.[5]

The dagger is an operator which takes the diagonal proposition and projects it onto the horizontal. If φ is the diagonal propositional determined by P, then $\dagger P$ expresses φ relative to all contexts. So if B is the propositional concept determined by my statement to O'Leary in the example above, the following matrix gives the propositional concept, $\dagger B$:

$\dagger B$	i	j	k
i	T	F	F
j	T	F	F
k	T	F	F

What $\dagger B$ says is roughly this: *What is said in S's utterance of* **You are a fool** *is true*, where the definite description, *What is said in S's utterance of* **You are a fool** may be a nonrigid designator—a description that refers to different propositions in different worlds. Notice that the dagger always yields a constant propositional concept as its value. That is, whatever the case with P, $\dagger P$ will always express the same proposition relative to every context. If P itself is already a constant propositional concept in this sense, then $\dagger P$ will express the same propositional concept as P.[6]

Compare this operator with a more familiar modal operator, propositional necessity. $\Box P$ expresses in any world the proposition that is true at that world if and only if the proposition expressed by P at that world is the necessary proposition—the one that is true in all possible worlds.

---

[5] The tense logic analogue of the dagger operator was, according to David Lewis, invented by Frank Vlach and is discussed in his UCLA PhD dissertation (Vlach 1973). The notation is Lewis's. See Lewis (1973: 63–4n).

[6] Another operator which has intuitive application is represented by Lewis as an upside-down dagger. What it does is to project the diagonal proposition onto the *vertical*, which, in effect, turns contingent truths into necessary truths and contingent falsehoods into necessary falsehoods. Hans Kamp (1971) proposed the temporal analogue of this operator as a representative of the sentence adverb *now*. *It is now true that A* said at time t expresses a proposition that is true at all times just in case A is true at t. The operator makes a difference when *now* is embedded in the context of other temporal modifiers. Using it, one can represent sentences like *Once, everyone now alive hadn't yet been born* without object language quantifiers over times. David Lewis and David Kaplan have suggested that this operator shows the semantic function of expressions like *actually* and *in fact*, as in *If I had more money than I in fact have, I would be happier*.

Propositional necessity is a one-dimensional operator in the following sense: The proposition expressed by □P at any point depends only on the proposition expressed by P at that point. To evaluate □P on any horizontal line, one need look only at the values of P on that line. This distinction between one- and two-dimensional operators parallels, on the next level up, the distinction between extensional and intensional operators. Compare the extensional negation operator: to evaluate ~P at any point, one need look only at the value of P at that point. Extensional operators take points (truth-values) into points; one-dimensional operators take horizontal lines (propositions) into horizontal lines; two-dimensional operators take the whole matrix (the propositional concept) into another whole matrix. Each kind of operator is a generalization of the kind preceding it.[7]

Let me mention one complex operator, square-dagger, which says that the diagonal proposition is necessary. This can be understood as the A PRIORI TRUTH operator, observing the distinction emphasized in the work of Saul Kripke between a priori and necessary truth. An a priori truth is a statement that, while perhaps not expressing a necessary proposition, expresses a truth in every context. This will be the case if and only if the diagonal proposition is necessary, which is what the complex operator says. I will illustrate this with a version of one of Kripke's own examples (1971: 273–5). Suppose that in worlds i, j and k, a certain object, a metal bar, is one, two and three meters long, respectively, at a certain time t. Now

---

[7] Although the dagger and the upside-down dagger are defined on propositional concepts, they can be generalized to any kind of two-dimensional intension. For example, they may be interpreted as operators on two-dimensional individual concepts, or on property concepts. Let a represent a definite description, say *the President of the United States*, and let i, j and k be three times, say 1967, 1971 and 1975. Matrix (i) below represents the two-dimensional intension of this definite description relative to these times. Matrix (ii) represents the rigid description, *the person who is in fact, or now, the President of the United States*. This is the two-dimensional intension of ↓a. David Kaplan (Kaplan 1989) discusses this operator on singular terms and compares it with Keith Donnellan's account of the referential use of definite descriptions.

(i)

	i	j	k
i	LJ	RN	GF
j	LJ	RN	GF
k	LJ	RN	GF

(ii)

	i	j	k
i	LJ	LJ	LJ
j	RN	RN	RN
k	GF	GF	GF

suppose an appropriate authority fixes the reference of the expression *one meter* by making the following statement in each of the worlds i, j and k: *This bar is one meter long*. Matrix C below represents the propositional concept for this statement. Matrix $\Box \dagger C$ represents the propositional concept for the claim that this statement is a priori true:

C	i	j	k
i	T	F	F
j	F	T	F
k	F	F	T

$\Box \dagger C$	i	j	k
i	T	T	T
j	T	T	T
k	T	T	T

The proposition expressed by the authority is one that might have been false, although he couldn't have expressed a false proposition in that utterance.

I have said how propositions are to be understood, and what propositional concepts are. The third notion I need is the concept of speaker presupposition. This, I want to suggest, is the central concept needed to characterize speech contexts. Roughly speaking, the presuppositions of a speaker are the propositions whose truth he takes for granted as part of the background of the conversation. A proposition is presupposed if the speaker is disposed to act as if he assumes or believes that the proposition is true, and as if he assumes or believes that his audience assumes or believes that it is true as well. Presuppositions are what is taken by the speaker to be the COMMON GROUND of the participants in the conversation, what is treated as their COMMON KNOWLEDGE or MUTUAL KNOWLEDGE.[8] The propositions presupposed in the intended sense need not really be common or mutual knowledge; the speaker need not even believe them. He may presuppose any proposition that he finds it convenient to assume for the purpose of the conversation, provided he is prepared to assume that his audience will assume it along with him.

It is PROPOSITIONS that are presupposed—functions from possible worlds into truth-values. But the more fundamental way of representing the speaker's presuppositions is not as a set of propositions, but rather as a set of possible worlds, the possible worlds compatible with what is presupposed. This set, which I will call the CONTEXT SET, is the set of possible

---

[8] I have discussed this concept of presupposition in two earlier papers, Stalnaker (1977) and "Pragmatic Presuppositions," reprinted in Ch. 2 of the present volume. Stephen Schiffer (Schiffer 1972: 30–42) and David Lewis (Lewis 1969: 52–60) have discussed concepts of mutual knowledge and common knowledge which resemble the notion of presupposition I have in mind. Paul Grice spoke, in the William James Lectures, of propositions having *common ground status* in a conversation (Grice 1989).

worlds recognized by the speaker to be the "live options" relevant to the conversation. A proposition is presupposed if and only if it is true in all of these possible worlds. The motivation for representing the speaker's presuppositions in terms of a set of possible worlds in this way is that this representation is appropriate to a description of the conversational process in terms of its essential purposes. To engage in conversation is, essentially, to distinguish among alternative possible ways that things may be. The purpose of expressing propositions is to make such distinctions. The presuppositions define the limits of the set of alternative possibilities among which speakers intend their expressions of propositions to distinguish.

Each participant in a conversation has his own context set, but it is part of the concept of presupposition that a speaker assumes that the members of his audience presuppose everything that he presupposes. We may define a NONDEFECTIVE CONTEXT as one in which the presuppositions of the various participants in the conversation are all the same. A DEFECTIVE CONTEXT will have a kind of instability, and will tend to adjust to the equilibrium position of a nondefective context. Because hearers will interpret the purposes and content of what is said in terms of their own presuppositions, any unnoticed discrepancies between the presuppositions of speaker and addressees is likely to lead to a failure of communication. Since communication is the point of the enterprise, everyone will have a motive to try to keep the presuppositions the same. And because in the course of a conversation many clues are dropped about what is presupposed, participants will normally be able to tell that divergences exist if they do. So it is not unreasonable, I think, to assume that in the normal case contexts are nondefective, or at least close enough to being nondefective.

A context is CLOSE ENOUGH to being nondefective if the divergences do not affect the issues that actually arise in the course of the conversation. Suppose for example that you know that Jones won the election, believe mistakenly that I know it as well, and are prepared to take the truth of this proposition for granted if the occasion should arise, say by using it as a suppressed premise in an argument, or by using the description *the man who won the election* to refer to Jones. On my dispositional account of speaker presupposition, if you are prepared to use the proposition in this way, then you DO presuppose that Jones won the election, even if you never have the opportunity to display this disposition because the subject does not come up. Since I do not know that Jones won the election, I do NOT presuppose it, and so the context is defective. But the defect may be harmless.

It will not necessarily be harmless: If the news is of sufficiently urgent interest, your failure to raise the subject may count as a display of your disposition to take its truth for granted. There will not be exactly a failure of

communication, but there will be a misperception of the situation if I
infer from the fact that you do not tell me who won that you do not know
either.

A conversation is a process taking place in an ever-changing context.
Think of a state of a context at any given moment as defined by the presuppositions of the participants as represented by their context sets. In the
normal, nondefective case, the context sets will all be the same, so for this
case we can talk of the context set of the conversation. Now how does an
assertion change the context? There are two ways, the second of which, I
will suggest, should be an essential component of the analysis of assertion.
I will mention the first just to set it apart from the second: The fact that a
speaker is speaking, saying the words he is saying in the way he is saying
them, is a fact that is usually accessible to everyone present. Such observed
facts can be expected to change the presumed common background knowledge of the speaker and his audience in the same way that any obviously
observable change in the physical surroundings of the conversation will
change the presumed common knowledge. If a goat walked into the room,
it would normally be presupposed, from that point, that there was a goat
in the room. And the fact that this was presupposed might be exploited in
the conversation, as when someone asks, *How did that thing get in here?*,
assuming that others will know what he is talking about. In the same way,
when I speak, I presuppose that others know I am speaking, even if I do
not assume that anyone knew I was going to speak before I did. This fact,
too, can be exploited in the conversation, as when Daniels says *I am bald*,
taking it for granted that his audience can figure out who is being said to
be bald.

I mention this commonplace way that assertions change the context in
order to make clear that the context on which an assertion has its ESSEN-
TIAL effect is not defined by what is presupposed before the speaker begins
to speak, but will include any information which the speaker assumes his
audience can infer from the performance of the speech act.

Once the context is adjusted to accommodate the information that the
particular utterance was produced, how does the CONTENT of an assertion
alter the context? My suggestion is a very simple one: To make an assertion is to reduce the context set in a particular way, provided that there are
no objections from the other participants in the conversation. The particular way in which the context set is reduced is that all of the possible situations incompatible with what is said are eliminated. To put it a slightly
different way, the essential effect of an assertion is to change the presuppositions of the participants in the conversation by adding the content of
what is asserted to what is presupposed. This effect is avoided only if the
assertion is rejected.

I should emphasize that I do not propose this as a DEFINITION of assertion, but only as a claim about one effect which assertions have, and are
intended to have—an effect that should be a component, or a consequence, of an adequate definition. There are several reasons why one cannot define assertion in terms of this effect alone. One reason is that other
speech acts, like making suppositions, have and are intended to have the
same effect. A second reason is that there may be various indirect, even
nonlinguistic, means of accomplishing the same effect which I would not
want to call assertions. A third reason is that the proposed essential effect
makes reference to another speech act—the rejection of an assertion,[9]
which presumably cannot be explained independently of assertion.

Our proposed effect is clearly not a sufficient condition for assertion. Is
it even a necessary condition? It might be objected that a person who
makes an assertion does not necessarily intend to get his audience to
accept that what he asserts is true. The objector might argue as follows:
Take one of your own examples, your statement to O'Leary that he is a
fool. You knew in advance that O'Leary would not accept the assertion,
so according to your account, you knew in advance that your assertion
would fail to achieve its essential effect. That example should be anomalous if your account were correct, but it is not anomalous. Would it not
be more plausible to characterize assertion as trying to get the audience to
accept THAT THE SPEAKER ACCEPTS the content of the assertion?[10] But this
Gricean twist is not required. My suggestion about the essential effect of
assertion does not imply that speakers INTEND to succeed in getting the
addressee to accept the content of the assertion, or that they believe they
will, or even might succeed. A person may make an assertion knowing it
will be rejected just as Congress may pass a law knowing it will be vetoed,
a labor negotiator may make a proposal knowing it will be met by a
counterproposal, or a poker player may place a bet knowing it will cause
all the other players to fold. Such actions need not be pointless, since they
all have secondary effects, and there is no reason why achieving the
secondary effects cannot be the primary intention of the agent performing
the action. The essential effects will still be relevant even when it is a fore-
gone conclusion that the assertion, legislative act, proposal, or bet will be
rejected, since one generally explains why the action has the secondary
effects it has partly in terms of the fact that it would have had certain
essential effects had it not been rejected.

[9] It should be made clear that to reject an assertion is not to assert or assent to the contradictory of the assertion, but only to refuse to accept the assertion. If an assertion is
rejected, the context remains the same as it was. (More exactly, rejection of an assertion
blocks the *second* kind of effect that assertions have on the context. The first kind of effect
cannot be blocked or withdrawn.)

[10] David Kaplan, in discussion, raised this objection.

One may think of a nondefective conversation as a game where the common context set is the playing field and the moves are either attempts to reduce the size of the set in certain ways or rejections of such moves by others. The participants have a common interest in reducing the size of the set, but their interests may diverge when it comes to the question of how it should be reduced. The overall point of the game will of course depend on what kind of conversation it is—for example, whether it is an exchange of information, an argument, or a briefing.

The game could be expanded by introducing other kinds of moves like making stipulations, temporary assumptions, or promises, asking questions, and giving commands and permissions.[11] Each of these kinds of linguistic action is presumably performed against a background of presuppositions, and can be understood partly in terms of the effect that it has, or is intended to have, on the presuppositions, and on the subsequent behavior, of the other participants in the conversation.

This is a very abstract, and a very simple, sketch of what goes on when someone says something to someone else. But there is enough in it to motivate some principles that are useful for explaining regularities of linguistic usage. I will mention three such rules which illustrate the interaction of context and content. Given the framework of propositions, presupposition, and assertion, the principles are all pretty obvious, which is as it should be. They are not intended as empirical generalizations about how particular languages or idiosyncratic social practices work. Rather, they are proposed as principles that can be defended as essential conditions of rational communication, as principles to which any rational agent would conform if he were engaged in a practice that fits the kind of very abstract and schematic sketch of communication that I have given.[12]

I will list the three principles and then discuss them in turn.

1. A proposition asserted is always true in some but not all of the possible worlds in the context set.

2. Any assertive utterance should express a proposition, relative to each possible world in the context set, and that proposition should have a truth-value in each possible world in the context set.

3. The same proposition is expressed relative to each possible world in the context set.

The first principle says that a speaker should not assert what he presupposes to be true, or what he presupposes to be false. Given the meaning of

---

[11] David Lewis (1979b) outlined a language game of commanding and permitting which would fit into this framework.

[12] The influence of Grice's theory of conversation should be clear from my discussion of the application of these principles.

presupposition and the essential effect ascribed to the act of assertion, this should be clear. To assert something incompatible with what is presupposed is self-defeating; one wants to reduce the context set, but not to eliminate it altogether. And to assert something which is already presupposed is to attempt to do something that is already done.

This rule, like the others, can be applied in several ways. If one could fix independently what was presupposed and what was said on a given occasion, then one could use the rule to evaluate the speaker's action. If he failed to conform the rule, then he did something that, from the point of view of the conversation, was unreasonable, inefficient, disorderly, or uncooperative. But one can also use the rule, or the presumption that the speaker is conforming to the rule, as evidence of what was presupposed, or of what was said. Perhaps as more than just evidence. The rules may be taken to define partially what is presupposed and what is said in a context by constraining the relation between them. So, if a speaker says something that admits of two interpretations, one compatible with the context set and one not, then the context, through the principle, disambiguates. If the speaker says something that seems prima facie to be trivial, one may take it as a clue that the speaker's context set is larger than was realized—that the context was defective—or one may look for another interpretation of what he said. There are thus three ways to react to an apparent violation of the rule: First, one may conclude that the context is not as it seems. Second, one may conclude that the speaker didn't say (or didn't mean) what he seemed to say (or to mean). Third, one may conclude that the rule was indeed violated. Since there is usually a lot of flexibility in both the context and the interpretation of what is said, the third reaction will be an unusual one, although it will not be unusual to use the rule to explain why some utterance would have been deviant if it had occurred in a given context.

The second principle concerns truth-value gaps, and connects semantic presupposition with pragmatic speaker presupposition. The principle implies that if a sentence x semantically presupposes a proposition φ (in the sense that x expresses a truth or a falsehood only if φ is true), then φ is presupposed by the speaker in the sense of presupposition discussed above.

There are two different ways that a truth-value gap may arise: a sentence may fail to express a proposition at all in some possible situation, or it may succeed in expressing a proposition, but express one that is a PARTIAL function—one that is undefined for certain possible worlds. Both kinds of truth-value gap are excluded from the context set by this rule.

The rationale for this rule is as follows: The point of an assertion is to reduce the context set in a certain determinate way. But if the proposition is not true or false at some possible world, then it would be unclear

whether that possible world is to be included in the reduced set or not. So
the intentions of the speaker will be unclear.

Again this principle can be used in any of the three ways: to interpret
what is said, as a clue to what is presupposed, or as a basis for evaluating
the action of a speaker.

The third principle, which says that an utterance must express the SAME
proposition relative to each possible world in the context set, is closely
related in its motivation to a fundamental assumption of the logical atom-
ists and the logical empiricist tradition. In Wittgenstein's terminology
the assumption is this: Whether a proposition (read: sentence) has sense
cannot depend on whether another proposition is true (cf. *Tractatus*,
Proposition 2.0211). Meaning and truth must be sharply divided, according to this tradition, in order that one be able to use language to communicate in a determinate way. One must be able to tell what a statement says
independently of any facts that might be relevant to determining its truth.
Now it has always been clear that this kind of principle requires qualification, since it is a matter of fact that words mean what they mean. And the
phenomena of context-dependence are evidence of other ways in which
what is said is a function of what is true. The framework of presupposition
and assertion at once provides a natural way to qualify this traditional
assumption so as to make it compatible with the phenomena, and a clear
explanation of why it must hold in the qualified version. To see why the
principle must hold, look at the matrix for the propositional concept D.
Suppose the context set consists of i, j and k, and the speaker's utterance
determines D. What would he be asking his audience to do? Something

D	i	j	k
i	T	T	T
j	F	F	T
k	F	T	T

like this: If we are in the world i, leave the context set the same; if we are in
world j, throw out worlds i and j, and if we are in world k, throw out just
world i. But of course the audience does not know which of those worlds
we are in, and if it did the assertion would be pointless. So the statement,
made in that context, expresses an intention that is essentially ambiguous.
Notice that the problem is not that the speaker's utterance has failed to
determine a unique proposition. Assuming that one of the worlds i, j or k
is in fact the actual world, then that world will fix the proposition unambiguously. The problem is that since it is unknown which proposition it is

that is expressed, the expression of it cannot do the job that it is supposed to do.[13]

As with the other principles, one may respond to apparent violations in different ways. One could take an apparent violation as evidence that the speaker's context set was smaller than it was thought to be, and eliminate possible worlds relative to which the utterance receives a divergent interpretation. Or, one could reinterpret the utterance so that it expresses the same proposition in each possible world. Consider an example: hearing a woman talking in the next room, I tell you, *That is either Zsa Zsa Gabor or Elizabeth Anscombe.* Assuming that both demonstrative pronouns and proper names are rigid designators—terms that refer to the same individual in all possible worlds—this sentence comes out expressing either a necessary truth or a necessary falsehood, depending on whether it is one of the two mentioned women or someone else who is in the next room. Let i be the world in which it is Miss Gabor, j the world in which it is Professor Anscombe, and k a world in which it is someone else, say Tricia Nixon Cox. Now if we try to bring the initial context set into conformity with the third principle by shrinking it, say by throwing out world k, we will bring it into conflict with the first principle by making the assertion trivial. But if we look at what is actually going on in the example, if we ask what possible states of affairs the speaker would be trying to exclude from the context set if he made that statement, we can work backward to the proposition expressed. A moment's reflection shows that what the speaker is saying is that the actual world is either i or j, and not k. What he means to communicate is that the diagonal proposition of the matrix E exhibited below, the proposition expressed by $\dagger E$, is true.

E	i	j	k
i	T	T	T
j	T	T	T
k	F	F	F

$\dagger E$	i	j	k
i	T	T	F
j	T	T	F
k	T	T	F

---

[13] Clarification is needed to resolve an ambiguity. The third principle says that the proposition expressed in any possible world in the context set must coincide *within the context set* with the proposition expressed in any other possible world in the context set. So, for example, if the context set is $\{i, j\}$, then an utterance determining the propositional concept represented below will not violate the principle. Even though the proposition expressed in i diverges from the proposition expressed in j, the divergence is outside the context set. David Lewis pointed out the need for this clarification.

	i	j	k
i	T	F	T
j	T	F	F
k	F	T	T

I suggest that a common way of bringing utterances into conformity with the third principle is to interpret them to express the diagonal proposition, or to perform on them the operation represented by the two-dimensional operator DAGGER. There are lots of examples. Consider: *Hesperus is identical with Phosphorus, it is now three o'clock, an ophthalmologist is an eye doctor*. In each case, to construct a context which conforms to the first principle, a context in which the proposition expressed is neither trivial nor assumed false, one must include possible worlds in which the sentence, interpreted in the standard way, expresses different propositions. But in any plausible context in which one of these sentences might reasonably be used, it is clear that the diagonal proposition is the one that the speaker means to communicate. The two-dimensional operator DAGGER may represent a common operation used to interpret, or reinterpret, assertions and other speech acts so as to bring them into conformity with the third principle constraining acts of assertion.

To conclude, let me show how this last suggestion can help to explain a puzzle concerning singular negative existential statements. The puzzle arises in the context of a causal or historical explanation theory of reference according to which proper names refer to their bearers, not in virtue of the fact that the bearer has certain properties expressed in the sense of the name, but rather in virtue of certain causal or historical connections between the referent and the speaker's use of the name.[14] According to this theory, the PROPOSITION expressed by a simple singular statement containing a proper name, like *O'Leary is a fool*, is the one that is true if and only if the individual who is in fact causally connected in the right way with the speaker's use of the name has the property expressed in the predicate. So the proposition is determined as a function of the individual named rather than as a function of the name, or the sense of the name.

What does this theory say about statements like *O'Leary does not exist*? If the statement is true (which this one happens to be), then there is no individual appropriately related to the speaker's use of the name, and thus no proposition determined as a function of such an individual. So at least for TRUE negative existential statements, it seems that proper names must play a different role in the determination of the proposition expressed from the role they play in ordinary predicative statements.

Perhaps a negative existential statement says, simply, that there is no individual standing in the right causal relation to the speaker's use of the

---

[14] The causal account of reference is defended, in general in Kripke (1972) and Donnellan (1971). Donnellan (1974) discusses the problem of singular negative existential statements in the context of this account of reference.

name.[15] This does seem to get the truth-conditions right for negative existential ASSERTIONS, but it clearly gets them wrong for some other kinds of singular negative existential constructions. Consider, for example, counterfactual suppositions, as in the antecedent of the conditional *If Aristotle hadn't existed, the history of philosophy would have been very different from the way it was.*[16] Clearly the proposition expressed in the antecedent of this conditional is not the proposition that our use of the name *Aristotle* is not appropriately connected with any individual. THAT proposition is compatible with Aristotle's existence. Furthermore, if Aristotle hadn't existed, then our uses of his name probably would not have existed either. The proper name seems to function in the antecedent of the counterfactual more like the way it functions in ordinary predicative statements: The proposition is determined as a function of the PERSON Aristotle; it is true in possible worlds where HE does not exist, and false in possible worlds where HE does exist.

So it seems that not only do proper names act differently in negative existential assertions than they do in singular predicative assertions, they also act differently in negative existential ASSERTIONS than they do in negative existential SUPPOSITIONS. What one asserts when he says *Aristotle does not exist* seems to be different from what one supposes when he says *Suppose Aristotle hadn't existed.*

Let us see how the pragmatic principle can account for these facts. Begin with the most straightforward semantic account of negative existential constructions: *Aristotle does not exist*, like *Aristotle was wise*, is a proposition about Aristotle. It is false in possible worlds whose domains contain the person WE call Aristotle and true in possible worlds whose domains do not contain that person. What if the name does not, in fact, refer? Suppose for example the statement is *Sherlock Holmes does not exist*. Then the proposition will be necessarily true, by the same rule, since the domain of no possible world contains the actual person WE call Sherlock Holmes.[17] Now let us use this straightforward semantic account to construct a propositional concept for an utterance of *Sherlock Holmes does not exist*. Let the world *i* be the actual world. Let *j* be a world in which a famous

[15] Donnellan's explanation of the *truth-conditions* for singular negative existential statements is roughly in accord with this suggestion, but he cautions that the rule he proposes "does not provide an *analysis* of such statements; it does not tell us what such statements mean, or what propositions they express. This means that in this case we are divorcing truth-conditions from meaning" (Donnellan 1974: 25). According to Donnellan, "no obvious way of representing propositions expressed by existential statements suggests itself" (ibid. 30).

[16] Kripke, in talks on this subject, has made this point about counterfactuals with negative existential antecedents.

[17] I believe this straightforward semantic account is the one that Kripke has defended in the talks mentioned in note 16.

detective named *Sherlock Holmes* lived in nineteenth-century London, and Sir Arthur Conan Doyle wrote a series of historical accounts of his cases.. Let world k be a possible world in which Sir Arthur Conan Doyle was a famous detective named *Sherlock Holmes* who wrote a series of autobiographical accounts of his own cases under the pseudonym *Sir Arthur Conan Doyle*. These stipulations determine the following two-dimensional matrix for the utterance:

G	i	j	k
i	T	T	T
j	T	F	T
k	F	F	F

Now suppose i, j and k are a context set (say a person has heard these three rumors about the origin of the Sherlock Holmes stories and does not know which is true). As the matrix shows, the utterance violates the third principle, and so a reinterpretation is forced on it. Diagonalization, or the dagger operation, brings the utterance into line with the principle, and yields the intuitively right result:

	i	j	k
i	T	F	F
j	T	F	F
k	T	F	F

But now contrast the case of the counterfactual. To interpret the statement *If Aristotle hadn't existed, the history of philosophy would have been very different from the way it was,* we do not need to diagonalize, since in any possible context appropriate to THAT statement, it will be presupposed that Aristotle does exist. So the proposition supposed is the one obtained by the straightforward rule.[18] Again, this is intuitively the right result.

We have not escaped the conclusion that the content of the assertion *Aristotle did not exist* is different from the content of the supposition *suppose Aristotle hadn't existed*. But we have explained that consequence using a single SEMANTIC account of singular negative existential construc-

---

[18] It is interesting to note that if the conditional were in the indicative mood, the result would have been different. This is because an indicative conditional is appropriate only in a context where it is an open question whether the antecedent is true. So to say *If Aristotle didn't exist* is to suppose just what is asserted when one asserts *Aristotle didn't exist*.

tions—the account which is most natural, given the causal theory of names—together with independently motivated pragmatic principles.

The general strategy which this explanation illustrates is to use pragmatic theory—theory of conversational contexts—to take some of the weight off semantic and syntactic theory. Some other problems where I think this strategy and this theory will prove useful are the explanation of presupposition phenomena,[19] the explanation of the differences between subjunctive and indicative conditionals,[20] the analysis of definite descriptions, and the behaviour of deictic and anaphoric pronouns. My hope is that by recognizing the interaction of some relatively simple contextual factors with the rules for interpreting and evaluating utterances, one can defend simpler semantic and grammatical analyses and give more natural explanations of many linguistic phenomena.

[19] This is discussed in Stalnaker (1977).
[20] This is discussed in "Indicative Conditionals", reprinted in Ch. 3 of the present volume.

5

On the Representation of Context

I. Introduction

It has for a long time been widely recognized that no satisfactory semantic theory—theory of the relation between linguistic expressions and what
they express—can ignore the role of the contexts in which expressions are
used and interpreted. Discourse is a dynamic interactive process in which
speech acts affect the situations in which they take place, and in which the
situation affects the way the speech acts are understood. More than forty
years ago philosophers from the British ordinary language tradition—
most influentially John Austin, Peter Strawson and Paul Grice—criticized
traditional semantic accounts that ignored the context of the use of language and the fact that speech was a kind of action. More recently, a lot
of high-powered formal machinery has been developed and deployed by
linguists and logicians for the study of contexts and the discourses that
take place in them—machinery that draws both on the ideas of the anti-
formalist Grice–Austin tradition and on the resources of the kind of formal semantics that those philosophers were reacting to. There is situation
semantics (Barwise and Perry, 1983), discourse representation theory and
file change semantics (Kamp and Reyle, 1993; Heim, 1982), update
semantics, dynamic predicate logic, dynamic Montague grammar
(Groenendijk and Stokhof, 1990, 1991), among others. Different frame-
works use different devices and apparatus, and use the apparatus in different ways to explain the phenomena. In some cases, such as discourse
representation theory, the theory is presented as a semantics for English,
or at least for some fragment of English, which provides an algorithm
matching sequences of sentences with structures that interpret them.
Dynamic predicate logic, on the other hand, is only indirectly relevant to
any natural language. It defines an artificial language with new kinds of
dynamic variable binding operations, obviously different from anything in

This paper grew out of material prepared for a seminar at MIT given jointly with Irene
Heim. I owe much to discussion with her, and to her writings. I would also like to thank
Kai von Fintel, Jason Stanley, Zoltan Szabo and several anonymous readers who com-
mented on an earlier version of this paper.

natural language, but presumably intended to model, approximately, some of the devices used in natural language. But all these theories are responding to some common themes, and are motivated by the same basic ideas. I think it will help to put the theories and the phenomena they are concerned with in perspective to look back at some of the basic ideas, and to try to describe the structure of discourse in a way that abstracts away from the details about the mechanisms and devices that particular languages may provide for doing what is done in a discourse. It helps, I think, to get clear about what language is for—what it is supposed to do—before explaining how it does it.

So my intention in this discussion of the representation of context is to talk about what discourses are and what goes on in them, while saying as little as possible about the grammatical apparatus that participants in them use. I want to emphasize that it is not my purpose to criticize any of the dynamic semantic theories, or to propose alternative ways of doing what they do. My concern is with the foundations. What I will do is to sketch some descriptive apparatus that helps to display some of the ways that context and content interact. The apparatus is schematic and idealized, and is to some extent familiar (see Stalnaker, 1978, 1988), but I think it is useful to keep looking back at some of the simple truisms that underlie the sophisticated semantic and pragmatic theories that have been developed.

In Section II, I will review the motivating ideas for the descriptive apparatus that I want to recommend, and give the outlines of the apparatus itself, the central notion of which is the concept of speaker presupposition. Then in the remainder of the paper, I will try to illustrate some ways in which the application of the apparatus might help to clarify and explain some phenomena about discourse. In Section III, I will discuss the phenomenon of accommodation, arguing that the phenomenon can be explained in terms of the structure of speaker presupposition, without invoking any special rules or mechanisms of accommodation. In Section IV, I will respond to an argument given by Hans Kamp that the kind of representation of context I am recommending is not rich enough to allow for an explanation of certain linguistic phenomena. Finally, in Section V, I will consider how the framework might help to clarify some issues concerning pronouns with indefinite antecedents.

II. What Is a Discourse Context?

I will start with two simple ideas that motivate the kind of representation of context that I will sketch. First, speech is action, and speech acts should be understood in terms of the way they are intended to affect the situation in which they are performed. Second, speech acts are context-dependent: their contents (and so the way they are intended to affect the situation) depend not only on the syntactic and semantic properties of the types of expressions used, but also on facts about the situation in which the expressions are used. These two simple observations point to two different roles that context plays: it is both the object on which speech acts act and the source of the information relative to which speech acts are interpreted. To explain the interaction of the two roles, we need a single conception of context that will represent the information about the situation that is relevant both to the role of context in determining content and to explaining how the content determined then acts on the situation. The point of a discourse—at least one central kind of discourse—is the exchange of information. Participants in a conversation begin with certain information in common, or presumed to be in common, and it is that body of information that the speech acts they perform are designed to influence. The content of an assertion will be a piece of information, and if the assertion is successful, then that information will become part of the body of information that provides the context for the subsequent discourse.

So both of the roles that contexts play require that they include a body of information: context-dependence means dependence on certain facts, but the facts must be available, or presumed to be available, to the participants in the conversation. So I propose to identify a context (at a particular point in a discourse) with the body of information that is presumed, at that point, to be common to the participants in the discourse.

Some of the common information that defines a context will be information about what the participants in the conversation are talking about: if the subject matter is the current American political scene, then speakers will take lots of familiar facts about that scene for granted (for example, that Bill Clinton is the President, and that he is running for reelection), assuming that everyone already knows them, and already knows that everyone already knows them. But the information presumed to be common will also include facts about the discourse that is currently taking place, since when one is engaged in a conversation, one can normally take for granted that speakers and hearers are aware that the conversation is taking place, that speakers are saying what they are saying in the way they are saying it. And one can take for granted that everyone is taking these things for granted. The interaction of the information of these two different kinds is a theme of much of the current work in discourse semantics and pragmatics, and it will be the central focus of my discussion here.

We can represent the information that defines the context in which a speech act takes place with a set of possible situations or possible worlds—

the situations that are compatible with the information. This set, which I have called the *context set* (Stalnaker, 1974) will include all the situations among which the speakers intend to distinguish with their speech acts. The presumed common information—what is presupposed in the context—is what all these possible worlds have in common. An assertion can then be understood as a proposal to alter the context by adding the information that is the content of the assertion to the body of information that defines the context, or equivalently, by eliminating from the context set—the set of possible worlds available for speakers to distinguish between—those possible worlds in which the proposition expressed in the assertion is false. The world, as Wittgenstein said, is all that is the case, and a possible world is all that would be the case if that world were actual. Every proposition, relevant or not, that is taken for granted by the participants in a conversation will be true in all of the possible worlds that define the context. Since speakers in the actual world take for granted when they are talking that they are talking, they will be talking not only in the actual world, but also in each of the possible worlds that define their context.[1] Within each possible world in the context set, a discourse is taking place, and it has a context represented by its own context set. If, when talking about American politics, I take for granted that Bill Clinton is the President, then it will be true in each possible world in the relevant context, not only that Bill Clinton is the President, but also that I am, in that world, taking for granted that he is. Facts about what is presupposed in a context are not only facts about the actual world in which the discourse is taking place (which may or may not be a member of the context set), but also facts about the worlds that define the context. There is no problematic circularity here, but just the familiar relational structure that one finds in modal semantics, and semantics for knowledge and belief operators. The structure of speaker presupposition can be represented by a Kripke semantics in which the accessibility relation is *serial, transitive*, and *Euclidean*,[2] but not necessarily *reflexive*. The requirement that the relation

---

[1] As Zoltan Szabo has pointed out to me, just what a speaker, or a writer, presupposes about the situation in which she is speaking or writing, will vary from case to case. While in an ordinary face-to-face conversation, the speaker will presuppose that her addressee hears her as she speaks, and knows the time of utterance, this won't be true for answering machine messages. To interpret a particular token of an answering machine message like "I can't come to the phone now," one needs a context in which the addressee, but not the speaker, is presumed to know the facts necessary to determine the content of the message.

[2] A binary relation R is serial if:

$(x) (\exists y) (Rxy);$

and it is Euclidean if:

$(x) (y) (z) ((Rxy \wedge Rxz) \rightarrow Ryz).$

be transitive and Euclidean reflects the assumption that speaker presupposition is transparent: speakers know what they are presupposing, so they presuppose that they are presupposing that P if they are, and that they are not if they are not. The requirement that the relation is serial is simply the assumption that the context set is always nonempty—there is always at least one possibility compatible with what is being presupposed.

The nonreflexivity of the relation reflects the important fact that the actual world in which a discourse takes place need not be compatible with the context of that discourse, which is just to say that some things presupposed by a speaker may be in fact false. This may happen for a number of different reasons. A speaker might be presupposing something false simply because he has a false belief, either about the subject matter of the discourse, or about the discourse itself. He might presuppose something false in order to deceive, or because of some mutually recognized pretense. Sometimes the most effective way to communicate something true is to presuppose something false. For example, if you are presupposing something false but irrelevant, I may presuppose it as well, just to facilitate communication. (You refer to Mary's partner as "her husband," when I know that they are not married. But I might refer to him in the same way just to avoid diverting the discussion.)

I have said that we should identify a context, or context set, with the set of possible situations that are compatible with what is presupposed, or taken to be common ground, by the participants in the discourse. But it is individuals who presume that something is or is not common information, and different participants in the same conversation may not in fact agree in what they presuppose. But even if actual presuppositions of speaker and addressee diverge, it is part of the idea of speaker presupposition that it is presupposed that the presuppositions of the different participants in the discourse are the same. To presuppose something is to presuppose that it is common ground, so if what is presupposed is not in fact common ground, then something false is being presupposed. So in those possible worlds compatible with what anyone is presupposing, all the participants (at least everyone that the speaker presupposes to be a participant) will be presupposing the same things. This fact about the concept of presupposition will be reflected in a constraint on the accessibility relations in the modal semantics for presupposition, in this case a constraint on the relation between the different accessibility relations for the different speakers. The following is the relevant condition: for any two participants i and j in the discourse, and any possible worlds x, y and z, if $R_i xy$, then $R_i yz$ iff $R_j yz$.

It would, of course, be unrealistic to assume that the participants in a discourse are always in fact presupposing exactly the same things, and the constraint I have proposed does not assume this. This presupposition, like any presupposition, may be false in the actual situation. We need not even assume that any participant *believes* that this presupposition holds, since this presupposition, like any presupposition, may involve the pretense that something is common ground when it is not. But the constraint is important, since it will help to explain some of the ways in which contexts change in response to events that take place in a discourse. Because it is presumed that shared information is shared, the presuppositions of different speakers will tend to adjust to an equilibrium position in which they are the same.

Discourse contexts, I have been suggesting, can be represented by the set of possible situations compatible with the information that is presumed, by the speaker, to be common ground, or information that is shared and recognized to be shared by all the relevant participants. This is a representation from the point of view of one of the participants in the context of what is common to all, and it is a representation of a context at a particular moment. This body of information is the information that is available for the interpretation of what is said in the context. If certain information is necessary to determine the content of some speech act, then appropriate speech requires that the information be presumed to be shared information at the time at which that speech act is to be interpreted. But exactly what time is that? The context—what is presupposed in it—is constantly changing as things are said. The point of a speech act—an assertion, for example—is to change the context, and since the way the speech act is supposed to change the context depends on its content, interpretation must be done in the prior context—the context as it is before the assertion is accepted, and its content added to what is presupposed. But the prior context cannot be the context as it was before the speaker began to speak. Suppose Phoebe says "I saw an interesting movie last night." To determine the content of her remark, one needs to know who is speaking, and so Phoebe, if she is speaking appropriately, must be presuming that the information that she is speaking is available to her audience—that it is shared information. But she need not presume that this information was available before she began to speak. The prior context that is relevant to the interpretation of a speech act is the context as it is changed by the fact that the speech act was made, but prior to the acceptance or rejection of the speech act. A successful statement will thus change the context in two different ways that need to be distinguished. First, the fact that the statement was made is information that is added to the context simply as a result of the fact that it is a manifestly observable event that it was made. Second (assuming the statement is not rejected), the content of the assertion will be added to the context. One might imagine a formal language game in which the two kinds of change take place successively: first, the addressee takes in and adjusts to the fact that a particular proposition has been asserted—that it has been proposed that a certain piece of information be mutually accepted; second, the addressee accepts or rejects the proposal, either adding the content of the assertion to the contextual information, or leaving the context as it was after the first change. But there is no reason why the two changes need take place at different times. In real conversations, particularly conversations that are exchanges of information by people whose authority is not in question, there need be no moment when the context has changed in the first way, but not yet in the second. Nevertheless, even when the two changes take place at once, the distinction between them is important, since the explanations will be different for the different kinds of changes. I will try to bring out the significance of the distinction by discussing, first, the concept of *accommodation*, second, by responding to an argument that the possible worlds representation of context is not sufficiently rich to account for some phenomena, and third, by looking at some simple examples of pronouns and indefinite reference.

III. Accommodation

Context changes of the first kind include the recognition of unproblematic observable events, such as that a certain person uttered certain words, but they also include the recognition of any facts that the hearer can infer from the occurrence of these observable events, with the help of standing information that is part of the prior context. We add to the context, not only the information that Phoebe uttered certain sounds, but also that she uttered an English sentence, and that she is saying something to us. And if it was part of the information presupposed before she began to speak that Phoebe is a cooperative and competent participant in our conversational enterprise, and if her utterance does not give us reason to give up this presupposition, then we can also infer that she is making whatever presuppositions are required to make her utterance intelligible and appropriate. The phenomenon is familiar: Phoebe says

(1) I can't come to the meeting—I have to pick up my cat at the veterinarian.

Her utterance is appropriate, let us suppose, only if it is presupposed, and so part of the presumed shared information, that Phoebe owns a cat. But suppose Phoebe had no reason to believe that her interlocutor knew about her cat before she made her statement. That does not matter, since Phoebe can reasonably assume that her interlocutor can infer that she has a cat, and that she is presupposing that she has a cat, from the prior presupposition that she will speak appropriately, and from the fact that her statement would be appropriate only if she were making that presupposition. This phenomenon, which David Lewis has labeled "accommodation," is just a case of inference from the observed fact that the utterance event takes place. Lewis, in setting out a dynamic model of a conversational game, described a distinctive kind of rule, a "rule of accommodation," that is characteristic of linguistic practices (Lewis, 1979). Such rules, he says, ensure that presuppositions "straightway come into existence" when they are required to render what someone says acceptable. Lewis distinguished context changes by accommodation from the simpler kind of change that takes place when "something conspicuous happens at the scene of a conversation, and straightway it is presupposed that it happened," but I do not think there is a distinction to be made here, or a reason to hypothesize a special rule or mechanism of accommodation. An utterance event is something conspicuous that happens at the scene of a conversation, and the presupposition that such an event occurred is the source of any accommodation.

To make this point clearer, let me sketch in a little more detail how the derivation of the accommodated presupposition might go. First, suppose that it is a prior standing presumption that Phoebe is a competent and cooperative speaker, so it is presupposed that her speech acts will be appropriate. Second, suppose it is also a prior standing presupposition that the definite description, "my cat" in the expression "I have to pick up my cat" presupposes that the speaker has a cat, in the sense that the use of this expression is appropriate only in a context in which the speaker is making this presupposition—presuming that it is shared information that the speaker has a cat. This, we can assume, is something that competent speakers of English know, and it is a standing presupposition in an ordinary conversation taking place between English speakers that they are all competent speakers. Now if these standing presuppositions remain in force when we add the new information that Phoebe uttered (1), then it will follow that Phoebe is presupposing that she has a cat. But since what is presupposed is what is presumed to be shared information, this implies that Phoebe is presupposing that her addressee is presupposing that she has a cat. (Not that her addressee was presupposing it before she began to speak, but that he is presupposing it after having taken in the fact that she made her statement.) So since it follows from the addressee's standing presuppositions together with manifestly observable facts that Phoebe is making this presupposition, he will presuppose that Phoebe is making it, and since it is presupposed that presuppositions are shared information, he will accommodate by presupposing it himself.

The last move in this derivation requires that the addressee be willing to suppose that if Phoebe is presupposing that she has a cat, then it is true that she has a cat, and so the appropriateness of Phoebe's presupposition will require that she be presupposing that the addressee will be willing to suppose this. If this assumption is not correct—if something controversial has been presupposed (either as a result of the speaker's misperception, or in a deliberate attempt to sneak something by the addressee)—then the context will become defective, and some backtracking and repair will be required. So our derivation helps to explain a familiar feature of accommodation: that (to quote Irene Heim), "assumptions to be accommodated are supposed to be uncontroversial and unsurprising. One may explicitly assert controversial and surprising things (in fact one should) but to expect one's audience to accept them by way of accommodation is not good conversational practice" (Heim, 1992: 212).

IV. On an Alleged Problem with This Representation of Context

Hans Kamp has argued that this framework for a representation of context is not rich enough to allow for some distinctions that are needed to account for some linguistic phenomena. I don't think his argument is correct, and I think the explanation of why it is not correct helps to bring out the significance of the two contrasting ways in which speech acts change the context. More generally, I think it will help to clarify the contrast between the descriptive apparatus that I am sketching and a theory of the mechanisms of a particular language, such as discourse representation theory. I will argue that while the example on which Kamp bases his argument does point to a fact about the language that needs explanation, it does not point to an inadequacy in the representation of context I have proposed, which is designed not to provide a solution to that problem, but to provide a framework in which the problem, and alternative responses to it, can be clearly formulated.

Kamp's argument (Kamp, 1988) begins with a pair of examples due to Barbara Partee. Consider these two contrasting sentence pairs:

(2) a. Exactly one of the ten balls is not in the bag.
    b. It is under the sofa.
(3) a. Exactly nine of the ten balls are in the bag.
    b. It is under the sofa.

Kamp asks us to assume that each discourse takes place in the same initial context. In each case, the first assertion changes the context, and the second assertion is made in the changed context. He then notes that the first statements of each pair, (2a) and (3a), are truth-conditionally equivalent—true in exactly the same possible worlds. So he concludes that if contexts are simply identified with sets of possible worlds, and if assertions simply add the truth-conditional content to the context, then the posterior context that results from the assertion of (2a) will be the same as the one that results from the assertion of (3a). But on the other hand, the contexts in which the second statement takes place must be different in the two cases, since (2b) is the same as (3b), yet they cannot receive the same interpretation. The "it" in (2b) can, and most naturally does, refer to the ball that is not in the bag, while the "it" in (3b) cannot refer to that ball. "We must conclude," Kamp says, "that no difference can be predicted if contexts are identified with sets of possible worlds. Therefore, a theory of meaning and context dependent interpretation of English must, if it is to handle such examples successfully, adopt a representation of contexts that goes beyond what sets of possible worlds are able to reveal" (Kamp, 1988: 158).

Now it is right that the abstract framework does not *predict* this difference, since it says nothing about the way pronouns work. This representation of context is not intended as a part of a theory of meaning for English, or any other language, natural or artificial, but as a piece of apparatus with which the phenomena might be described and explanatory hypotheses stated. But does the framework permit a distinction between the contexts for (2b) and (3b), given that the prior contexts for (2a) and (3a) are the same? Kamp's claim is that the representation of context by a set of possible worlds is not sufficiently rich to allow the phenomena to be explained, but this is not correct. One cannot conclude from the fact that the prior context (the context as it was before the speaker began to speak) is the same for (2a) and (3a), and the fact that the truth-conditional content of (2a) and (3a) are the same, that the resulting contexts (the contexts for (2b) and (3b)) must also be the same. The assumption that one can draw this conclusion ignores the first way in which a speech act changes the context. Since it is a manifestly observable fact that, in each case, a certain sentence was uttered, this fact, together with any additional information that follows from that fact, conjoined with standing background information about linguistic and speech conventions, is available to distinguish the two posterior contexts, the contexts relative to which (2b) and (3b) are interpreted.

A pronoun such as "it" presumably requires a context in which a certain individual of the appropriate kind is uniquely salient, or in some way available for reference. The abstract framework, by itself, says nothing about which particular facts make salient, or available for pronominal reference, an individual who inhabits the domains of the possible worlds that define the context. Among the facts that might be relevant are facts about the words used to express certain propositions in the discourse, since these are facts that are available to the participants in the discourse, and so are reflected in each of the possible worlds that are members of the relevant context set. So long as we make the minimal assumption that information can be relevant for the determination of content only if it is presupposed by the speaker to be information that will be available to the addressee, then we can be sure that the set of possible worlds that defines what is presupposed will suffice to represent a context.

I want to emphasize that I am not suggesting that Partee's example does not pose a real problem: the problem of explaining just what the relevant difference is between (2a) and (3a), the difference that is responsible for the fact that (2a) makes a certain individual available for pronominal reference, while the truth-conditionally equivalent (3a) does not. Discourse representation theory and dynamic predicate logic each have something to say about what the mechanisms that explain the difference might be. But whatever the explanation, it will appeal to facts about English, or about the practice of speaking English, that can be presumed to be available to competent English speakers, and so they will be facts that distinguish the possible worlds that define the different contexts.

I also want to emphasize that in giving this response to Kamp, I am not proposing to add anything new to the possible worlds that define a context, and am not proposing any alteration in the straightforward account of the content of sentences such as (2a) and (3a). I am simply observing something obvious: that when a speech act takes place, it is a manifest fact, and so at that point presumed shared information, that it takes place. It is simply an obvious fact that an assertion changes the context, not only by adding the information that is the content of the speech act (the same information in the case of (2a) and (3a)), but also by manifesting the fact (different in the utterances (2a) and (3a)) that the event itself takes place.

V. Pronouns and Indefinite Reference

To try to get clearer about the way a context might make individuals available for reference, I will look at some simple examples of pronouns with indefinite antecedents. Start with the following unproblematic opening move in a conversation.

(4) I met an interesting woman at the dinner last night. She was a member of Clinton's cabinet.

One fact about the context that results from the acceptance of the first of these two statements (a fact about the subject matter of the discourse) is that in all of the possible worlds in the context set, the speaker met an interesting woman. No particular woman was specified, so it need not be the same interesting woman that the speaker met in each possible world in the context, and nothing rules out the possibility that the speaker met several interesting women in some of the possible worlds compatible with the information. A second fact (a fact about the discourse) that is presupposed after the first statement has been made is that a woman that the speaker met at the party last night is uniquely available to be the referent of the pronoun "she" in the conversation in question. At least that must be true if the second statement is to discriminate in a determinate way between the possible situations that define the context. But if there are possible worlds compatible with the context in which the speaker met two interesting women at the dinner, what makes one or the other of them the referent of "she" in that world?

Presumably, in this particular example, the speaker has a particular woman in mind,[3] but since the audience knows nothing about the women at the dinner except what the speaker tells them, and since the speaker has so far given them only general information, it cannot be a fact about the context—about what is presumed to be common knowledge—that any particular woman is salient, or available to be referred to in the subsequent conversation. We can, however, say that it is a fact about the individual possible worlds that are the members of the set that defines the context that a certain person is available to be the denotation, in that world, of a pronoun. This will be a fact about the conversation, and not about the subject matter. There might be two possible worlds compatible with the context that are indistinguishable with respect to the events that happened at the dinner, but different with respect to which of the two interesting women is the potential denotation of the pronoun "she." Suppose it is compatible with the context, after the first of the two statements, that the speaker met an interesting woman who was a member of Clinton's cabinet, and also an interesting woman who was not. Then there will be two possibilities corresponding to this situation: one in which the first interesting woman is marked as the potential referent, and one in which the second is. When the speaker goes on to make the second statement, its content eliminates the second of these possibilities. While this difference between possibilities does not concern facts about the subject matter, it is

---

[3] Just what it means to say that one has a particular person or thing in mind is, of course, notoriously difficult to pin down. It is obviously itself a highly context-dependent notion. I don't take the phase to imply that one has a very intimate knowledge of the individual, or that one has the capacity to identify the individual, by description, or by observation. Even if our speaker would now be unable to distinguish the woman he is talking about from another woman he met at the party, it might still be true that there is a particular woman he is talking about, presumably the causal source of his beliefs about her.

a factual difference: the fact that distinguishes the two possible worlds is a fact about the discourse which is taking place, not only in the actual world, but also in each of the possible worlds compatible with the context. Specifically, it is a fact about the interpretation of certain potential continuations of the discourse.

The recognition of the possibility that the speaker met two interesting women might be quite explicit in the context. Suppose the speaker had begun his conversation this way:

(5) I met two interesting women at the dinner last night. Let me tell you about one of them.

Here the second speech act conveys no information about the events at the dinner. All it does is to make available one of the two women for reference by a pronoun. Which one? One of them in some possible worlds compatible with the context, and the other in others. But what sort of fact about the world is it that determines which of the women it is? It is clear enough how the facts determine whether what is presupposed or said about the events at the dinner is correct or not. The speaker either did or did not actually meet an interesting woman who was a cabinet officer. But if the speaker really did meet two interesting women, in a certain possible world, how do the facts about that world determine which of them is the denotation of the speaker's "she"? At least in this particular example, it seems reasonable to say that this is up to the speaker. Suppose the actual facts are these: one of the two interesting women that our gullible and politically unaware speaker met was a professor of philosophy who was introduced to him by a practical joker as the Secretary of Defense. The other was in fact the Secretary of Health and Human Services, but the speaker was ignorant of this fact—he thought she was a talk show host. So the speaker correctly believes that he met exactly one interesting woman who was a cabinet officer, but he is mistaken about which of two women it was. The facts about which the speaker is mistaken will not affect what he presupposes, or how what he says changes the context, but it will affect how his statements are assessed, and how they might be corrected. A participant in the conversation who was aware of the relevant facts might correctly respond to our speaker's second statement by saying

(6) She wasn't a member of Clinton's cabinet—that was a joke.

So it seems clear that if the facts were as described, the speaker's second statement would be false. In contrast, if he had instead told his story in a single statement, saying

(7) I met an interesting woman who was a member of Clinton's cabinet at the dinner last night

then he would have spoken truly, even if only by a lucky accident. But as he did tell it, it seems to me that he said something false.[4]

In early work on formal pragmatics by Richard Montague and some of his colleagues, contexts were identified with *indices*, n-tuples that included all the features of the situation on which the extensions of expressions might depend. So an index would contain a speaker, an addressee, a time, a place, a possible world, and other things such as "indicated object" coordinates to determine the referents of demonstrative pronouns. Meanings were identified with functions from such indices to extensions (see Montague (1974), Lewis (1970, 1981)). David Kaplan's work on demonstratives suggested that meaning plus context should determine content, rather than extension: meaning takes context to content, and content takes circumstances to extension. But contexts were still represented by n-tuples of elements (speaker, time, indicated objects, etc.)—everything other than meaning that is needed to determine content. Context, on this account, was constituted by those elements required to determine what was being said with a sentence, but nothing was explicitly said in the theory about the epistemic status of such a context. If, however, we assume that the speaker presupposes that the addressee will know what is being said, then we will be assuming that the addressee knows what the relevant index is, which implies that the "indicated objects" must be salient, or that the speaker must be assuming that everyone knows which individual a pronoun denotes. But all that is really required for content to be determined, and for it to be known in the context how it is determined, is for there to be a unique available "indicated object" in each possible situation compatible with the context. What the context must determine, for the interpretation of a pronoun, is a function from worlds in the context set to individuals.

So to return to our example of an opening conversational gambit, the idea is that the first statement of (4) changed the context in two ways: by adding the purely existential information, and by making, in each possible world compatible with the resulting context, a certain individual available for future reference by "she." If the statement is rejected, then the change induced by the existential information will not take place, but in some cases, this will not prevent the other change—the making available for

---

[4] Kai von Fintel pointed out to me that (6)—the correction—would be an appropriate response to (7) as well as to (4), and so it is not clear that (7) is true. I agree that the correction would be appropriate in either case, and true in both cases, but while I think the truth of (6) shows that the second statement of (4) is false, I don't think it shows that (7) is false. When the speaker of (6) says "she wasn't a member of Clinton's cabinet," he directly contradicts the second statement of (4), "she was a member of Clinton's cabinet." So if (6) is true, the second statement of (4) must be false. But while (6) gives a reason to reject (7), it doesn't follow that it contradicts it. Compare the Strawson correction example discussed below.

future reference of a certain individual. Consider a famous example of Peter Strawson's (1952: 187):

(8) X: A man jumped off a bridge.
    Y: He didn't jump, he was pushed.

In this dialogue, X succeeds in making a certain man available for reference (by Y) in the subsequent context, even though the statement that accomplished this was rejected by Y. It was the fact that the statement was made, and not the fact that it was accepted, that did the job.

It is the speaker introducing the individual into the context, and not necessarily the individual using the pronoun, whose intentions are relevant to determining the referent of the pronoun. In Strawson's correction dialogue, Y's "he" refers to the person X had in mind. The dialogue might take the following turn: After Y says "he didn't jump, he was pushed," X corrects the correction:

(9) No, I didn't mean that man. I agree he was pushed, but the one I was talking about really did jump.

Even though Y had a particular person in mind who he believed to be the referent of his "he," it is the person X had in mind to whom he refers, and that is why Y can be corrected. (But notice that even though Y's correction is rejected, he succeeded in changing the context by making a different man available for reference by X.)

It will of course not always be true that a speaker making an existential statement has a particular individual in mind. Suppose Z says:

(10) I predict that a woman will be nominated for President in 2000. Furthermore, I predict that she will win.

Suppose (to Z's surprise and delight) both parties nominate women in 2000. Naturally, one wins and one loses. Was Z's statement true or false? It would seem churlish to say that her prediction was anything but completely correct, but it is not clear that our semantic intuitions, strictly speaking, support this judgment. There does not, in this case, seem to be any fact that makes one or the other nominee the referent of the speaker's "she." Perhaps, in this case, the speaker was presupposing that at most one woman would be nominated, if only because the alternative did not occur to her. If that is true, then the second statement will have a determinate truth-value in each possible world in the context set, and so will change the context in a determinate way, but it will not have a determinate truth-value in the actual world.

Linguists sometimes distinguish specific from nonspecific indefinite noun phrases, corresponding roughly to the case where the speaker has someone or something in mind, and cases where he does not. The problem has always been to understand what difference this distinction makes for the truth-conditions of statements containing the indefinite expression, and how facts about the speaker's state of mind that were unavailable to the audience could be relevant to the semantics of what was being said. The account I am sketching suggests that this difference matters, not to the interpretation of the indefinite expression itself, but only to the evaluation of subsequent statements made with pronouns anaphoric to the indefinite expression.

Assertions, I have suggested, are proposals to change the context by adding the information that is their content. We might contrast assertions with a different speech act, supposition, that has a similar effect, but a different point. A supposition—what one does, for example, with the antecedent of a conditional—is different from an assertion in two obvious ways: first, the intention is to add the content expressed in the supposition to the context only temporarily; second, an act of supposition does not represent its content as something the speaker believes, and is not subject to criticism on the ground that it is false. But since it alters the context, at least while it is in effect, in the same way as a successful assertion, one should expect to find parallels in the behavior of the two speech acts, and one does. One also finds some contrasts, which I think can be explained in terms of the two obvious differences between the speech acts. Suppositions change the context in the same two ways that assertions do, but in the case of supposition, while the change induced by the content is temporary, the preparatory change—the change induced by the fact that the supposition was made—is not. We can, for example, make a particular individual salient by referring to him in a supposition, and he may remain salient even after we are no longer making the supposition. So I can say, for example,

(11) If Colin Powell runs for President, I will be surprised. I won't, however, be surprised if he is nominated for Vice President.

Even when an individual is introduced into the context by an indefinite reference in a supposition, an individual may sometimes be made available beyond the scope of the supposition. Consider:

(12) If a man with a Scandinavian accent calls, tell him about the leak in the drain pipe under the kitchen sink. He's the plumber. I left a message on his answering machine.

The situation here parallels the Strawson example of correction. Just as, given the right background information, an individual introduced in an assertion may remain available for reference even when the assertion is rejected, so in some contexts an individual introduced in a supposition may remain available for reference after the supposition is no longer in force.

In the case of suppositions made for the purpose of contingency planning or hedged predictions, the content of the supposition is simply added, temporarily, to the context; no presuppositions are subtracted, or suspended. But with counterfactual suppositions, one requires a new temporary context set, disjoint from the primary one. One crucial difference between an ordinary context and a counterfactual or derived context—a context brought into play either by a counterfactual supposition or some other embedded expression of a proposition, such as a belief attribution—is that in the possible world compatible with a derived context the discourse itself need not be taking place. If X says to Y, "Suppose I had never met you," the possible worlds compatible with what is being supposed are not worlds in which their conversation is taking place. So derived contexts do not change in the same two ways in the course of the conversation. If an individual in the possible worlds in a derived context is uniquely available for reference, this will have to be a fact about the conversation taking place in the possible worlds in the primary context. In interpreting speech acts with embedded sentences, the interplay between information represented by primary and derived context sets can help to clarify phenomena concerning intentional identity and *de re* belief attributions. But that is a discussion for another time.

VI. Conclusion

My main aim in this paper has been to redirect attention from the details of the devices and mechanisms of particular natural languages to the general structure of the practices in which natural languages are used to serve the ends of speakers and listeners. The hope is that if we get clearer about the structure and purposes of discourse, we can better distinguish the idiosyncratic features of particular conventional devices from more general features of the practice that follow from assumptions about what people engaged in it are trying to do. With a framework for representing the general features of discourse, we should be able to describe in a perspicuous manner the problems that alternative semantic theories are addressing, and the alternative hypotheses about how different languages and discourse practices work. And perhaps if we are clearer about the general structure of discourse this will help us defend simpler semantic analyses. The general strategy is like the one proposed by Paul Grice and spelled out in the beginning of his William James lectures about thirty years ago. Grice's more specific project at that point was to reconcile traditional semantic analyses of logical expressions—those offered by truth-functional logic—with the diversity of facts about the uses of such expressions by invoking some simple maxims of conversation, maxims that assumed little more than that conversation was a rational and cooperative activity whose primary purpose was the exchange of information. The semantic theories for natural language available today are considerably more complex and sophisticated than those that Grice was concerned to defend, and a lot more has been said since then—much of it inspired by Grice's ideas—about the general structure of conversation. But I think the general Gricean strategy of trying to reduce the burden on semantics by explaining as much of the phenomena as possible in terms of truisms about conversation as a rational activity remains as fruitful and promising as it was when he first proposed it.

PART II

Attributing Attitudes

6

Semantics for Belief

When we attribute a belief by saying something of the form *x believes that P*, we say that a certain relation, expressed by *believes*, holds between *x* and an object of belief—something denoted by the sentential complement, *that P*. There are lots of theories about what these objects of belief are: some say they are structured complexes made up of senses or concepts; others argue that they are sentences themselves, or sets of sentences; they have been held to be *sui generis* primitive objects—unanalyzed propositions. Perhaps they are sets of possible worlds, or possible and impossible worlds, or sets of situations or partial worlds. A defense of any such account of the object of belief should be motivated by a general theoretical account of the nature of the belief relation—one that can contribute both to a philosophical explanation of intentionality, and to empirical accounts of cognitive states and processes. It must also be able to contribute to an explanation of the semantic facts about belief attribution. There is some tension between these two requirements for an adequate account of the object of belief. The facts about belief attributions suggest that the objects of belief should be individuated very finely: for almost any two distinct sentential clauses, *that P* and *that Q*, one can find a context where it seems plausible to say that someone believes that *P*, but disbelieves that *Q*. Such facts tend to push one to take the objects of belief to be sentences, or close copies of sentences. But any theoretical account that tries to explain belief and other cognitive states as capacities and dispositions to interact with the extra-linguistic world will tend to motivate a more coarse-grained conception of content. Whatever the details of such an account, belief will relate a believer, not to a sentence, but to the information that a sentence conveys; it may be difficult to come up with a conception of information or informational content that distinguishes sentences that the facts of belief attribution seem to distinguish.

The account of the object of belief that I want to defend faces this tension in a particular acute form. Theoretical considerations, I have argued,

An earlier version of this paper was written while I was a National Endowment of the Humanities Fellow at the Center for Advanced Study in the Behavioral Sciences in Stanford. I am grateful to both institutions for support.

motivate a coarse-grained conception of informational content, a conception that individuates contents in terms of their truth-conditions.[1] Such a conception of content is appropriate both to solve philosophical problems about the nature of intentionality, and to give an adequate characterization of the capacities that a science of cognitive processes seeks to explain. But the assumption that sentential clauses in belief attributions refer to coarse-grained informational contents—contents that are identical if they are necessarily equivalent—seems to have consequences that are obviously false. It is obvious that anyone who is less than deductively omniscient will fail to believe everything necessarily equivalent to what he believes.

We need three assumptions to get a particular case of this kind of conflict: first, we need to assume the general account of objects of belief that says that necessarily equivalent objects of belief are identical. Second, we need to assume that some specific sentences P and Q are necessarily equivalent. Third, we need the intuitive judgment that it is possible to believe that P while disbelieving that Q. The most common response is to take the examples to refute the general account. The main burden of this response is to give and motivate some alternative theoretical account. A second more heroic response is to reject the intuitive judgments about beliefs, arguing that we don't really believe what we seem to believe. The main burden of this response is to explain away the appearances. My strategy will be different from both of these. I will question the second assumption, that sentences that appear to be necessarily equivalent really are, in the relevant context, equivalent. There is, I will suggest, more complexity and flexibility—and more context-dependence—in the relationship between sentences or sentential complements and the propositions they express or denote. Sentences necessarily equivalent in one context may be only contingently equivalent in another.

The task of defending the coarse-grained conception of informational content is a large one; in this paper I will concentrate on only a small part of it. I will adopt, as a working hypothesis, the hypothesis that objects of belief are individuated by their truth-conditions, as represented in the possible worlds framework, taking for granted the theoretical considerations that motivate this conception of content. Thoughts or propositions, I will hypothesize, are functions from possible worlds into truth-values. My task will be to sketch a general strategy, and some particular devices, for reconciling this conception of content with the phenomena concerning belief attribution.

The examples I will focus on will be examples of necessary and impossible propositions, since this is where the apparent divergence between

[1] In Stalnaker (1984).

theory and fact becomes most dramatic. That is, I will focus on examples of statements of the form *x believes that P* or *x wonders whether P* that are problematic in the following way: on the one hand, straightforward and well-motivated semantical rules imply that the complement, *that P*, denotes a necessary truth or a necessary falsehood; on the other hand, the complement seems intuitively to denote a possible object of belief or doubt. Given our working hypothesis, necessary truths and falsehoods are not possible non-trivial objects of belief or doubt, so there is a prima facie conflict in such an example. My strategy for discovering a resolution of the conflict will be this: first, ignoring the semantical rules for a moment, try to characterize a context for the belief statement and a *contingent* possible worlds proposition defined on that context that seems intuitively to be what the statement says that the believer believes. If one can do this, it is plausible to conclude (given our working hypothesis) that that proposition is the one denoted by the sentential complement. Now comes the second and the harder part of the problem: to find a systematic way of connecting the proposition that the belief statement seems to be saying the agent believes with the semantical rules for the sentential complement that seems to be expressing that proposition; that is, to find a systematic explanation for the fact that the complement denotes, in that context, that proposition.

For example, suppose we begin with the statement *O'Leary believes that Hesperus is Mars*. Our semantical theory tells us that the proposition *that Hesperus is Mars* is necessarily false—true in no possible world. Yet clearly we can easily imagine a story in which the belief attribution seems intu-itively to be true. The first task, according to the strategy I will follow, is to try to tell such a story in the language of the possible worlds framework. To do this, we ask, is there a way the world might be such that to believe that Hesperus is Mars is to believe that the world is that way? If so, then we can characterize a contingent proposition—the one that would be true if and only if the world were the way O'Leary thinks it is—that seems to be the content of O'Leary's belief. Then we can go on to attack the second, harder question: how is it possible for the expression, *that Hesperus is Mars* to denote the contingent proposition that our intuitive inquiry tells us it must denote? If we can show how to provide answers to these two kinds of questions—answers that generalize to cover all the standard problematic examples—then, I think, we will have reconciled our working hypothesis with the phenomena concerning attributions of belief.

The same strategy can be applied to a simpler but parallel problem. Consider, not belief attributions, but simple assertions; not *O'Leary believes that Hesperus is Mars*, but O'Leary's assertion, *Hesperus is Mars*. The problem, in the case of this example at least, is essentially the same:

given our hypothesis, there is a conflict between the theoretical conclusion that the assertion expresses a necessary falsehood and the intuitive judgment that the assertion conveys a coherent, if incorrect, piece of information. To resolve the conflict, we need to answer two questions corresponding to the two questions asked about the belief example: first, what contingent proposition seems to represent the information conveyed? Second, how can that sentence convey that information?

I will look first at the assertion question, which I have discussed in more detail elsewhere,[2] since it is easier, and it should help answer the question about belief. It should help because it is natural to assume that the information O'Leary conveys when he says *Hesperus is Mars* is the same as the information that is the belief content reported in the statement *O'Leary believes that Hesperus is Mars*. And it is also natural to assume that the explanation of how that assertion can convey that information will correspond to an explanation of how the belief attribution can attribute that belief. But the parallel is not perfect; there are some additional problematic features of belief contexts, and a solution to the assertion problem will take us only part of the way toward a solution to the problem about belief.

To help characterize assertions and their contexts, I will need to introduce and explain a piece of descriptive apparatus: the notion of a *propositional concept*. I will first define this notion in the abstract; second, I will say how I want to apply this notion to the description of assertions in context; third, I will contrast the notion of propositional concept with a different semantical notion with which it has been sometimes confused. This contrasting notion is formally somewhat similar, but plays a quite different role in the explanation of linguistic phenomena.

A propositional concept is a function from possible worlds into propositions. Since, on our working hypothesis, propositions are themselves functions from a domain of possible worlds, a propositional concept may be thought of as a two-dimensional proposition. If, for purposes of exposition, we assume a small finite number of possible worlds, we can represent propositions by simply enumerating the truth-values for the different possible worlds. For example, if i, j and k are the relevant possible worlds, the following represents a proposition:

$$i \quad j \quad k$$

T	F	T

To represent a propositional concept in an analogous way, just write a line of truth-values like this for each possible world as follows:

---

[2] "Assertion", reprinted in Ch. 4 of the present volume.

	i	j	k
i	T	F	T
j	F	T	T
k	F	T	F

Each horizontal line represents the value of the propositional concept for the argument written to the left of that line.

To see how propositional concepts are applied to the description of assertions in context, recall two simple and, I hope, uncontroversial facts. First, acts of assertion (and all other speech acts) are performed in a context in which certain information is taken for granted as the presumed common background against which the speech act is interpreted. Second, among the items of information taken for granted or presupposed in this way by the speaker will be the proposition that the act of assertion itself is taking place. Now we can represent the presumed background information as a set of possible worlds—the possible worlds compatible with the background information. This set of alternative possibilities is the set of possible situations between which the speaker intends to distinguish with his speech acts.

In terms of this representation of the presumed background information, the second of the uncontroversial facts mentioned above comes to something like this: in every possible world that is compatible with the background information the assertion in question is taking place. When O'Leary says *the cat is on the mat*, he is speaking not only in the actual world but also in all the other possible worlds compatible with the beliefs, presumptions and presuppositions of those who believe, presume, or presuppose that O'Leary is speaking. In particular, he is speaking in all those possible worlds compatible with the background presuppositions that O'Leary himself is making as he speaks.

Given these facts, it follows that when someone makes an assertion, his words determine not only a proposition, but a propositional concept, relative to the possible worlds compatible with the speaker's presumed background information. We can describe various features of the speech situation, and state various constraints on the relation between assertions and their contexts, in terms of the properties of the propositional concept determined in this way. For example, some propositional concepts will be constant relative to the context, and others will not be. If the point of an assertion is to convey the information contained in the proposition expressed, then it is clear that an appropriate assertion will determine a constant propositional concept.

Now let me contrast propositional concepts with a different two-dimensional semantical object: what David Kaplan, in his work on demonstratives, has called *character*.[3] Characters are like propositional concepts in that they are functions from something into content, where content is, or determines, a function from possible worlds into truth-values. Thus character, like propositional concept, suggests a two-stage process of semantic evaluation. But the arguments of Kaplan's character functions are (or may be) different from the arguments of propositional concepts, and they play a different role in semantic description and explanation.

In Kaplan's theory of demonstratives, a *context* is represented by an index—an n-tuple that specifies all the features of the situation in which a discourse takes place on which the content of the expression of some specific pragmatic language might depend. For example, if the language contains tenses, the content of some sentences will depend on time of utterance, and so one element of the index must be a time; if the language contains first and second person pronouns, the content of some sentences will depend on who is speaking, and to whom, so the index must have places specifying a speaker and an addressee. The semantical rules for such a language will assign to the sentences a function from indices into propositions; these functions are the characters of the sentences to which they are assigned. So, for example, the character of *I love you* might be a function taking an index, $\langle a,b,t \rangle$ into the proposition that is true (in a given possible world) if and only if a loves b at time t in that world.

So a character is a kind of meaning: it is associated by the semantic theory of a specific language with expression *types*. Sentences have the content they have, in a given context, *because* they have the character they have. In contrast, a propositional concept is not a kind of meaning, and is not associated with expression types of a language by the semantic theory for that language. Propositional concepts are determined by particular utterance *tokens* and their contexts. The same sentence type, with the same meaning, used in different contexts may determine different propositional concepts. And utterances don't have the content they have *because* they determine a certain propositional concept. This gets things backwards. Rather, an utterance determines a certain propositional concept because it has the content it has in the various possible worlds in which that particular concrete utterance token exists.

Not only is a propositional concept not a meaning, it is not even a function of the meaning of the sentence whose utterance determines it. To determine the relevant propositional concept, one needs to know, not only

---

[3] Kaplan (1989).

what the sentence used in fact means—what it means in the actual world—but also what it means in the various alternative possible worlds in which the utterance takes place. Since meaning may vary from world to world, an eternal sentence (a sentence that, in Kaplan's terminology, has constant character) may determine a variable propositional concept, and may determine different propositional concepts on different occasions of use.

So, despite some superficial similarities, character and propositional concept are quite different notions. They belong to different theories—theories that are applied at different stages in the explanation of speech. And they are not competing notions: neither can do the job that the other was designed to do.

Now with the notion of a propositional concept at hand to help us describe the situation, let us apply the strategy outlined above to the assertion problem. Consider O'Leary's assertion, *Hesperus is Mars*. If we approach the question, "What is O'Leary saying?" not by asking about the semantical rules for the sentence O'Leary is using, but instead by asking what the world would be like if what O'Leary seems intuitively to be saying were true, then an answer is not hard to find. There are possible worlds that resemble the actual world with respect to the way the heavens appear to the untrained eye, but in which the solar system is quite differently arranged. The solar system in these worlds has the same planets as our world has, and they have the same names. But in these counterfactual worlds, Mars appears in the evening at the very place where Venus in fact appears, and it has quite the same appearance as Venus in fact has (at least to the untrained eye). Ancient astronomers in these worlds called this planet that appears in the evening (not of course knowing that it was a planet) by a name from which descends the name *Hesperus*—a name used by the modern English speakers of these counterfactual worlds to refer to that planet.

Now a man like O'Leary, who has the superficial knowledge of the solar system that most of us have, and who is inclined sometimes to misremember what he has read or heard, might well believe that a world of the kind I have described is the actual world. If he did believe this, he might express his belief by saying "Hesperus is Mars." And if he did say this, I think we would all conclude that he was saying that the world was something like the world I have described.

Call the actual world *i* and some representative from the class of counterfactual worlds I have described *j*. The conclusion I am claiming we all should reach is that the content of O'Leary's assertion seems to be the contingent proposition that is false at *i* and true at *j*.

Now let us look at the semantical rules for the sentence *Hesperus is Mars*. Both *Hesperus* and *Mars* are proper names. Suppose Kripke has convinced us all that proper names are rigid designators—singular terms that refer to the same individual relative to all possible worlds. Assume also that *is* express identity in this context. From these assumptions, together with the assumption that Hesperus is, in fact, distinct from Mars, it follows that the content of O'Leary's assertion is the proposition that is necessarily false—false even at *j*, the possible world that is the way O'Leary seems to be saying that the world is. So the result of applying otherwise well-motivated semantical rules conflicts with our holistic intuitive judgment.

To resolve the conflict, let us look not just at the proposition determined, but at the whole propositional concept: ask not just, what does *Hesperus is Mars* say (according to the semantical rules)—what is its truth-value at various alternative possible worlds—but also what *would* it say if it were said in various alternative possible worlds. If we consider just the two possible worlds I have labeled *i* and *j*, the propositional concept is this one:

	i	*j*
i	F	F
j	T	T

In *j*, "Hesperus" rigidly designates Mars, and so the sentence *Hesperus is Mars* expresses (according to the semantical rules we are assuming) the necessary truth.

Note that while neither of the horizontal propositions that make up this propositional concept is the contingent proposition that O'Leary seems to be expressing, there is a proposition determined by the propositional concept that is the intuitively right one: this is the *diagonal proposition*—the one that for each possible world is true if and only if the horizontal proposition expressed in that world is true at that world. This suggests the following hypothesis: *Under certain conditions, the content of an assertion is not the proposition determined by the ordinary semantical rules, but instead the diagonal proposition of the propositional concept determined.* To make this hypothesis precise, we need only spell out the conditions under which the operation is to be performed. I have tried to go some way toward doing this in Chapter 4. The general strategy is a Gricean one.[4] There are various independently motivated pragmatic maxims governing discourse. When a speaker seems to be violating one of these in a blatant way, a cooperative conversational strategy may require that the addressee reinterpret what is said in a way that makes it conform to the maxims. One way to

---

[4] See e.g. Grice (1989).

reinterpret—a way that is appropriate to the violation of a particular pragmatic maxim—is to diagonalize: to take the assertion to express the diagonal proposition of the propositional concept determined by the utterance
and its context. This operation yields intuitively plausible results, and it
helps to reconcile semantical rules that work well in most contexts with
apparently recalcitrant phenomena.

I want to turn now from the assertion problem to the problem about
belief. The main problem concerns the way beliefs are attributed to others:
that is, it concerns the relationship between the sentential complement
used by a speaker to attribute a belief to someone and the proposition that
the subject of the attribution is said to believe. But let us look first at belief
from the believer's point of view. Propositional concepts can help us to
understand the relationship between the content of a belief and the way
that a believer might represent his belief to himself. Imagine O'Leary, not
asserting anything about the solar system, but just thinking about it. He
might be out on a clear evening, looking up at that so-called star he has
seen so often, thinking to himself, *that's Mars*. The content of that
thought is obviously something like the contingently false proposition
described above. An hypothesis similar to the one sketched above for the
assertion example will explain how that mental event—that act of
thought—can have that content.[5]

Finally, let us look at belief attribution: statements of the form *x believes
that P*. There is an additional problem that arises here, a problem that pre-
vents us from simply generalizing, in a mechanical way, the explanation of
the problematic assertions to an explanation of problematic attributions
of belief. The problem arises from the following difference between the
assertion case and the belief attribution case: in the case of assertion, the
speaker—the person who chooses the words to be uttered—is the same
person as the one whose attitudes the words are chosen to express. We have
only one point of view to contend with—that of the speaker. But in the
belief case, the speaker's point of view will normally be different from that
of the subject to whom the attitude is attributed. The subject's language, if
any, may be different from the speaker's; the background information
against which the speaker's utterance is to be evaluated may be very different from the information that might be exploited by the subject whose
belief is described in the utterance. So the means available to the subject
for putting his belief into words might be very different from the means
available to the speaker.

---

[5] In "Indexical Belief", reprinted in Ch. 7 of the present volume, I consider in more detail
some now familiar problems concerning belief from the believer's point of view, applying
the diagonalization strategy to them.

This contrast between the points of view of speaker and subject affects the possibility of the diagonalization explanation in belief attribution cases because it makes it difficult to construct an appropriate propositional concept, and difficult to generalize about when a sentential complement should be interpreted by a diagonal proposition. In the assertion case, it is relatively clear how a sentence determines a propositional concept, relative to the possible worlds compatible with the presuppositions of the speaker. It is clear because of the fact that it will be presupposed by the speaker (that is, it will be true in all possible worlds compatible with the speaker's context) that the utterance event is taking place. But to extend the kind of explanation I am proposing to the belief attribution case, we need to define a propositional concept not just for the possible words compatible with the presuppositions of the speaker, but also for the possible worlds that are, or might be, compatible with the beliefs of the subject of the attribution.[6] When the beliefs of the subject are very different from the presuppositions of the speaker, it is not always obvious how this is to be done.

Consider the example with which we began: *O'Leary believes that Hesperus is Mars*. Suppose this is said by Daniels to me. Of course Daniels and I both know that Hesperus is Venus, and not Mars. There are no possible worlds compatible with the background presuppositions of *our* conversation in which the solar system is arranged so that Mars appears where Venus in fact appears in the evening. And O'Leary—the subject—is not participating in our conversation, and does not know about it. We cannot ask, what proposition the complement of Daniels' statement about O'Leary expresses in each of the possible worlds compatible with O'Leary's beliefs. We cannot ask this since that statement does not exist in all of those possible worlds. Nevertheless, if required to extend the propositional concept, to define it for those possible worlds, it is intuitively pretty clear, at least for this example, how we should do it. We ask something like the following question: If Daniels were to utter the sounds he is uttering in a possible world compatible with O'Leary's beliefs, what would the content of those sounds be? If the solar system were arranged so that Mars appears in the evening where Venus in fact does, then Daniels and I, as well as O'Leary, would use the name *Hesperus* to refer to Mars. And so,

---

[6] The possible worlds compatible with what the speaker presupposed define the basic context for the interpretation of the speaker's speech act. In the case of a belief attribution, the possible worlds that may, for all the speaker presupposes, be compatible with what the subject of the attribution believes define what I have called the *derived context*. This is the context relative to which the sentential complement is interpreted. In "Belief Attribution and Context", reprinted in Ch. 8 of the present volume, I argue that some of the same pragmatic maxims that constrain the relation between speech acts and basic contexts will constrain the relation between content attribution clauses and derived contexts.

according to the semantical rules in that world, Daniels' sentential complement, *that Hesperus is Mars*, expresses a necessary truth. If we extend the propositional concept in this way, defining it for the situations that might, for all Daniels and I are presupposing, be compatible with O'Leary's beliefs, then the diagonal of that propositional concept will be the proposition that seems, intuitively, to be the one O'Leary is said to believe.

What if O'Leary speaks some language other than English? That will make no difference to the explanation, so long as he has some acquaintance with Venus as it appears in the evening, either through having seen it, or through having acquired some name that denotes Venus because Venus appears where it does in the evening. The propositional concept we construct is the one not for the sentence as O'Leary would use or understand it, but for the sentence as the speaker and addressee would use and understand it if they were in the possible worlds relative to which the propositional concept is being defined. Because *our* name *Hesperus* would denote Mars if the solar system had been differently arranged in a certain way, *we* can use the clause *that Hesperus is Mars* to refer to the proposition that the solar system is differently arranged in that way.

O'Leary's belief about Hesperus and Mars is a belief about the solar system, and not a belief about the English language. But the diagonalization explanation will also work for cases where the belief in question is a linguistic belief, expressed in the material mode. Consider this example, adapted from an argument of Alonzo Church and discussed by Tyler Burge[7] *Alfred believes that a fortnight is a period of ten days.* It is intuitively clear that if what this statement says is true, then in possible worlds compatible with Alfred's beliefs, *fortnight*, in English, means *period of ten days*. The proposition Alfred is said to believe, it seems plausible to suppose, is the one that is true in possible worlds with that rule of English, and false in others. That proposition is the diagonal of the appropriate propositional concept.

Church, in his discussion of a related example, notes the failure of a translation test.[8] Whatever the example sentence says, it is clear that its translation into German cannot say the same thing. German has no word for *fortnight*, so the German translation of that word would have to be the same as the translation of the phrase *period of fourteen days*. Church, as I understand him, uses this failure to argue for the conclusion that the example sentence does not succeed in saying what it seems to be saying. It ought, Church suggests, to be reformulated in explicitly metalinguistic terms. But we can explain the failure of the translation test without

---

[7] Burge (1978).   [8] Church (1954).

drawing this conclusion. According to the kind of account I am suggesting, belief attributions are, in cases requiring diagonalization, highly context-dependent. Translation into another language will alter the possible contexts of use for a sentence, and may do so in ways that affect the possible interpretations of the sentence. In the example sentence, it is essential to the context of use that the language being spoken be English, and this is why translation into German yields a sentence that cannot be used to say what the English sentence says.

Of course we do not always diagonalize, and where we do not, we can use language and concepts not available to the subject to attribute belief. If Alfred believes that Bernard will be gone for fourteen days, we can truly say *Alfred believes that Bernard will be gone for a fortnight*, whatever Alfred's beliefs about the word *fortnight*. We can also, in *de re* or relational belief attributions, use referring expressions not available to the subject. So, for example, if O'Leary and I can see that there is one and only one man in the room wearing a faded denim leisure suit, and if that man is in fact van Fraassen, and if Daniels believes that van Fraassen is a spy, then I can truly say to O'Leary, *Daniels believes that the man in the faded denim leisure suit is a spy*, even if Daniels is not present, and does not know that van Fraassen even owns a faded denim leisure suit.

The situation gets slightly more complicated with examples that are *de re* belief attributions, but that also require diagonalization. Consider the following examples borrowed and adapted from a paper by Bas van Fraassen.[9] *Daniels believes that the man in the faded denim leisure suit is Kaplan* (said by me to O'Leary in circumstances like those described above), and *Daniels believes that I am Kaplan* (said by van Fraassen). What would the world be like if the belief that these statements seem to attribute to Daniels were true? (I assume that both statements attribute the same belief to him.) It would be a world in which Daniels' use of the name *Kaplan*—the particular use that in fact refers to David Kaplan, Professor of Philosophy at UCLA and author of a monumental but still unpublished manuscript on demonstratives—referred instead to Bas van Fraassen. That is, it would be a possible world in which the correct historical explanation of Daniels' use of the name *Kaplan* (in cases where *in fact* it refers to David Kaplan) involves, in the relevant way, van Fraassen instead of Kaplan. We will get the proposition that is true in just those possible worlds if we diagonalize the propositional *function* concept for the predicate *being Kaplan*, and then predicate the result of van Fraassen. In this way, we can apply the diagonalization strategy to *de re* or relational belief attributions as well as to *de dicto* or notional attributions.

---

[9] See van Fraassen (1979). This is a descendant of an unpublished paper that suggested these examples.

It is interesting to compare these last two examples with examples obtained by reversing subject and predicate in the complements. *Daniels believes that Kaplan is the man in the faded denim leisure suit*, and *Daniels believes that Kaplan is I*. Despite the symmetry of identity, these sentences seem clearly to say something different from the ones they were derived from. I think the first would normally be appropriate only if Daniels were present, and true only if he were aware of someone wearing the outfit described. I am not sure what the second sentence would be trying to say.

The procedure I am proposing for extending propositional concepts so that the diagonalization strategy can be applied to problematic belief attributions takes examples case by case. It is not, as yet, very satisfactory if we are looking for a systematic way to explain why the complements of belief attributions denote the propositions that they seem to denote. But if, using this procedure, we can find a possible worlds proposition that is a plausible candidate to be the object of belief being attributed in the various problematic examples, then we will at least have a good way of answering the first of the questions that our working hypothesis suggested that we ask. That is, if we can do this, we will be able to reconcile the hypothesis with the phenomena by finding possible worlds propositions for the recalcitrant examples. And it will not be completely mysterious how these propositions can be expressed by the sentences that seem to express them.

7

Indexical Belief

There is, or appears to be, a conflict between, on the one hand, some received doctrines about propositional attitudes and their objects, and on the other hand, the existence of attitudes that seem to be essentially indexical. It is often assumed that belief, for example, is a relation between a person and some kind of abstract object which is timelessly true or false. But it is difficult to see how to explain many of a person's beliefs about himself—about who or where he is—in terms of a relation to such an abstract object. The conflict was diagnosed and discussed some years ago in a series of papers by Hector-Neri Castañeda.[1] More recently, John Perry[2] and David Lewis[3] have written on the conflict, each suggesting, in different ways, that we must modify or reject some of the received doctrines in order to account for the existence of essentially indexical attitudes. I will argue that despite the appearance of conflict, one can reconcile the doctrines with the phenomena in question, although the reconciliation I will suggest yields a conception of the object of attitudes which is rather different from the traditional one.

I will begin by stating the received doctrines about propositions and propositional attitudes (I) and reviewing some of the examples that raise problems for the doctrines (II). Then I will sketch the responses to the problem that Perry and Lewis have proposed (III), followed by my own proposal and some reasons for thinking it gives a better account of the situation (IV).

It is at least initially plausible to assume that O'Leary's believing that pigs can fly is a relation between the man O'Leary and an abstract object—call it a proposition—which is denoted by the expression *that pigs can fly*. To make this assumption is not to say very much about what sort of things propositions are: they might be complexes made up of concepts and objects, sentences of some ideal language of thought, equivalence classes of sentence tokens, functions from possible worlds into truth-

---

[1] See Castañeda (1966, 1967).
[2] See Perry (1977, 1979).   [3] See Lewis (1979a).

values. The doctrine that causes the problem we are concerned with is independent of the details of one's theory about the nature of propositional objects; all that is essential is that propositions have truth-values that do not vary from time to time, person to person, or place to place. If propositions are identified with sentences or meanings of sentences, they must be eternal sentences, or meanings of eternal sentences. If propositions are identified with functions taking truth and falsity as values, they must take possible worlds as their arguments, and not indices that may have different values in the same world.

The received doctrine may be summed up in two theses:[4]

1. Belief is a relation between an animate subject and an abstract object which we will call, without prejudging its nature, a proposition.
2. Propositions have truth-values, and their truth-values do not vary with time, place, or person.[5]

II

Here are four examples, all derived from examples discussed by Perry and Lewis, of the phenomenon that creates the problem.

1. Rudolf Lingens is an amnesiac lost in the Stanford Library. He has found and read a biography of himself, and so knows quite a bit about Rudolf Lingens. He knows, for example, that Lingens is a distant cousin of a notorious spy. But he does not know that *he* is Lingens—that *he* is a distant cousin of a notorious spy. No matter how complete the biography, it will not by itself give him the information he lacks. Even if the book includes the fact that Lingens is an amnesiac lost in the Stanford Library, this may not be enough. He can use this information only if he knows, or has reason to believe, that *he* (and no other amnesiac) is lost in the Stanford Library.[6]

2. Heimson is mad. He believes that he is Hume. Hume, of course, having been sane, and no amnesiac, also believed that he (himself) was Hume. Hume and Heimson disagreed about who was Hume, but they agreed that

---

[4] Perry (1979), lists three theses which together constitute what he calls the doctrine of propositions. Perry's first two theses are essentially the same as the two I have listed. The third (roughly, that propositions cannot be identified with truth-values) is part of any plausible doctrine of propositions, but is not relevant to the problem.

[5] This thesis need not be taken to exclude the possibility that some propositions may lack a truth-value. What is essential is that they not ever change truth-values (or change from not having a truth-value to having one).

[6] This is Perry's example, discussed in Perry (1977). The character, Rudolf Lingens, first appeared in Frege's "The Thought".

Hume lived in Edinburgh, that Hume wrote a history of England, that Hume was acquainted with Voltaire. They might (if Heimson was both mad enough, and sufficiently well informed about Hume) have agreed about all the facts about Hume that could be stated in a neutral, impersonal way.[7]

3. O'Leary has somehow managed to lock himself in the trunk of his car. He knows that no one will be able to hear his cries for help until morning, so he goes to sleep. He wakes up when the town clock tolls, but isn't sure whether it rings three or four times. "I wonder what time it is," he thinks. "I wonder whether it is now three, or whether it is four."[8]

4. There are, according to a distinguished theologian, two gods. One lives on the tallest mountain and throws down manna, while the other lives on the coldest mountain and throws down thunderbolts. Both, it is alleged, are omniscient with respect to knowledge of propositions. Each knows, down to the last detail, exactly which possible world is actual. But neither knows which God he is. It may even be, the theologian has conjectured, that their omniscience helps explain their ignorance of who they are, since omniscient beings lack the kind of limited perspective that most of us have from which they might infer their own identities.[9]

The problem with these examples is not simply that a belief is reported or expressed with an indexical or context-dependent sentence—a sentence whose truth-value may vary over different speakers, times and places of utterance. Proponents of the received doctrines about propositions have long recognized that sentences may be context-dependent, but they take this to show that the propositional content of a sentence may vary from context to context. Different utterances of the sentence "I am happy" have different truth-values, but this is because the sentence is used to express different timeless propositions on different occasions, and not because it expresses a proposition whose truth-value may vary from occasion to occasion. Context-dependent sentences may have the same *meaning* from use to use, even when the truth-value changes, but meaning cannot, in general, be identified with content. The meaning of a sentence (or at least one aspect of the meaning) is something like a function about contexts of use into propositional content.[10]

So, according to this standard way of reconciling the received doctrines with context-dependence, the variation is in the means of expressing

---

[7] This example is also from Perry (1977).

[8] O'Leary is my own character, but the example is essentially the same as examples discussed by Perry and Lewis.

[9] The theologian in question is David Lewis. The example is from Lewis (1979a).

[10] See "Pragmatics", reprinted in Ch. 1 of the present volume, for an informal discussion of this conception of meaning, and Kaplan (1989) for a theoretical development of it.

propositions, and is not integral to content. The same thought which might most easily be expressed with tenses and personal pronouns could, in principle, always be expressed in a neutral, impersonal way.

The examples cited above are problematic because in these cases there seems to be no way to eliminate the indexical element in the expression or report of the attitude without distorting the content. As we said, Lingens knows that *Lingens* is a cousin of a spy, but still does not know that he himself is one. The beliefs and doubts in question in these examples are self-locating attitudes. They seem to be beliefs and doubts, not about the way the world is, but about the agent's place in it at the time at which he has the belief or doubt. It is not obvious how to express such attitudes in terms of a relation between a person and some timelessly true or false proposition.

III

I want now to sketch two responses to the problem—one by John Perry and one by David Lewis. Each responds by rejecting one of the two received doctrines: Perry denies thesis 1; Lewis denies thesis 2.

Propositions of the traditional kind—abstract objects that conform to thesis 2—play a role in Perry's account of belief, but according to him, belief is more than a relation between a person and such an object. A person believes a proposition in virtue of being in a certain belief state, but belief states must not be confused with *objects* or *contents* of belief—with *propositions* of the traditional kind. A particular instance of a belief state will determine a proposition, but it cannot be identified with it. The same proposition might be determined by different belief states, and the same belief state may, in different circumstances, determine different propositions.

Perry's notion of a belief state, as I understand it, is modeled on the notion of sentence meaning alluded to in section II above: meaning as a function from context into propositional content. Roughly, two people are in the same belief state if their beliefs might correctly be expressed with sentences with the same meaning, in this sense. So, for example, Hume and Heimson are in the same belief state because each could correctly express his belief with the sentence "I am Hume." But the propositions they believe—the object of their beliefs—are of course different since what Hume believes is true while what Heimson believes is false.

It seems that Lingens believes that Lingens is a cousin of a spy, but not that *he* is. So does he believe of Lingens that he is a cousin of a spy or not? Perry's answer is that he is in one belief state that determines the proposition that Lingens is a cousin of a spy; but fails to be in a different belief state that also determines the same proposition. Were Lingens to learn that he was Lingens, he could infer that he was a cousin of a spy. In doing so, he would not come to learn a new proposition; he would come to learn the same proposition in a new way—relative to a new belief state.[11]

Lewis's account treats belief as a relation to a single abstract object, but the object is not a proposition. Lewis argues that so-called propositional attitudes should be understood as attitudes to *properties* rather than to propositions. To have a belief is to ascribe a property to oneself. Heimson's belief that he is Hume consists in his ascription of the property *being identical to Hume* to himself. Lingens does not know that he is a distant cousin of a notorious spy because he doesn't ascribe the property *being a distant cousin of a notorious spy* to himself.

The suggestion fits the problematic examples very nicely, but what about the more familiar cases? How, for example, are we to understand Lingens's belief, based on his reading, that Lingens is a cousin of a spy as the self-ascription of a property? Lewis's answer is that to believe that Lingens is a cousin of a spy is to ascribe to oneself the property of being in a possible world in which Lingens is a cousin of a spy. Any attitude which might be explained as a relation between a person and a proposition can as well be explained as the self-ascription of a property in this way. To believe the proposition that p is to believe that one is in a world in which p.

This account of attitudes to impersonal propositions may seem artificial at first, but Lewis uses an analogy between location in physical space and location in logical space to motivate it. There are not two kinds of beliefs, self-locating beliefs and propositional beliefs: *all* beliefs are self-locating. Overtly self-locating beliefs are beliefs about one's location in space and time within the actual world. Beliefs that appear to be attitudes to more objective, impersonal propositions are beliefs about one's location in logical space—in the space of possible worlds. Unlike most of us, the gods of Lewis's story know precisely where they are in logical space—they know

---

[11] I initially interpreted Perry's account to imply the following: statements of the form *x believes that p* assert that *x* stands in a relation to *two* abstract objects, a proposition and a belief state, both of which are determined by the sentential clause, *that p*. But this, I have been told (John Perry, personal communication), is a mistake. According to the intended interpretation of Perry's account, sentences of the form *x believes that p* assert that the person *x* is in some belief state or other which determines the proposition *that p*. So Perry is not really disagreeing with the doctrine of propositions if that doctrine is taken to be a doctrine about the semantics of belief attributions. According to this interpretation of Perry's account, it is not strictly correct to say that Lingens believes that Lingens is a cousin of a spy, but not that *he* is. He *does* believe that *he* is, even though it would be misleading to put it that way.

what world they are in. What they fail to know is their location within that world—what mountains they are on. Both what they know and what they fail to know can be seen as information about their own place in the overall scheme of things. The problem with the received doctrine, according to Lewis's account, is that it focusses exclusively on one kind of self-locating belief. The examples show that we need to generalize the idea, which is what the shift from propositions to properties does.

IV

I want now to try to reconcile the two theses about propositions and propositional attitudes with the examples, and to compare this reconciliation with the proposals of Perry and Lewis. To do this, I need to say a little more than is said by the received doctrine about what I take propositions to be. Propositions, according to the account I will sketch, are functions from possible worlds into truth-values. Equivalently, but more informally, they are ways of dividing a space of possibilities—ways of picking out some subset from a set of alternative ways that things might be. The intuitive idea behind this conception of proposition is an old one: it is the idea that what is essential to propositional or informational content is that certain possibilities be excluded. To say or believe something informative is to rule something out—to say or believe that some of the ways the world might have been are not ways that it is. The *content* of what one says or believes should be understood in terms of the possibilities that are excluded.

According to this conception, propositions are not structured entities with concepts, objects or senses as parts; they are not complexes which reflect the grammatical or semantic structure of the sentences that express them. The content of a sentence will of course be a function of what is expressed or denoted by the constituents of the sentence, and of its structure, but concepts, objects, senses and semantic structure are part of the means by which content is determined, and not components of the content itself. The same proposition might be expressed in very different ways; different expressions with very different logical forms might divide the same set of alternative possibilities in the same way.

This conception of propositional content is compatible with various different accounts of the alternative possibilities that propositions are said to distinguish between. One might, like Carnap, take them to be linguistic entities—state descriptions in some ideal language. One might, like David Lewis, take them to be concrete universes, other universes similar in kind

to, and as real as, our own universe, where "our own universe" refers to
ourselves and our total environment.[12] Or one might take the alternative
possibilities relative to which propositions are defined to be abstract but
non-linguistic objects—something like maximal properties that the world
might have, or might have had. I will assume, and have argued elsewhere,
that the third kind of explanation is the appropriate one.[13]

One might ask, are there such things as possibilities, or possible worlds,
in this sense? I doubt that it is plausible to believe that there is, independent of context, a well-defined domain of absolutely maximally specific
possible states of the world, but I do not think the proposed conception of
propositional content requires a commitment to such a domain. The alternative possibilities used to define propositions must be exclusive alternatives which are maximally specific, relative to the distinctions that might
be made in the context at hand. But one can make sense of this requirement even if there is no ultimate set of possibilities relative to which any
possible distinctions might be made. One might think of possible worlds
as something like the elements of a partition of a space, rather than as the
points of the space. The space might be partitioned differently in different
contexts, and there might be no maximally fine partition. (This is only a
rough analogy. And the space itself may also differ from context to context.)

If the alternative possibilities there are vary with context, then so do the
propositions which are, according to the conception of content I am
sketching, just ways of distinguishing between the alternative possibilities.
One can make sense of questions about the identity and difference of the
propositions expressed in different utterances or acts of thought only
given a common context—a common set of possibilities that the propositions are understood to distinguish between. This yields a conception of
proposition which is less stable than, and very different from, the traditional conception, but it is, I think, more adequate to the phenomena of
speech and thought.

If this is what propositions are, then how are we to understand the
beliefs and doubts of the characters in the examples sketched above as attitudes to propositions? The account of propositional content suggests an
intuitive strategy for answering this question. In general, to understand
the content of a person's belief, ask what the world would be like if the
belief were correct. What is the world like, according to the person's conception of the way the world is? If we can give a coherent account, in our
own terms, of a way, or a set of ways, that things might have been which

[12] See Lewis (1973: 84–91). This passage is reprinted in Loux (1979).
[13] See Stalnaker (1976a) and also the other papers in Loux (1979) for discussions of the
philosophical status of possible worlds.

seems intuitively to represent correctly the person's own conception of the world and his place in it, then we will have explained his beliefs as attitudes to propositions—objects which conform to the received doctrines.

I will approach the question holistically. That is, I will not begin by looking at the sentences which express or ascribe the belief and ask what proposition seems to be determined by the semantical rules for such sentences. Instead I will ask what alternative possible situations seem, according to the story as a whole, to be compatible with the agent's beliefs. If we can get a plausible answer to this question, then we can turn to the different question about the means by which that proposition was expressed or ascribed. We can ask, how is it that the sentences used to express and ascribe the belief are able to express and ascribe that belief.

So what is the world like according to Lingens? When the question is put this way the answer is fairly clear. In all possible worlds compatible with Lingens's beliefs, there is a person named "Lingens" about whom a biography was written which was read by Lingens, who is an amnesiac lost in a library. In all of these possible worlds, the subject of this biography is a distant cousin of a notorious spy. Who is this person? Is he Lingens himself—the same Lingens that the biography is in fact about, the man who is in fact an amnesiac lost in the Stanford Library? In some of the alternative possible worlds compatible with Lingens's beliefs the person named "Lingens" is Lingens, but in others of the possible situations he is a different person. (I am assuming that in the original story, Lingens does not believe that he is *not* Lingens. He doesn't have an opinion one way or the other about who he is.)

According to this characterization of Lingens's state of mind, his belief that Lingens is a cousin of a spy seems not really to be a belief *about* Lingens; it is a belief about whoever falls under a certain general concept, the concept of being the person named "Lingens" who is the subject of a certain biography. But, one might object, aren't proper names rigid designators? Isn't the proposition that Lingens is a cousin of a spy the proposition that is true in possible worlds in which the man Lingens is a cousin of a spy, and false in worlds in which that same man is not a spy? If Lingens's cousin were not a spy, wouldn't we say that Lingens's belief was false, even if some different person named "Lingens" were the subject of the biography, and were a cousin of a spy?

This objection points to a clash between the answer to the holistic question about Lingens's state of mind and the straightforward answer to the more analytical question, what proposition results from applying independently plausible semantical rules to the sentence with which the belief is expressed or ascribed. To get clearer about the relation between the answers to the two questions let me look more closely at what the semantical rules tell us about the proposition expressed by the sentence, "Lingens is a cousin of a spy." In asking about this, I will continue to presuppose that propositions are functions from possible situations into truth-values. I will begin by describing three possible situations, and then ask what function from these possible situations into truth-values is determined by a straightforward semantic account of the sentence in question. The semantic account will presuppose that "Lingens" is a rigid designator, that "is a cousin of a spy" expresses a property (a function from possible worlds into classes of individuals), and that the proposition expressed is the one that is true if and only if the individual designated has the property expressed.

First, the three possible situations: Situation i is the actual situation. Lingens, the amnesiac, is the subject of the biography, and is a cousin of a spy. But in situation j, the biography correctly describes, and was written about, a different person—call him "Lingens 2." Our Lingens, the amnesiac, has a different name, and is not a cousin of a spy in situation j. Situation k is just like situation j, except that in k the biography of Lingens 2 makes some false claims. Lingens 2's cousin is not a spy in k.

We are interested in what the semantic account sketched above tells us about the proposition expressed by a certain token of the sentence "Lingens is a cousin of a spy," the token that occurs in the biography that is read by Lingens, and accepted by him. But note that this token exists, not only in the actual situation, but also in the other two possible situations I have described. So we may ask a more general question: not just, what proposition is *in fact* expressed by that sentence token, but for each of the possible situations, what proposition is expressed by the token as it occurs in that situation.[14] If proper names are, as Kripke and others have argued, rigid designators whose reference is determined by the causal explanation of the relevant uses of the name, then the answer to this question will be different for the different possible situations.

According to the straightforward semantic account, in situation i, the name "Lingens" rigidly designates Lingens—our Lingens, the amnesiac. This person is a cousin of a spy in situation i, but is not a cousin of a spy in j or in k. So the proposition expressed by the sentence is the one that is true at i, but false at the other two situations. But in situation j, the occurrence of "Lingens" in question rigidly designates a different person, Lingens 2. This man is a cousin of a spy at j, but presumably does not exist at all at i, and is not a cousin of a spy in k. Hence the proposition expressed by the token as it occurs in j is the one that is false at i, true at j, and false

---

[14] Some may dispute my assumption that the same token exists in the different situations. I think it is plausible to say that it does, but it is enough for my purposes that the tokens in different possible situations are epistemic counterparts for Lingens.

at k. In k, the name also rigidly designates Lingens 2, so the same proposition is expressed as is expressed in j. The following two-dimensional matrix, representing what I have called a *propositional concept*, summarizes these facts.[15]

	i	j	k
i	T	F	F
j	F	T	F
k	F	T	F

The horizontal lines of Ts and Fs represent the propositions expressed, according to the semantic account we are presupposing, by the sentence "Lingens is a cousin of a spy" as it occurs in each of the three alternative possible situations. Propositions are represented simply by enumerating their truth-values at each of the relevant possible situations. Note that the truth-value, in situation j, of the proposition that is *in fact* expressed by the sentence in question (that is, the one that is expressed in situation i) is different from the truth-value, in j, of the proposition that *would* have been expressed if j had been actual (that is, the one that is expressed in situation j).

Now it is clear from the description of the example that Lingens does not know whether he is in situation i or situation j, although he does believe that he is not in k, since he believes that what the biography says is true. It follows that he does not believe either of the two propositions represented by the rows of the matrix. It also follows that he does not know which of the two propositions the sentence in the biography expresses. But he does believe this: whichever proposition the sentence expresses, it is a true one. This is why he can safely assent to the statement in the biography.

The proposition that the sentence in question expresses a truth is the proposition that is true at i and at j, but false at k. This is a different proposition from either of the ones represented by rows of the matrix, but it is represented in the matrix: it is the *diagonal proposition*, the proposition that is true at x (for each x) if and only if the proposition expressed in x is true at x. This proposition, I suggest, is the belief that Lingens expresses when he says "Lingens is a cousin of a spy," and the belief we ascribed when we wrote that Lingens believes that Lingens is a spy in describing the example.[16]

[15] Propositional concepts are discussed and applied to the explanation of identity statements and negative existentials in "Assertion", reprinted in Ch. 4 of the present volume.

[16] In making this suggestion, I am not proposing a general account of the semantics for belief. In particular, I am not proposing the hypothesis that in general *x believes that p* is true if and only if *x* believes the diagonal proposition of the propositional concept for the expression *that p*. All I am suggesting is that in this example, the belief we seem, intuitively, to be attributing to Lingens coincides with the one determined by the diagonalization

So the objector to whom we are replying is right in a sense: Lingens's belief is not simply about Lingens; it is about whoever plays a certain role in the world, and that role is played by different people in different alternative possible situations. But we need not reject the causal chain account of reference, or the thesis that names are, in their normal uses, rigid designators. The role in question is defined by the kind of causal relationship described by causal theories of reference; the proposition in question is a function of the propositions determined, in various alternative possible situations, by the semantic account which assumes that names are rigid designators.

Am I saying that the belief in question is essentially metalinguistic—that it is a belief about the semantic value of a certain sentence? No, I am saying only that the content of the belief in question is the diagonal proposition of a certain propositional concept. One way to express the proposition unambiguously is to refer to a certain sentence , but propositions, on the account we are presupposing, are independent of the means by which they are expressed. The facts that distinguish the possible situations in which the proposition is true from those in which it is false are not primarily linguistic facts; they are facts about where people are in the world, and what they have done.

My description of the possible situations compatible with Lingens's beliefs assumes that Lingens knows who he himself is in the following sense: in each of these situations, one and the same person—Lingens himself—is the person denoted by "I."[17] What he does not know is who the subject of the biography is: the person occupying this role varies from situation to situation. But, one might object, why not describe the situation in the opposite way? Wouldn't it be more natural to say that Lingens knows who *Lingens* is, but does not know who he himself is. That is, why not say that in all possible situations compatible with Lingens's beliefs, Lingens himself is the subject of the biography, but the amnesiac—the person referred to by "I"—is a different person from situation to situation.

This alternative description is, I think, perfectly coherent, and fits the example as well as the one I have offered. The difference between the two accounts is in how individuals are identified across the possible situations which define a state of belief. I am inclined to think that there may be no

operation. The question, "What compositional semantic rules will explain, in general, the truth conditions of *x believes that p* as a function of the semantic value of its parts?" is not a question I am trying to answer here. If I am right about the examples, and about what propositions are, then the answer to this question will be more complicated than has sometimes been supposed since the relation between the meaning of the clause *that p* and the proposition it denotes may be highly context-dependent.

[17] This account of "knowing who" is Jaakko Hintikka's. See Hintikka (1962: 131f). See Boër and Lycan (1975) for an interesting and thorough discussion of "knowing who."

fact of the matter about which of the descriptions is correct—that they are essentially equivalent.[18] To try to make this plausible, let me digress briefly to make some general remarks about the question of the identification of individuals across this kind of possible situation.

Consider an example which, unlike the ones we have been discussing, is relatively unproblematic. I believe that Daniels was once an iceman in Chicago. My belief is, I think it is reasonable to say, really *about* Daniels; I know him fairly well, and am not inclined to confuse him with anyone else. Others might correctly ascribe this belief to me by referring to Daniels himself ("See that bald guy talking to the tall woman by the bar? Stalnaker believes that he was once an iceman in Chicago"). The reason that my belief can be ascribed in this way is that in each of the possible situations which define my state of belief, the very same person—Daniels himself— is a former Chicago iceman. But what, we might ask, is it about my state of mind that makes it correct to identify that person with our Daniels? Why is that person Daniels rather than someone else with the same name and similar characteristics?

The question I am asking here is something like the kind of question that Kripke has taught us to view with suspicion. Kripke argued that when I make a counterfactual supposition—when I say, for example, "suppose Daniels had become a concert pianist," then I do not need to answer the question, "what is it about the person in your supposed counterfactual situation which makes him *Daniels*?" We don't need a criterion of identity to make counterfactual suppositions about particular individuals. So long as I am able to refer to Daniels in the actual world, then I can put *him* into my story. The person is Daniels simply because I say that he is.

Kripke's argument is persuasive, but my question is not quite the same as the one he rejects. I am asking, not about stipulated counterfactual situations, but about possible situations which characterize a state of belief. The question is, how must I be related to Daniels in order that my beliefs be about *him*? It won't help to answer *this* question to say that the person is Daniels because I say that he is, since my ability to say that he is—to refer to Daniels—is presumably dependent on the fact that I can have beliefs about, and intentions toward, *him*.

The question is a large and difficult one, but it is easy to point in a general way to the kind of considerations that should go into an answer. My belief is about Daniels partly because of the role that Daniels played in causing my state of mind to have the character which it has, and partly because the actions that my beliefs dispose me to perform are actions that involve Daniels. If Daniels had looked different, or had done

---

[18] Jaakko Hintikka has argued that there may be alternative equally correct ways to identify individuals across possible worlds. See e.g. Ch. 2 of Hintikka (1975).

different things, then the former Chicago iceman in the possible situations
which define my state of belief would have been different in corresponding
ways. And when I meet Daniels at an APA meeting, my behavior toward
him can be explained in part in terms of the characteristics that the former
Chicago iceman has in the possible situations that define my beliefs. That
is why he is Daniels.

Now however this kind of answer is filled out, it would be highly
implausible to expect that there should always be a nice one-one correspondence between certain individuals in the actual world and those who
inhabit the possible worlds that define a state of belief. As Bernard J.
Ortcutt taught us long ago, one and the same actual person may be
responsible for the existence and character of two distinct individuals in
the possible situations that define some state of belief. And equally well,
two distinct actual individuals may merge together in someone's mental
representation of the world. In these cases, questions such as "which individual in the belief world is the real Ortcutt?" may have no determinate
answer. In cases where two individuals in a possible situation have equal
claim to be identified with an individual in the actual world (or the reverse)
how the identification is made may depend more on the context of belief
ascription that it does on the character of the belief state itself.

In the world as Lingens thinks it might be, there are two individuals
both of whom are appropriately related to Lingens. Each one would be
said to be Lingens himself it if weren't for the other. It does not really matter, I think, which we say is the real Lingens. If I had described the case differently, saying that the subject of the biography was the real Lingens in
situation *j*, while some different person was the one reading the biography,
then the propositional concept for the statement "Lingens is a cousin of a
spy" would have been different from the one described above. But the *diagonal proposition* of the propositional concept—the proposition that I said
was the content of Lingens's belief—would have distinguished between the
situations *i, j* and *k* in exactly the same way.

My account of the Lingens example treats it as a special case of a more
general problem about *de re* belief. The problem is essentially the same,
according to my explanation, as the old problem of Ortcutt, the man
whom Ralph knows in two different guises. Ortcutt, you recall, is the "man
in a brown hat whom Ralph has glimpsed several times under questionable
circumstances," and also "a gray-haired man vaguely known to Ralph as
rather a pillar of the community."[19] In both the Lingens and the Ortcutt
cases, the problem is that two distinct individuals in the possible situations
used to characterize a state of mind correspond to the same individual in

---

[19] Quine (1966: 185).

the real world. In the case of Lingens, the relevant real world individual is the same as the one with the state of mind in question, but this does not seem to make very much difference to the explanation.[20] What does make a difference, in both cases, is that the subject of the attitudes in question, and the thoughts that he is having, are things that exist not only in the actual world, but also in the possible situations that define the subject's attitudes. As Descartes might remind us, when Lingens is wondering who he is, he knows at least that he (or someone) is wondering this—that his particular act of asking himself "who am I?" exists. What this means, according to the conception of content I am presupposing, is that a person thinking that thought will be an inhabitant in each of the possible situations compatible with his knowledge. It is this fact which makes it possible to find a propositional concept for the sentences used to express and ascribe the problematic beliefs, and so to explain how those sentences can be used to express and ascribe the right attitudes.

Let me apply the strategy I am using to two more examples, and then compare my explanation with the proposals of Lewis and Perry.

What is the world like according to O'Leary, the man who has locked himself in the trunk of his car? There are two relevantly different possible situations compatible with O'Leary's beliefs. In both of them, O'Leary is locked in the trunk of his car thinking to himself, "what time is it?" In one of these situations, this thought occurs at three o'clock in the morning, while in the other it occurs at four o'clock. The propositions that O'Leary wonders about are the ones that distinguish between these two possible situations.

O'Leary might express his doubt by asking "Is it now three o'clock?" If we follow a standard semantic account according to which both the indexical "it" and the name "three o'clock" are rigid designators of times, the propositional concept for the affirmative answer to the question will be as follows:

	i	j
i	T	T
j	F	F

(i is the situation in which O'Leary's thought occurs at three, and j is the situation in which it occurs at four). Again, it is the diagonal proposition of this propositional concept that is the content of the proposition that O'Leary would learn if he received an affirmative answer to his question.

[20] cf. Boër and Lycan (1980) where it is argued that the problem of the essential indexical is just a special case of the general problem of *de re* belief. The authors do not say, however, very much about how they would deal with the general problem.

It is essential to a correct account of this case that we be referring to the particular thought token that O'Leary is thinking. For suppose O'Leary thinks *both* at three and at four, "I wonder what time it is?" Suppose further that he knows, somehow, that he will think this at just these two times, although he knows that at four he won't remember having thought it at three. In this case, both of the relevant possible situations will be ones at which O'Leary wonders what time it is at both times. But he still doesn't know, at three, whether *this* token of that thought is the one that occurs at three. In this embellished example, the two possible situations are indiscernible: no qualitative features of the situations distinguish them. One who believes that indiscernible but distinct possible situations are impossible will find my explanation unacceptable, but I take the states of mind that are described in these examples to provide a context in which we can make sense of such possibilities.

The case of the two gods, as I would describe it, is also a case of ignorance of which of two indiscernible possible worlds is actual. One of these possible worlds is the actual world (assuming that the theologian's story is true), while the other is like it except that the god who is *in fact* on the tallest mountain is instead on the coldest mountain, with all the properties that the god on the coldest mountain in fact has. Thus the gods are not really omniscient with respect to propositional knowledge, although they are omniscient with respect to purely qualitative features of the world. When the god on the tallest mountain looks down on the world in whatever way nearly omniscient beings look upon the world, and wonders, "am I *that* one—the one on the tallest mountain?" he is wondering which of these two possible worlds is actual.[21]

Lewis considers this way of responding to his story and rejects it for two reasons. First, he rejects it because he believes that the identification of individuals across possible worlds must be explained in terms of counterpart relations that depend on qualitative similarities between individuals. For this reason, he rejects the coherence of qualitatively indiscernible but distinct possible worlds. But second, Lewis argues that the explanation won't work anyway, even for one who admits such possibilities. "Let's grant, briefly," he writes,

that the world *W* of the gods has its qualitative duplicate *V* in which the gods have traded places. Let the god on the tallest mountain know that his world is *W*, not *V*. Let him be omniscient about *all* propositions, not only qualitative ones. How

---

[21] cf. N. Wilson's famous example in which we are asked to imagine Julius Caesar to have all the properties of Marc Antony, and vice versa. Wilson, arguing that such a world is not really distinct from the actual world, remarked that the two worlds would look exactly the same. Arthur Prior replied that they might look the same to most of us, but they would look very different to Caesar and Antony. See Wilson (1959) and Prior (1960).

does this help? Never mind V, where he knows he doesn't live. There are still two different mountains in W where he might, for all he knows, be living.[22]

But this just begs the question. One cannot just stipulate that the god knows that he is in W, and not in V, for on the proposed explanation, that amounts to the assumption that he knows which mountain he is on. Lewis's argument may get some specious plausibility from the metaphor of location in logical space. Imagine a map of logical space divided into large sections corresponding to possible worlds, with each large section subdivided into smaller sections representing locations within possible worlds. Obviously, we could tell someone exactly which large section he was in without telling him where within it he was located. This may be an apt picture for an extreme realist about possible worlds—one who thinks that possible worlds are other universes like our own rather than alternative representations of our universe, but for the actualist it is a misleading picture. Knowing where you are within a country is a different thing from knowing which country you are in, but it is not so clear that knowing where you are in the world is not a case of knowing something about which world is the actual world. Consider counterfactual suppositions: it is natural to think of my supposition that I am now somewhere else in the world—say in Paris—as the supposition that a different possible world, or possible situation, is actual. Lewis himself must admit this in the case of ignorance of the spatial location of others. My doubt about whether Jimmy Carter is now in Washington must be explained as my doubt about whether I inhabit a world in which Jimmy Carter is now in Washington.

One might think that it is but a short step from the account I am proposing to Lewis's. One might think that instead of talking of indiscernible possible worlds, I should talk of what Lewis (following Quine) calls *centered worlds*. A centered world is an ordered pair consisting of a world and a designated individual in that world.[23] What I am calling distinct but indiscernible worlds might better be identified as distinct centered worlds with the same world, but different centers. And, as Lewis points out, to identify objects of attitudes with sets of centered worlds is equivalent to treating them as properties. I agree that the possible situations in terms of which intentional states and processes are defined are normally, perhaps essentially, centered in the sense that they all contain a representation of

[22] Lewis (1979a: 523).
[23] Lewis (1979a: 531–2). Quine originally defined centered worlds as pairs consisting of a world and a space-time point. Lewis suggested that we might replace the space-time point with an individual to avoid making the assumption that no two individuals can be in the same place at the same time. To handle the temporal cases, Lewis's centered worlds should probably be triples: a world, an individual and a time.

the mental state or process itself. But I think the identification of such possible situations with centered worlds in Lewis's sense, would make it more difficult to give an adequate account of the relations between different states of mind. Specifically, it would make it more difficult to compare past with present beliefs, and, more important, to explain the relations between the beliefs of different persons—relations that are essential to a natural explanation of the exchange of information. To bring this out, I will consider sequels to two of our examples.

O'Leary is rescued from the trunk of his car at nine the next morning. As he thinks back over his ordeal, he recalls the question he asked himself at three in the morning. "I still wonder," he thinks "what time it was *then*." I think O'Leary is asking himself the same question that he asked before. If he learns, somehow, that it was then three o'clock, the doubt that he had then will be resolved. This is because the same possible situations—ones in which a certain act of thought occurs at one of two different times—are involved. The centers of these situations have shifted in the sense that the act of thought whose location in time O'Leary wonders about is no longer the same as the act of wondering about it, but this shift does not require a shift in the possible situations used to characterize the propositions that define O'Leary's state of mind.

Even the embellished example according to which O'Leary wondered what time it was at both three and four might be followed by this sequel. Even if the event of O'Leary wondering what time it is at three was indistinguishable, to O'Leary, from the event of his wondering what time it was at four, it still might be that it is the first of these that O'Leary is recalling when he wonders, at nine, what time it was *then*.

How would this case be described on Lewis's account? He must say that at three, O'Leary was wondering about his present temporal location in the actual world, rather than about what possible world he inhabited. But at nine, what he wonders about is something quite different. Now he wonders whether he inhabits a world at which a certain thought occurred at three, or a world at which that thought (or its counterpart) occurred at four. This seems unnecessarily complicated.

Lingens, still lost in the Stanford Library, meets Ortcutt. "I've lost my memory and don't know who I am," says Lingens. "Can you tell me? Who am I?" "You're my cousin, Rudolf Lingens," replies Ortcutt.

This seems to be a simple case of direct and successful communication. Lingens requested a certain piece of information; Ortcutt was able to provide it, and did. Ortcutt was sincere—he believed what he said—and Lingens believed what he was told. Furthermore, Ortcutt's reply was direct: he did not just say something from which Lingens was able to infer the right answer to his question. He *told* him the answer.

If we take the objects of speech acts and mental states to be propositions, then our theoretical account of this act of communication can be as straightforward as the case seems to demand. Ortcutt's answer expresses a proposition that distinguishes between the relevant possible situations (the possible situations that define the presumed common knowledge of the two participants in the conversation) in a way that answers Lingens's question, and resolved his doubt. But Lewis's account of the case must be more complicated. If Lewis holds that the objects of speech acts, as well as of attitudes, are properties—that to make an assertion is also to ascribe a property to oneself—then he will have to describe the case in something like the following way: Lingens asks which of a certain set of properties is correctly ascribed to himself. Ortcutt responds by ascribing a *different* property to *him*self. Lingens is then able to infer the answer to his question from Ortcutt's assertion. (I am not sure just what property Ortcutt ascribes to himself. Perhaps it is the property of being someone who is talking to Lingens.) The answer to the question is thus quite indirect, and this is not a special feature of this example. The account I am putting into Lewis's mouth must hold that *all* answers to questions are indirect in this way. If assertions are always self-ascriptions of properties, then people talk only about themselves. Alternatively, Lewis might hold that speech acts, unlike attitudes, have propositions rather than properties as objects. But then he must deny that speech is a straightforward expression of thought—that what a person says, when he believes what he says, is what he believes. If Lewis makes this move, then he may save the intuition that Ortcutt's reply is a direct answer to Lingens's question, but he cannot say that the content of the answer is the information that resolves Lingens's doubt.

I think this last example also points to a limitation of Perry's account, the account that distinguishes belief states from belief contents. The problem, I will argue, is that neither a belief state nor a belief content, in Perry's sense, is an adequate representation of the *informational content* of Ortcutt's answer.

There is, as Perry points out, an analogy between the two objects Perry distinguishes to help account for indexical belief, and the two kinds of meaning that David Kaplan distinguishes to help account for indexical speech. The *character* of a sentence type, according to Kaplan, is a function from context into content, where content is something which determines a proposition in the sense we have been using the term. The character of "I am a cousin of a spy" will be a function taking a certain individual, the speaker, into a content that is true if and only if that individual is a cousin of a spy. Sentences with different characters (such as "I am a cousin of a spy," "you are a cousin of a spy") may, in different

contexts, have the same content. And different utterances of sentences
with the same character (such as two utterances of "I am a cousin of a spy"
by two different people) may have different contents. Perry's notion of a
belief state is something like a mental analogue of a character. In the
example of the conversation between Lingens and Ortcutt, the two men
are in different belief states, even after Lingens accepts what Ortcutt has
told him, but the two states determine the same content—the same object
of belief. Someone other than Lingens who believed himself to be a cousin
of a spy would be in the same belief state as Lingens, but the object of his
belief would be different.

The motivation for the distinction, in Kaplan's theory, as I understand
it, is something like this: we need to distinguish the information conveyed
or represented from the means by which it is conveyed or represented. The
information conveyed in an utterance—what is said—is of course dependent on the meaning of the sentence uttered, but one cannot identify content with meaning since what is said may depend on other things as well;
specifically, what is said may depend on information available in the environment of the utterance. Perry describes his distinction between objects of
belief and belief states in a similar way as a distinction between *what* is
believed and the *way* it is believed. But the point of Perry's distinction
must be different, since the lesson of the examples of essentially indexical
belief—the examples that motivate Perry's account—is that indexicals are
essential to the information itself and are not just part of the means used
to represent it. So, on Perry's account, objects of belief cannot be the same
as the informational content of a belief, or as the information that is
exchanged in a conversation.

It is true that, on Perry's account, when Ortcutt says "you are Rudolf
Lingens," the content of his statement, and of the belief he expresses, is the
same as the content of the belief Lingens comes to have when he accepts
what he is told, a belief he would express by saying "I am Rudolf Lingens."
But this common content cannot be identified with the information conveyed in the communication since the common content of Ortcutt's and
Lingens's belief is, according to Perry, the apparently trivial proposition
that Lingens is Lingens. Lingens already believed *that* propositional
object, in at least one way. The change, when he received the new information, was that he came to believe it in a new way.

Belief states are too subjective to represent informational content, since
the relevant belief state Ortcutt is in is a different one from the one Lingens
comes to be in when he receives Ortcutt's information. But belief objects
or contents, in Perry's sense, are (at least in the problem cases) too extensional to represent information conveyed in an act of communication. We
need an intermediate entity, and the notion of proposition we have been

using—propositions as ways of dividing a set of alternative possibilities—supplies an appropriate one. If we identify objects of belief with this kind of entity, then we can reconcile the examples of essentially indexical belief with the received doctrines about propositions and propositional attitudes. And, I think, we can give a simpler and more natural account of thought and speech than Lewis's or Perry's accounts can give.

8

Belief Attribution and Context

The semantics of belief attribution seems, at a certain level of abstraction at least, very simple: the transitive verb *believe* expresses a relation between a person or other animate thing denoted by the subject term and a proposition denoted by the sentential complement that is the object of the verb. "Phoebe believes that fleas have wings" seems to say that Phoebe stands in the belief relation to the proposition *that fleas have wings*. I think that the semantics of belief really is as simple as it seems. Furthermore, I will assume that the objects of belief—the propositions—are relatively simple unstructured things: that they are, just as truth-conditional semantics would like to assume, entities that are individuated by their truth-conditions. And I will assume that the semantics by which sentential complements are related to the propositions they denote is essentially the same as the semantics by which ordinary sentences are related to the propositions they express. If you know how to tell what is said by the sentence *fleas have wings*, then you know, roughly at least, how to tell what is denoted by the clause *that fleas have wings*.

So why is the explanation of belief attribution such a complicated and difficult business? Many of the problems, I want to suggest, arise from the context-dependence of belief attribution; their solution belongs to a pragmatics of belief. And many of them arise from the complexities of the belief relation itself and will be solved only when we are clear about some philosophical issues concerning the nature of belief. In this paper, I will try to do some preliminary ground-clearing that is necessary before attacking these problems, and to sketch some ideas that may help provide a pragmatic account of belief attribution. I will begin by saying just a little about the kind of account of the nature of belief that I think is right, and that motivates the framework I will sketch. Then I will make some remarks about context and context-dependence in general, and about the line

An earlier version of this paper was read at the University of Amsterdam, Princeton University, the University of Minnesota and Tufts University. In the discussions on these occasions, and at Oberlin, I received helpful comments and suggestions from many people including Barbara Partee, David Lewis, Scott Soames, William Hanson, Michael McKinsey and Hans Kamp.

between semantics and pragmatics. Third, I will discuss some of the ways in which belief attributions are context-dependent, and sketch a framework in which they might be represented. Finally, I will make some suggestions about how the framework might help to clarify one familiar cluster of problems concerning belief attribution: problems about so-called *de re* ascriptions of belief.

One might hope that philosophical problems about the nature of belief could be separated from linguistic problems about the semantic structure of sentences ascribing beliefs, just as, presumably, one can and should answer questions about the semantics and pragmatics of constructions involving the words *good* and *right* without solving philosophical problems about the nature of morality. But the meaning and reference of the word *believe* is more intimately connected to the foundations of semantics than the meaning and reference of *good* and *right*, and so substantive assumptions about belief may have consequences for more general questions about how semantics should go. The objects or contents of belief are also the objects or contents of speech acts, and it is the central task of semantics in general to say how utterances are related to the objects or contents of the speech acts they are used to perform. Different conceptions of the nature of the objects of speech and thought will imply different conceptions of what this central task is. This is why the problem of the semantics of belief attribution is a problem not just about a limited kind of construction, but about the semantic values in general that semantic theory should assign to sentences.

For this reason, I think it is a mistake to look for a purely technical solution to the problem of characterizing the objects of belief, a solution that is not motivated by some conception of the nature of thought. What I mean by a purely technical solution is one that moves too quickly from facts or apparent facts about inferences among belief sentences to conclusions about the identity conditions for objects of belief. If examples suggest that one can believe that P while not believing that Q, for some P and Q, then, the technical strategy suggests, find a kind of semantic value for sentences that is finely enough individuated to distinguish P from Q. If P and Q are, according to a straightforward semantic account, necessarily equivalent or intensionally isomorphic or synonymous, then the examples show that necessary equivalence, intensional isomorphism or synonymy is not sufficient for the identity of propositions. Following this procedure will inevitably lead to a very fine-grained notion of the objects of belief; they will have to be mirrors of the sentences that express or denote them. Such an account of the objects of belief may make it easier to explain certain facts about belief attribution, but it will make it much more difficult to give a plausible general account of the function of speech acts and

mental attitudes, an account that explains how representational objects
and states represent. To give an adequate account of belief attribution, we
need to look not just at sentences attributing belief, but also at the foundations of semantics in general.

What is the alternative to the technical strategy? I will not suggest that
we ignore or deny the familiar facts about belief sentences, or that we
explain a divergence between theory and fact by a distinction between
idealized semantic competence and actual performance. If it is true that
Phoebe believes that P, and false that she believes that Q, then one must
say that *that* P and *that* Q denote different propositions in the relevant
contexts. But examples of this kind need not lead to any particular
account of the identity conditions for propositions. The technical strategy
assumes a simple and inflexible connection between sentences and propositions, concluding that propositions are complex, fine-grained objects. An
alternative is to assume a simpler and more straightforward conception of
the object of belief—one that is motivated by a general account of the
nature of representation and the foundations of semantics—and to locate
the complexity in the relation between sentence and proposition.

The assumption I will make, but not defend here, about the objects of
speech and thought is that the possible worlds analysis of a proposition is
correct. Propositions are functions from possible worlds into truth-values,
or they may be thought of as sets of possible worlds. The term "possible
world" is perhaps misleading for what I have in mind. A set of possible
worlds may be a space of relevant alternative possible states of some
limited subject matter determined by a context in which some rational
activity (deliberation, inquiry, negotiation, conversation) is taking place.
Although the kind of abstract account of speech and thought that I will
presuppose takes possible worlds for granted, it need not take on the metaphysical burdens that the picturesque terminology suggests. All that is
assumed is that agents who think and talk are distinguishing between possibilities, that their so distinguishing is essential to the activities that constitute their thinking and talking, and that we can usefully describe the
activities in terms of the possibilities they are distinguishing between.[1]

The intentional or representational character of states of belief should
be explained, I shall assume, in terms of two things: first, the way those
states tend, under normal conditions, to be caused; second, the actions
that those states tend to dispose the believer to perform. Very roughly, to
believe that P is to be in a state that is sensitive to the information that P,
and that disposes the agent to do what would best satisfy his desires if P
(together with his other beliefs) were true. This is very crude, and obvi-

---

[1] I develop this defense of possible worlds in Stalnaker (1984: ch. 3) and in Stalnaker
(1986).

ously needs to be qualified, refined and explained; my aim here is just to give a rough idea of the general kind of philosophical account of belief that I will be assuming. Any development of this rough idea (I have argued elsewhere)[2] will provide a rationale and a foundation for the conception of propositional content that I will be using, and also for the following familiar abstract account of belief states: a belief state may be represented by a set of possibilities—the possibilities that are not excluded by the agent's conception of the way things are. The set of propositions believed, relative to a belief state, is the set of propositions that are true in all of those possibilities. The propositions believed, on this kind of account, are not components or constituents of a belief state; there need not be an internal representation of some kind corresponding to each proposition believed. Instead, propositions believed are properties of a belief state. To say that Phoebe believes that fleas have wings is to characterize Phoebe's belief state, or one of them, as a belief state that is included in the set of possible worlds in which fleas have wings.

This kind of abstract account is, I think, simple, powerful, and well motivated philosophically, but there are obvious and familiar prima facie counterexamples which many theorists have taken to be decisive against it. Since my strategy for replying to the counterexamples will claim that belief attributions are highly context-dependent, I need to say something in general about pragmatics and context-dependence.

The line between pragmatics and semantics has been drawn in two quite different ways, and there are different things one can mean by a characterization of a phenomenon, a distinction, an anomaly or an ambiguity, as pragmatic. Sometimes, a pragmatic fact is one that is independent of truth-conditions or content. A pragmatic implication is one that is compatible with the truth of the premise and the falsity of the conclusion. A pragmatically anomalous statement is one that is conversationally inappropriate, but may still be true. This distinction between pragmatic and semantic is most commonly invoked to fend off apparent counterexamples to philosophical or semantic analyses. An analysis may imply that some obviously deviant statement is true, or that something that seems intuitively to be implied by a statement is not a consequence of it. Then the analysis is defended by providing an alternative pragmatic explanation for the deviance, or the implication: the statement violates conversational maxims rather than truth-conditions; the implication is a conversational implicature rather than a semantic entailment. Part of the task of pragmatic theory is to develop some systematic way of defending and evaluating such patterns of explanation.

[2] Stalnaker (1984: ch. 1).

The second way of contrasting semantics with pragmatics is to distinguish the aspects of the interpretation of a speech act which are determined by *meaning* from those that are determined by *context*. Two kinds of information are relevant to determining the content of a speech act: on the one hand there is specifically semantic information—information which any competent speaker of the language must know; on the other hand there is information about the circumstances in which the speech act was performed, or more generally, extra-linguistic information which the speaker presupposes that the addressee can use to determine what he is saying. Semantics, on this way of drawing the line, is concerned only with meaning: with the rules for determining content, relative to contextual information.

The two ways of distinguishing pragmatics from semantics cut across one another. On the one hand, some facts about usage that are independent of truth-conditions (for example the fact that sentences including words such as *even* and *but* have the presuppositions that they have) are explained in terms of the meanings of particular words. Such facts are pragmatic in the first sense, semantic in the second. On the other hand, a distinction or ambiguity may be a distinction of content, but one that is to be explained by a difference in context rather than meaning or syntax. (For example, the difference between two tokens of "the President is a Republican," one uttered in 1974, the other in 1983.) Such a distinction will be semantic in the first sense, pragmatic in the second.

These differences reflect two different roles that the notion of *context* plays in the explanation of linguistic phenomena. On the one hand, context is the general setting in which communication takes place. Linguistic phenomena are facts about what utterances get produced in what circumstances. One can't explain why people produce the utterances they produce simply in terms of a theory of the semantic content of those utterances. One also has to take account of the point of saying what the utterances say, of the role of linguistic action in a more general rational activity. A representation of context must represent the background of presumed beliefs and purposes that give linguistic action its point.

On the other hand, context must include the information that speakers and hearers use to interpret context-dependent utterances—to determine what is said. If the language contains personal pronouns and tenses, then context must be something that tells us who is speaking, to whom, and when. If the interpretation of quantifiers and modal auxiliaries depends on domains of individuals and possible worlds, then such domains must be determined by a representation of context.

These are not too different notions of context, but two roles that a notion of context must play. It is important that a single notion of context play both roles if we are to explain the interaction of context and speech, and the patterns of reasoning by which people interpret each other's linguistic performances. Common assumptions and beliefs about the overall structure and point of a conversation may be the source of information necessary for the interpretation of context-dependent utterances. To take a very simple example, suppose Jones, in a conversation with Smith and Brown, says, "How was your trip to South America?" Suppose it is common knowledge among the three that Smith has recently been to South America, while Brown has not. Smith infers that she is the addressee from the fact that the question would be appropriate only if addressed to her. The same familiar Gricean patterns of reasoning used to derive conversational implicatures may also be used to determine what has been said when what is said depends on context.

In the setting of the possible worlds framework, the kind of representation of context that we need to play both of these roles is provided by a set of possible worlds representing the presumed common background knowledge of the participants in the conversation. I have called such a set the *context set*.[3] These possibilities will be the live options that speakers will be distinguishing between, and that hearers will take speakers to be distinguishing between, in the conversation. This presumed common background knowledge will also include any information that the participants assume is available to be exploited in interpreting each other's utterances.

The context set is of course continually being updated in the course of a conversation. The speech acts performed alter the context, and this is their point: they do it explicitly by putting forward a piece of information (in an assertion or a supposition) to be accepted and so added to the available background information; they also alter the context implicitly by saying something that would have a point, or be interpretable or appropriate only if the context were adjusted in some way. In such a case, hearers accommodate, to use a term of David Lewis's,[4] by assuming that the appropriate things were common ground even though they previously were not, or that certain things were not common ground which a hearer previously thought were. Such accommodation takes place innocently when participants in a conversation correct mistakes about what each other knows or agrees about, or it takes place by design when a speaker smuggles assumptions into a conversation by presupposing things that he knows his audience will be able to tell he is presupposing. There are all degrees of openness to such implicit communication. The pretense that a piece of new information was common knowledge can be mutually recognized for what it is, or the speaker may intend to deceive his audience

---

[3] See "Assertion", reprinted in Ch. 4 of the present volume.   [4] See Lewis (1979c).

about what he takes them to know or assume. Either way, the pattern of reasoning is the same.

One more general remark before turning to belief, a remark about how semantics and pragmatics fit together. The main task of *semantics* is to provide rules for the determination of the propositions expressed by sentences. And propositions, I have said I will assume, are functions from possible worlds or possible situations into truth-values. What the context provides is the domain of possible worlds that propositions distinguish between. Semantics in general gives us rules for picking a subset of possible situations from such a domain. On this kind of account, context is not just information that mediates between utterance and proposition; it is the material out of which propositions are constructed.

Now, finally, let's look at belief. According to the straightforward semantic analysis, a sentence of the form *x believes that P* expresses a proposition that is a function of another proposition, the one denoted by *that P*. But our pragmatic account tells us that, in general, to express a proposition is to select a subset of a set of possible situations given by the context. This will be true of embedded sentences as well as sentences uttered on their own. For embedded sentences, we need an embedded, or as I will call it, a *derived context*.

For many sentences that have sentences as parts, the derived context set will be the same as, or a subset of, the basic context set. For example, it seems clear that for indicative conditionals, the context set for the consequent is the intersection of the basic context set with the proposition expressed in the antecedent. But for other cases the situation will be more complicated, and more interesting. For subjunctive conditions, for example, the antecedent creates a new context which will normally be disjoint from the basic context—that's what it is for a conditional to be counterfactual. But this is not simply a case of a context shift, as when one begins presupposing something previously presupposed to be false. After making a counterfactual supposition, the information in the basic context is still there to be exploited and to guide interpretation. One has two contexts either or both of which may play a role in the interpretation of the consequent. One may for example use pronouns to refer to individuals who inhabit the possible worlds of the basic context even if they are absent from those of the derived context, or the other way around. On the one hand, one can say "If Copernicus hadn't existed, someone else would have proposed the theory *he* proposed." On the other hand, one can say "If a woman had proposed the theory Copernicus proposed, *she* would have been ignored."

Belief attributions are cases of the more interesting kind—cases in which the derived context may be different, often disjoint, from the basic context. What Phoebe believes, or is assumed to believe, may be different from, or incompatible with, what a speaker talking about Phoebe's beliefs believes or assumes. The relevant derived context will be determined by the basic context in the following way: for each possible situation in the basic context, Phoebe will be in a definite belief state which is itself defined by a set of possible situations—the ones compatible with what Phoebe believes in that possible situation. The union of all the possible belief states will be the set of all possible situations that might, for all the *speaker* presupposes, be compatible with Phoebe's beliefs. This set of possible situations is the derived context for interpreting the clauses that are intended to express the contents of Phoebe's beliefs.

In an extended conversation about what Phoebe does or does not believe, the derived context may become a stable part of the background. Like the basic context, it will be updated as the conversation proceeds, explicitly when explicit belief attributions are made, and implicitly when accommodation is required in order to make sense of what is being said. Like the information in the basic context, the information in this derived context will be available to guide the interpretation of utterances. All of the ways that ordinary contextual information constrains and guides the interpretation of assertions and other speech acts will also be ways in which derived contexts constrain and guide the interpretation of embedded sentences that ascribe or deny beliefs. Just to see how the pattern goes, let me give three very simple examples of kinds of pragmatic constraints on basic contexts, and parallel constraints on the derived contexts for belief attributions. First, presupposition requirements: Just as "Harry regrets accepting the bribe" is appropriate only in a context in which it is presupposed that a bribe was offered, and that Harry accepted it, so the statement "Phoebe believes that Harry regrets accepting the bribe" requires a derived context in which it is presupposed that a bribe was offered and that Harry accepted it. That is to say, it must be presupposed—taken by the speaker to be common ground—that Phoebe believes that a bribe was offered, and that Harry accepted it. Second, pronominal reference: One can use *he* to refer to someone only if there is a unique most salient male in each of the possible situations in the context set. In a belief attribution, one needs such an individual in each of the possible situations in the derived context set. So we may say "Phoebe thought she heard a prowler in the vegetable garden last night. She believed that he probably came to steal one of her prize-winning zucchinis."[5] For all the speaker assumes or implies, there may really have been no such prowler, but the pronoun *he* can still be appropriately used to "refer" to the prowler, since

[5] Peter Geach brought this kind of example to the attention of linguists and philosophers in Geach (1967).

he inhabits each of the possible situations in the derived context set. For this reason, a definite proposition is determined by the embedded sentence (assuming the constraint is met), and a determinate belief is ascribed. Third, the familiar Gricean patterns of accommodation and conversational reasoning apply to derived contexts as well as to basic ones. Here is an example that fits a well-known pattern: A disjunction is appropriate only if both disjuncts are compatible with the context. So if O'Leary says "Daniels is either on vacation or in prison," he conversationally implicates that he has at least some reason to think that Daniels may be in prison. Accommodation requires that a possible situation in which Daniels is in prison be included in the basic context. In the same way, if O'Leary says, "Phoebe believes that Daniels is either on vacation or in prison," he implicates that he has some reason to think that it may be compatible with Phoebe's beliefs that Daniels be in prison. This is because accommodation requires us to include a possible situation in which Daniels is in prison in the derived context set.

All of this is straightforward once we adopt a certain conception of what belief states are, and of the way sentences determine propositions relative to contexts. The repertoire of pragmatic devices for explaining how context influences what is said, or meant, carries over to the explanation of what is expressed or implied in the sentential complement of a belief attribution. But there are some differences between basic and derived contexts. One difference is that basic contexts, but not derived contexts, always contain a speaker and a speech act. Each possible situation in the basic context set contains the speaker saying what he is saying. But an act of counterfactual supposition may create a context in which that act does not take place, and a derived belief context—the possible situations that might, for all that is presupposed, be compatible with Phoebe's beliefs— may not include the conversation about Phoebe's beliefs. Because of this there will be some constraints on assertions and other simple speech acts that do not correspond to constraints on belief attributions and counterfactual suppositions. For example, one cannot appropriately assert things that conflict with the possibility of one's asserting them, but one can perfectly easily suppose things that imply that one is not supposing them. If I say, as I reveal certain sensitive information to you, "I'm not telling you any of this," you know what I mean, and it's not what I say. But if I say "suppose I hadn't told you any of this," or "Phoebe believes that I'm not telling you any of this," you can understand me in a straightforward literal way. A second related difference: A derived context is always one of at least two contexts whose information is available to be exploited, and information may be imported from one into the other. A speaker may use personal pronouns, demonstratives or other referential devices to pick out individuals in the basic context, and use those individuals to express propositions that alter the derived context. Consider, for example, "Phoebe believes you are in Australia this month," or "If that man [pointing] weren't here, the party would be a lot livelier." It is the mixing of information from different contexts that accounts for Russell's notorious yacht, which may be believed or supposed to be longer than it is.

That is the general framework that I hope can help to clarify belief attribution. The final thing I want to do here is to look in a little more detail at one phenomenon that involves the interaction of basic and derived contexts, the phenomenon of *de re* or relational belief ascription. I will first set the stage by saying why philosophers have found the phenomenon puzzling, and describing two contrasting strategies for resolving the puzzles. Then I will consider how the phenomenon looks from the point of view of the framework that I have been sketching.

Quine, in his classic paper "Quantifiers and Propositional Attitudes,"[6] first focussed attention on the phenomenon of *de re* belief attribution. The problem, from his point of view, was something like this: Belief attribution contexts are opaque—substitution of co-referential names in them may not preserve truth-value. And, Quine had argued, quantification into opaque contexts is a mistake based on confusion of use and mention. Opaque contexts are like quotation contexts, and one obviously cannot coherently quantify into quotation contexts. But we do quantify into belief contexts, and such quantifications seem, intuitively, to be intelligible. Quine was content to dismiss quantifications into *modal* contexts as a metaphysical mistake with its source in philosophers' confusions, but felt a need to make sense of the more common and familiar quantifications into proposition attitudes. It was clear that "Ralph believes someone is a spy" is ambiguous, with one sense meaning that there is a particular person believed by Ralph to be a spy. And if that existential statement is true, then there must be a true instantiation of it—a particular person (in this case Bernard J. Ortcutt) that Ralph believes to be a spy. But if, as Quine believed, believing is to be understood in terms of a relation between a believer and a *sentence*, then how are we to understand a concept of belief that relates the believer to objects in the world, and not just to their names? Quine's problem can be seen more directly by considering what happens when a believer knows an individual in two different ways without realizing that it is the same individual. Ortcutt is the man Ralph sees on the beach whom he takes to be a pillar of the community, and at the same time the man in the brown hat that he takes to be a spy. Is Ortcutt believed to be a spy or not? The Ortcutt situation is essentially the same as the

---

[6] Quine (1966).

situation of Kripke's bilingual Pierre who says "Londres est jolie" while denying "London is pretty" because he doesn't realize that the English city he learned in France to call "Londres" is the same as the one he learned in England to call "London".[7]

Quine's solution to these problems was to distinguish two concepts of belief, notional and relational belief, and to explain the second in terms of the first. Relational or *de re* belief attributions do not attribute particular beliefs to persons. Rather, they say that the believer has a belief meeting a certain condition, but without saying what particular belief it is. Roughly, the pattern of analysis of relational belief in terms of notional belief (belief that takes a sentence as object) goes like this: to say that x believes *of* a certain individual that it is F is to say that x believes-true a sentence of the form *a is F*, where *a* denotes the individual. On this kind of analysis, *de re* belief is not a special kind of belief. Rather, it is a special way of describing a belief. The analysis reconciles a sentential conception of belief with quantification into belief contexts, and also solves the Ortcutt problem by giving *de re* belief sentences a different logical form. Despite appearances, "Ralph believes Ortcutt to be a spy" and "Ralph believes Ortcutt not to be a spy" do not ascribe conflicting beliefs to Ralph any more than "someone is a spy" and "someone is not a spy" predicate conflicting properties of someone.

A contrasting strategy, which I will call the semantical strategy, begins by rejecting the assumption that belief is at bottom a sentential attitude. Propositions, it assumes, are the objects of belief; *de re* belief is belief with a distinctive kind of proposition as its object: a singular proposition. To believe of Ortcutt that he is a spy is to believe the singular proposition that ascribes spyhood to Ortcutt. Different versions of this strategy will give different accounts of what a singular proposition is. For those who take propositions to be structured objects with properties, relations, truth-functions and quantifiers as constituents, singular propositions will be propositions with individuals themselves (rather than individual concepts) as constituents. For those who adopt the possible worlds conception of a proposition, a singular proposition will be a proposition whose truth in any given possible world depends on the properties of some particular individual. What is common to these accounts and essential to the idea of a singular proposition is that the identity of a singular proposition is a function of an individual rather than of some concept or mode of presentation of the individual.

The semantical strategy is simpler in the abstract and less *ad hoc* than the Quinean strategy: it takes *de re* belief ascriptions to be, as they seem

---

[7] See Kripke (1979).

intuitively to be, ascriptions of particular beliefs. But this strategy raises problems in application. What is it to believe a singular proposition? What is it to believe that Ortcutt himself is a spy, and not just to believe that the person fitting a certain description, or presented to the believer in a certain way, is a spy? And this strategy needs a solution to the Ortcutt problem. Given that Ralph knows Ortcutt in two different ways, which singular propositions about Ortcutt does he believe?

It is often supposed by proponents of the semantical strategy that believing a singular proposition requires a special kind of relation between the believer and the individual the proposition is about: one must be *acquainted* with the individual in some special way. To be in a position to believe that the man on the beach (whoever he might be) is a spy, one need only have general concepts of men, beaches, and so forth. But to believe *of* that man that he is a spy, one must be acquainted with the man himself, and not just with some concept that picks him out. The main task of developing the semantical strategy is to spell out the relevant notion of acquaintance.

The first strategy was criticized for making *de re* belief too easy. It seemed intuitively wrong, for example, to say that Poirot believes the butler to have done it simply in virtue of the facts that the butler did it and that Poirot believes that the person who did it did it. But the second strategy threatened to make *de re* belief too difficult. How does this line avoid the conclusion that Ralph, who is acquainted with Ortcutt in two different guises, has contradictory beliefs? One way is to strengthen the required acquaintance relation to the point where mistakes of identity are impossible. But the problem is that mistakes of identity are almost always possible. It is perhaps implausible, but surely conceivable, for example, that poor Phoebe does not realize that her husband and her lover are one and the same person, a man who heroically preserves his marriage and keeps his wife unwittingly faithful by serving, in disguise, her need for extracurricular adventure. If *de re* belief rules out the possibility of mistakes of identity, then perhaps the only thing one can be intimately enough acquainted with to have *de re* beliefs about is oneself.

Even if this extreme conclusion could save the semantic strategy from contradiction, it obviously has consequences that clash with intuitions about examples. Intuitively, it seems clear that *de re* belief attribution is altogether natural in cases where the believer's relation to the object of belief is no more intimate than it is in the puzzle cases. There is a familiar form of argument—one might call it the divide and conquer argument—that has been used to bring this out. Begin by telling each half of the Ortcutt story separately. In one story, Ralph sees Ortcutt in the brown hat, but never sees him on the beach. In the other, he sees him on the beach, but not in the brown hat. Now it is obviously perfectly appropriate and unproblematic to say that Ralph believes Ortcutt to be a spy in the first story, and that he believes him not to be a spy in the second. But there does not seem to be any reason why we cannot put the two stories together without taking back any belief attributions. There is no reason why Ralph need change his mind about the man in the brown hat just because he meets a man, who he takes to be a different man, on the beach. So, the argument concludes, it is difficult to deny that in the original Ortcutt story, Ralph both believes Ortcutt to be a spy, and believes him not to be a spy.[8]

There are intermediate strategies. David Kaplan, in his paper "Quantifying In,"[9] developed a kind of compromise between the two accounts I have contrasted. He followed Quine in assuming that *de re* belief ascriptions do not ascribe particular beliefs, but rather are to be analyzed as existential quantifications. But he followed the semantical strategy in holding that *de re* belief ascriptions were true only if the believer stood in a special acquaintance relation to the individual in question. His analysis followed Quine's pattern, but strengthened the requirement that the name denote the individual. To believe Ortcutt to be a spy, according to Kaplan's account, one must believe-true some sentence of the form *a is a spy*, where *a* not only denotes Ortcutt, but also meets certain other conditions, conditions relating both to the internal content expressed by the name, and also to the causal relations among the name, the individual named, and the believer. But these conditions might still be met by two different names that the agent does not recognize as names of the same individual, and so it will be possible, on Kaplan's analysis as well as Quine's, to believe Ortcutt to be a spy, and also to believe Ortcutt not to be a spy, without any inconsistency in one's beliefs. This avoids the Ortcutt problem, and also the counterexamples which showed the Quinean analysis to be too liberal. But it seems an *ad hoc* compromise. In the context of the semantical strategy, the acquaintance requirement has a motivation: in general, one cannot believe a proposition without grasping the concepts in terms of which it is defined. Similarly, it seems plausible to say that one cannot grasp, and so cannot believe, a singular proposition unless one is acquainted with the individual in terms of which it is defined. But the requirement loses this motivation when the acquaintance requirement is grafted onto the Quinean strategy. Also, Kaplan's analysis retains the artificial conclusion that *de re* belief ascriptions do not ascribe particular beliefs, and it is tied to the sentential conception of the object of belief.

---

[8] Kripke, in his discussion of the Pierre example, uses the divide and conquer argument effectively.

[9] In Kaplan (1969).

For this strategy to work, beliefs must at least be sentence-*like* objects, with name-like parts as constituents.

None of these accounts seems to me entirely successful. I think we can give a more natural account of *de re* belief attribution if we recognize that propositions believed are not constituents of belief states, but simply ways of characterizing them, and that belief states themselves—the sets of possible worlds compatible with a person's beliefs—are defined relative to a context of relevant alternative possible situations. The strategy I am pursuing faces its own version of the persistent philosophical problems about the relation between representational mental states and the individuals they are about, but I think the strategy will help to bring those problems into sharper focus, and to clarify the relation between philosophical problems about the nature of mental representation on the one hand and pragmatic and semantic problems about the way we describe mental representation on the other.

The pragmatic strategy maintains, with the semantic strategy, that *de re* belief ascriptions ascribe particular beliefs, but it does not say that the beliefs ascribed are a particular kind of proposition, nor does it require some strong acquaintance relation with the individuals the beliefs are about. Propositions, I am assuming, are subsets of a set of relevant alternative possibilities given by a context. The individuals referred to in a *de re* belief ascription, or in an ordinary predication, are not constituents of a proposition denoted or expressed; they are resources available for the expression of a proposition, things that propositions may be determined as a function of. In general, the task of a propositional expression (a sentence or sentential clause) is to pick out in a determinate way a subset of the relevant context set. The constraints on *de re* belief attribution, like the constraints on any kind of proposition expressing act, will derive from the simple requirement that the act succeed in this task.

Let me quickly describe the phenomenon of *de re* belief in terms of the apparatus of basic and derived context sets, and then look at the Ortcutt problem.

This much is agreed by all: in *de re* belief attribution, one refers to an individual, and uses the individual to characterize a belief. The way the speaker refers to the individual is independent of the way the believer is said to think of the individual. In terms of the apparatus I have sketched, this suggests two different sets of pragmatic constraints. First, reference is made in the *basic* context, and the pragmatic conditions that must be met for reference to succeed are conditions on the basic context. For example, if a definite description is used, it is presupposed that a unique most salient individual fits the description: in each possible situation in the basic context set, there must be such an individual. If a personal pronoun or demonstrative is used, there must be an individual presupposed in the basic context to be in the appropriate role. But second, the derived context must meet certain conditions in order for the individual picked out to be able to be used to characterize the believer's belief state in a determinate way. A proposition must be determined, relative to the *derived* context set, as a function of the individual, which is to say that the individual determined must exist as a single individual in each of the possible situations in the derived context set.

Even if this is clear enough in the abstract, it does not tell what it is for an individual found in the actual world, or located in a speaker's basic context set, to be in a possible world compatible with a believer's beliefs. In the world as Ralph believes it to be there is a person in a brown hat who behaves in a suspicious manner, and is a spy. Is that person Ortcutt? The kind of answer that I think should be given to this question goes roughly like this: Ralph is in a mental state of a certain kind that tends, under normal conditions, to be sensitive to facts about the world. If the facts the state tends to be sensitive to are facts about Ortcutt, then Ralph has beliefs *about* Ortcutt. This needs to be spelled out in terms of nested counterfactuals: *if* conditions were normal, then *if* Ortcutt were different in this or that way, then Ralph's mental state would be different in corresponding ways. For example, if Ortcutt were fatter, then (in the absence of distorting influences of some kind) Ralph's representation of the man in the brown hat would be a representation of a fatter man.

If something like this is right, then belief about an individual will require some kind of causal relation between the believer and the individual the belief is about, a causal relation in virtue of which the counterfactual dependencies hold. But this relation will be different in several ways from the kind of acquaintance relation required by the semantical strategy. First, the relevant relation is a special case of a more general relation between believers and propositions. In general, for a representational mental state to represent the world as being such that P, the state must be one that, under normal conditions, tends to carry the information that P, which means that if various alternatives to P were true, then the believer would be in various corresponding alternative states. Where the alternatives are alternative states of a particular individual, then the representational states will be representations of the individual. Second, the relevant relation is highly context-dependent. It is defined in terms of a notion of normal or optimal conditions, and a set of contrasting alternative states of the world, both of which may depend on the context in which a belief is attributed. This is a deep kind of context-dependence: it is not only that belief ascriptions—the way a speaker describes a belief state—may be influenced by the context in which he speaks. More than this, the belief relation itself—the relation between the believer and the propositions which are the contents of his beliefs—can be defined only in terms of parameters which may be influenced by the context in which questions about the believer's beliefs arise. Third, the relevant causal relation between a believer and an individual that his beliefs are about need not be a particularly strong relation of acquaintance. My beliefs might, for example, be sensitive in the appropriate way to facts about an ancient king I know little about, a person passingly glimpsed, a city known only from one sentence in a guide book (perhaps, "Londres est jolie"). In such cases, my beliefs could be informatively described (in some contexts at least) by referring to the individual in question and characterizing a proposition as a function of that individual.

If the causal relation necessary for correct *de re* belief attributions is not a particularly strong one, then it will be all the easier to find cases of the Ortcutt problem. What if, as seems to be the case in Quine's story, facts about *two* individuals in the world as Ralph believes it to be are sensitive to facts about Ortcutt? If Ortcutt were fatter, two individuals in the world as Ralph takes it to be would be fatter. The properties of those two individuals might not be sensitive to exactly the same facts, but it does seem clear that Ralph's representations of both of them tend to carry information about Ortcutt. Which one is the real Ortcutt? Several answers to this question are possible, and I'm not sure which is right: perhaps both men are Ortcutt. I think one can defend the thesis that what is one thing in one possible world may be two or more in some other possible world, but that is a long story. Perhaps it is indeterminate which man is Ortcutt. This is not to say that some possible worlds are inhabited by individuals of indeterminate identity; rather, it is to say that it is indeterminate which of two sets of possible worlds is the one compatible with Ralph's beliefs. Now whichever of these answers one gives, it will be clear that the pragmatic conditions for *de re* belief attribution are not met, since in possible situations compatible with Ralph's beliefs, there are two individuals who are, or might be, Ortcutt, and so no proposition will be determined as a function of Ortcutt. Suppose we are discussing Ralph's beliefs in a context in which it is mutually recognized that Ralph believes there are these two distinct individuals, one of which he sees on the beach, the other of which he has glimpsed in a brown hat, but nothing is presupposed about what Ralph thinks about either of them being involved in espionage. In this case, the derived context set will contain possible situations in which both are spies, situations in which neither are, situations in which the first man is a spy and the second not, and situations in which the second man is a spy and the first not. These are the possible situations that might, for all that is presupposed, be compatible with Ralph's beliefs. The speaker's job, in attributing a belief to Ralph, is to cut this set down in a determinate and correct way. It is clear that saying "Ralph believes Ortcutt to be a spy" just won't do the job, nor will saying "Ralph believes Ortcutt not to be a spy." It's not that Ralph isn't intimately enough acquainted with Ortcutt. Rather, the problem is that in the relevant context, no proposition is determined by applying the propositional function expressed by "is a spy" to the individual Ortcutt.

The situation might be different in a different belief attribution context, even if Ralph's state of mind were no different. Suppose, for example, that in a different discussion it is again presupposed that Ralph believes there are these two distinct individuals, but this time it is also presupposed that Ralph does *not* believe that the man on the beach is a spy. Nothing is presupposed about what Ralph thinks about the man in the brown hat. In this situation, it might be okay for the speaker to say "Ralph believes Ortcutt to be a spy" since accommodation will force the interpretation that identifies Ortcutt with the man in the brown hat.

Notice that the divide and conquer argument discussed above is ineffective against the pragmatic strategy I am defending. The key assumption of that argument was that Ralph does not lose any beliefs in the change from the divided stories to the combined story. But this assumption is not enough when we recognize the context-dependence of belief attributions. In general, even when the belief state of the believer remains the same, the belief attributions that are appropriate or correct may change with a shift in the context of attribution. In the Ortcutt example, it is clear that, and how, the combining of the two halves of the story changes the context in relevant ways.

In general, what the pragmatic strategy suggests is a change in perspective. If we focus on the function of a belief attribution—to describe correctly and informatively a belief state by distinguishing between relevant alternative possibilities given by a context—then we can get a clearer picture of what is wrong with *de re* belief attributions in Ortcutt situations, and more generally, a clearer picture of the way we attribute beliefs and other representational mental states.

PART III

Externalism

9

On What's in the Head

"Cut the pie any way you like, 'meanings' just ain't in the head!"[1] So Hilary Putnam taught us some years ago. He made the point with some compelling examples all fitting a now familiar pattern: first we are asked to imagine a counterfactual person exactly like some actual person with respect to all purely internal psychological and physical properties, but situated in a counterfactual environment which differs from ours in some subtle way. For example, where we have aluminum, they have a metal that resembles aluminum superficially, but that has a different chemical structure. We are the invited to note that despite the intrinsic similarities of the two doppelganger, their utterances have different semantic properties. When the earthling says "Aluminum is used in the construction of airplanes," she say something that differs in content from what her twin says when she utters the same sounds. Since what is in the heads of the two is the same, while what they mean when they use certain words is different, the meanings of those words must depend on something other than what is in those heads. Tyler Burge developed this kind of example in more detail and extended the point in several ways.[2] First he argued that it is not just meaning and other semantical properties, but also intentional psychological properties that are shown to depend on external conditions: beliefs, desires, hope and fears ain't in the head either. Second, he argued that social conditions—facts about the linguistic practices of members of the agent's community—were among the external conditions on which intentional mental states depend. Third, he emphasized that the dependence on external conditions was a pervasive phenomenon, one not restricted to some narrow range of concepts and expressions. It applies not just to *de re* attitudes or to attitudes expressed with proper names, indexical expressions and natural kind terms, but to *de dicto* attitudes and to all kinds of concepts and expressions. Burge called the thesis he was attacking—the thesis that intentional mental states are intrinsic properties of the individuals who are in those states—*individualism*.

In retrospect, it seems that we should not have been surprised by the

---

[1] Putnam (1975: 144).   [2] Burge (1979).

conclusions of Putnam and Burge. Isn't it obvious that semantic properties, and intentional properties generally, are *relational* properties: properties defined in terms of relations between a speaker or agent and what he
or she talks or thinks about. And isn't it obvious that relations depend, in
all but degenerate cases, on more than the intrinsic properties of one of the
things related. This, it seems, is not just a consequence of some new and
controversial theory of reference, but should follow from any account of
representation that holds that we can talk and think, not just about our
own inner states, but also about things and properties outside of ourselves.
But the conclusions were surprising, and they remain controversial. One
reason is that the anti-individualistic thesis seems to have some paradoxical consequences. If what we mean or think is not in the head, it would
seem that we cannot know, or at least cannot be authoritative about, what
we mean or think.[3] Another reason is that this thesis seems to be incompatible with the explanatory role that intentional mental states are thought
to play. We explain why people behave the way they do in terms of what
they believe and want. In fact, it is often assumed that belief and desire
states are to be defined in terms of the behavior they dispose the agents in
those states to engage in. But how can such states be causally relevant if
they are relational states—states that depend on things outside of the
agent?

One response to the anti-individualist thesis is to grant it, but to deny its
significance. If our ordinary concepts of belief, desire, and meaning are
relational concepts that individuate mental states in a non-individualistic
way, this only shows that our ordinary concepts are inappropriate for the
purpose of the explanation of behavior. But, this response suggests, the
revisions needed to render intentional concepts individualistic are not very
radical. What such a revision must do is to factor out the "organismic contribution" to an intentional mental state—that component of the state
that is dependent or supervenient on the internal states of the agent.

The revisionist response makes a negative and a positive claim. The negative claim is that no systematic explanatory theory of behavior will be
tenable unless it is individualistic. The positive claim is that although
ordinary intentional psychological concepts are not individualistic as they
stand, they can be revised in a way that renders them individualistic while
preserving the basic structure of intentional explanation. Jerry Fodor has
defended both claims; Daniel Dennett has proposed ways to defend the
positive thesis, and Stephen Stich and P. M. and P. S. Churchland have

---

[3] It is not clear that this is right. What does follow is that the intrinsic state of the head
is not authoritative: that is, it does not follow from the head's being in the intrinsic state it
is in that it has certain specific beliefs. But unless we assume the kind of individualism that
is being denied, this does not imply that *we* are not authoritative.

defended the negative thesis while rejecting the positive claim. In this paper, I want to explore both parts of the revisionist doctrine, beginning with the positive side. After trying to get clear about what is required in general to define an individualistic analogue of a relational concept, I will look at two proposals for defining narrow content—a kind of content that is intended to render intentional states purely internal. Then I will turn to the negative side of the case, discussing a number of formulations of the negative thesis and a number of arguments in its defense. I will be arguing, first, that it is harder than some have assumed to define narrow content, and second that ordinary wide content is less mysterious than some have assumed.

A number of quite different issues are involved in the revisionist doctrine: some are relatively abstract questions concerning concept formation, methodology, and the distinction between intrinsic and relational properties; others are more specific questions concerning the nature of intentional concepts and the psychological mechanisms that underlie their application. To help separate these different issues from each other, I will begin by exploring an analogy: I will look at a very simple causal-relational concept—a concept that should be relatively transparent and uncontroversial—and consider what is involved in the attempt to define a narrow or purely intrinsic version of it. Then I will look back at the intentional concepts themselves and at the proposals for carving out narrow content.

Consider the concept of a *footprint*. This is a causal-relational concept: something is a footprint in virtue of the way it was caused. One might make the point that a footprint is not intrinsic to the sand or mud in which it is located by telling a Twin Earth story: imagine a beach on Twin Earth which is, at a certain moment on July 4, 1985, exactly like Jones Beach in every intrinsic detail. The difference is that the counterpart on Twin Earth of a certain footprint on Jones Beach was caused, not by a foot, but by the way the waves happened to fall some hours earlier. So something on Twin Earth that is intrinsically indistinguishable from a footprint is not a footprint. A philosopher with a gift for coining slogans might sum up the lesson of this thought experiment this way: *Cut the pie any way you like, footprints just ain't in the sand!*

The revisionist replies that this may be true of our ordinary folk concept of a footprint, but explanatory science is interested only in states that *are* intrinsic to the sand. So let us define a new concept that individuates the relevant state of the sand in a way that is independent of its causal history and environment: let us say that a *narrow footprint* is a foot-shaped indentation, whatever its cause. Can't we, in this way, isolate that component of the state of containing a footprint that is intrinsic to the medium that is in that state? The anti-individualist will note that the new concept is still a relational one. Footprints in the new sense no longer depend on the *particular* cause of the indentation, but they still depend on general facts that are extrinsic to the sand. An elaboration of the Twin Earth story makes the point: suppose that on Twin Earth feet have a different normal shape. If this is true, the indentation in the sand there will not only fail to be an ordinary footprint because of its different causal history, it will also fail to be a *narrow* footprint because normal footprints are differently shaped there, and so the indentation on the beach is not even shaped like a foot.

This pattern of conceptual revision—replacing a dependence on a specific causal interaction with dependence on a general regularity in the environment—is exemplified in less artificial cases. It seems reasonable to say that in defining dispositional properties, for example, we begin with a kind of causal interaction (a substance dissolves, or an object is observed). We then use suitably hedged counterfactuals to get at a stable property of one of the things involved in the interaction—a property that the thing has independently of the fact that the interaction took place. A sugar cube is soluble if it would dissolve if put in water (under normal conditions). An object is observable if it would be observed if a normal observer were suitably placed. Some such dispositional properties (such as solubility in water) may be purely intrinsic, but others will not be. Whether something is observable may depend on the capacities of normal observers, perhaps also on the lighting conditions that in fact obtain, or at least on the lighting conditions that normally obtain. The concept of belief may be this kind of narrowed version of the concept of knowledge, replacing a dependence on more specific causal relations between the fact known and a state of the knower with more general patterns of causal relations between facts and internal states.

One might further narrow our revised concept of footprint by taking the phrase "foot-shaped indentation" in a reference-fixing way. That is, by a narrow footprint we mean an indentation that is shaped the way feet are *actually* shaped. So whatever shape feet have on Twin Earth, the counterpart on Twin Earth of the footprint on Jones Beach is still a narrow footprint. Now, it seems, we have succeeded in isolating a purely internal state of the sand.

The pattern of concept formation now looks like this; we begin with a concept that classifies states of a thing in terms of a relational property—specifically, in terms of the way those states are caused. We then focus on the intrinsic properties of the states the concept picks out, classifying them in a new way: as states that share those intrinsic properties. This pattern too seems to be exemplified in less artificial cases. Consider, for example, the concepts of *mass* and *weight*. Weight is the quantity that is closer to the surface—more directly observed and measured. But it is a relational concept: what you weigh depends on the gravitational field you are in. Mass is the quantity that a body has, independently of its gravitational field, that explains why it weighs what it does in different gravitational fields. Even at an initial stage of inquiry when we may not know very much about the relevant intrinsic properties, we can still use this strategy of concept formation to point at the properties, whatever they are, that play a certain role in the explanation of a thing's behavior.[4]

Our definition of narrow footprint may make use of a sound strategy of concept formation, but the success of this kind of definition will always depend on a substantive presupposition: that the things picked out by the relational property are similar to each other in an appropriate way. The substantive presupposition will never be plausible unless one idealizes a bit: there are deformed feet, and distorting conditions that may give rise to footprints of an unusual shape. These will certainly be footprints, but if our definition of narrow footprint is to succeed, they, and other indentations shaped like them, must be excluded. By foot-shaping indentations we mean indentations that have the *normal* or *characteristic* shape that feet make under *normal* conditions. This kind of qualification is a familiar part of characterizations of dispositional properties: a thing is soluble in water if it would dissolve if put in water *under normal conditions*. The point of the qualification is to ensure that what is defined is a stable property that we can generalize about. It might be that a thing would not dissolve if put in water in a particular situation because of anomalous environmental conditions even though the thing is intrinsically similar to soluble things. But we don't want to say that the thing loses its solubility under the abnormal external conditions. The qualification allows us to say that the thing remains soluble even though, in this case, it would not dissolve if put in water.

Even given such qualifications, a definition of this kind may fail. If the concept of footprint we begin with is the concept of a print made by a human bare foot, then the concept of a narrow footprint is perhaps well-defined, since there is a relatively well-defined shape that prints have, in normal cases, when they are made by such feet. But suppose we start with a more general notion: by "footprint" we mean a print made by a foot of some animal or other. This concept includes prints made by cloven

---

[4] There is a rough but useful analogy between this strategy of concept formation and a popular account of the way natural kind terms acquire their content. According to that account, one kind of property—a cluster of superficial properties—determines a set of things—say a set of animals—and then this extension is used to determine a different type of property—structural or explanatory or essential properties. The relevant properties of this type are the ones shared by the things in the extension.

hooves, webbed feet, and the paws of dogs as well as human feet, and it is not clear that these footprints have any one characteristic shape at all. If they do not, then our concept will collapse when we try to abstract away from the causal origin of the indentations we want to pick out. Or at best we will be left with a wildly disjunctive concept that will be of no interest.[5]

The moral of the story is that the narrowing of causal-relational concepts exemplifies a legitimate pattern of concept formation, but not a pattern that will in all cases yield a well-defined purely internal property. First, the pattern may succeed in eliminating a dependence of a property on specific interactions with other things, while leaving a dependence on general facts about the environment. Second, whether the pattern succeeds at all will depend on substantive presuppositions about the intrinsic similarities of things that share the causal-relational property. To evaluate the positive part of the revisionist thesis we need to see just what the presuppositions are in the case of intentional mental concepts, and to consider whether we have good reason to accept them.

The defense of the positive part of the revisionist thesis requires more than just the definition of narrow analogues for particular belief properties such as the property of believing that aluminum is used in the construction of airplanes; what is needed is a narrow analogue of belief in general. Like ordinary belief, narrow belief must be expressed as a relation between the believer and some kind of *content*. This is essential since the project is to explain mental states as internal states *while preserving the structure of intentional explanations*. The strategy is to change the notion of content in a way that makes belief states purely internal. But however content is explained, how is it possible for belief to be both a relation between a person and a content and also a purely internal state? To answer this we need to distinguish two ways in which a concept can be relational. Consider again the quantities weight and mass: a Twin Earth thought experiment will show that weight is a relational property. William weighs three hundred pounds, but his twin on the less massive Twin Earth weighs less. Mass, in contrast, is intrinsic; Twin William is equally massive. But both weight and mass are relational in another sense: they are both *semantically* relational concepts. There is a relation—weight (or mass) in pounds—that William bears to the number three hundred and that Wilma

---

[5] One might argue that concepts, such as the general concept of footprint, that collapse when we try to abstract away from causal origins are just the concepts that are of no interest to science. But this need not be true. It is conceivable, for example, that there be ecological generalizations about the role of footprints in the behavior of certain kinds of predators and their prey even if there were no interesting generalizations about the shapes of the relevant footprints. If there can be functional theories at all, then there can be theories that generalize about causal roles in abstraction from the intrinsic properties of the states that realize those roles.

bears to one hundred and two. Both weight and mass are concepts expressed by using a relational *predicate* together with a number to pick out a property. It is the fact that the family of properties—weight or mass properties—has a certain structure that makes it possible for them to be expressed in this way. But this is compatible with the properties being intrinsic in the sense that whether a thing has one of them is not contingent on anything external to the thing. The revisionist project requires a concept of belief that is semantically relational, but that expresses belief properties that are ontologically intrinsic; it proposes to accomplish this by changing or restricting the contents that are used to pick out the properties. Belief is to be narrowed by narrowing content.

So how is narrow content to be explained? The first answer I will consider is Jerry Fodor's.[6] Let me sketch, first Fodor's diagnosis of the problem—his explanation of the fact that content, in the ordinary wide sense, is not in the head—and then say how he proposes to revise the notion of content to get it back into the head where it belongs. The problem, Fodor says, derives from the following constraint on the identity conditions for content: beliefs that are true under different conditions have different contents. It is because the Earthling's thought or statement, "Aluminum is used in the construction of airplanes" could be true in possible circumstances in which her twin's corresponding statement or thought is false that we are required to conclude that the two have different content. Narrow contents cannot differ in this way, but if narrow content is not constrained by truth-conditions, how can it be a notion of content at all? The solution, Fodor proposes, it not to give up the connection between content and truth-conditions, but rather to relativize this connection to context. Narrow content will be something that determines the truth-conditions of a belief or utterance as a function of the external environment of the believer or speaker. The model for this account of narrow content is David Kaplan's account of the semantics for demonstratives and indexicals. Kaplan makes a distinction between *meaning* (or what he calls *character*) and *content*, and this distinction provides the model for Fodor's distinction between narrow and wide content. According to Kaplan's account, when Daniels and O'Leary both say "I am bald," they say something with the same *character*, but with different *content*. Daniels's statement says that Daniels is bald, whereas O'Leary's says that O'Leary is. Character is explained as a function from context to content. The pronoun "I" has a constant character: it always refers to the speaker. But because different speakers use that pronoun, the same sentences containing it may be used to say different things. In general, the character of a sentence of

---

[6] Fodor (1987: ch. 2).

the form "I am F" will be a function taking a context in which x is the speaker into the proposition that is true if and only if x has the property expressed by "F." Narrow content, on Fodor's account of it, is a generalization of character in Kaplan's sense, where the context includes any fact external to the believer that is relevant to the determination of wide content.[7]

Fodor suggests that once we are clear about the general nature of narrow content, "it's quite easy to see how the required principles of individuation should be formulated."[8] Here is his explanation of the "extensional identity criterion" for narrow content:

> There is presumably something about the relation between Twin-Earth and Twin-me in virtue of which his "water"-thoughts are about XYZ even though my water-thoughts are not. Call this condition that's satisfied by [Twin-Me, Twin-Earth] condition C. . . . Similarly, there must be something about the relation between me and Earth in virtue of which my water-thoughts are about H₂O even though my Twin's "water"-thoughts are not. Call this condition that is satisfied by [me, Earth] condition C'. . . . Short of a miracle, it must be true that if an organism shares the neurophysiological constitution of my Twin *and satisfies C*, it follows that its thoughts and my Twin's thoughts share their truth conditions. . . . But now we have an extensional identity criterion for mental contents: two thought contents are identical only if they effect the same mapping of thoughts and contexts onto truth conditions.[9]

This argument tells us what kind of thing narrow content should be: a mapping from context into truth-conditions; and it shows that *if* we succeeded in specifying such a mapping, it would have the right properties: it would be *narrow* (intrinsic) and it would be like *content* in the crucial way: it would determine the semantic or intentional properties of the thought (relative to context). But the argument tells us less than it seems about how such mappings are to be specified, and it obscures the fact that it is a substantive hypothesis that the internal states of believers contain thoughts that determine such mappings.

It is surely right that if the context (C or C') includes all information external to the believer that may be relevant to the determination of truth-conditions, then context, together with the internal states of the believer, will determine truth-conditions. That is only to say that truth-conditions are determined by the conditions that are relevant to determining them. But pointing this out does not tell us what function from context to content narrow content is supposed to be, or explain how it is that the relevant function is determined by what is in the believer's head. If the abstract

---

[7] An explanation of narrow content based on this analogy was developed in some detail in White (1982).

[8] Fodor (1987: 30).   [9] Ibid. 48.

procedure outlined in the argument could, by itself, show how to narrow content, then it could be used to define a narrow analogue of any relational property.

Consider this parody of Fodor's characterization of the criterion for narrow content: Take the property of being exactly three miles from a burning barn. Suppose I have this property, even though my counterpart who is located at exactly the same place in a certain counterfactual situation does not. He, let us suppose, is instead exactly three miles from a snow-covered chicken coop. Now there is presumably something about the relation between my counterpart and his world in virtue of which he is three miles from a snow-covered chicken coop even though I am not. Call this condition C. Similarly, there is something about the relation between me and my world in virtue of which I am three miles from a burning barn, even though my counterpart is not. Call it C'. Whatever these conditions are, we *do* know this: short of a miracle, it must be true that anyone in the location that both I and my counterpart are in our respective worlds would be three miles from a snow-covered chicken coop if condition C obtained, and three miles from a burning barn if instead C' obtained. But this does not help us identify a specific function that takes condition C' into the property of being three miles from a snow-covered chicken coop and also takes C into the property of being three miles from a burning barn—a function that is supposed to represent the contribution that an individual's location makes to the relational property. There are many such functions, and no reason to identify any of them with the contribution that my intrinsic location makes to the specific relational property. My counterpart cannot reasonably say, "I did my part toward being three miles from a burning barn by going to a place where, if conditions C' had obtained instead of C, I would have been three miles from a burning barn." *Every* location is such that for some external conditions, if those conditions obtain, then anything in that location is three miles from a burning barn.

The exclusive focus of Twin Earth situations makes it look easier than it is to factor out the contribution that the external environment makes to the possession of some relational property. In a Twin Earth story, we are asked to consider a possible situation in which an individual shares *every* intrinsic property with its actual counterpart. So if the actual individual has the relational property in question, we can be sure that its Twin Earth counterpart will have whatever property is supposed to be the purely intrinsic component of that relational property. But the story does not help us to identify the relevant intrinsic property. If we were to consider, not *Twin* Earths, but say *Cousin* Earth stories in which an individual resembles its counterpart in some but not all internal ways, it would be

clearer that this strategy for defining intrinsic properties in terms of rela-
tions may leave many questions unanswered. Suppose, for example, that
Cousin Earth contains both H_2O and XYZ. In this world the two substances are easily distinguished. Their superficial properties are somewhat
different from the superficial properties that H_2O has on Earth, and that
XYZ has on Twin Earth, and also somewhat different from each other.
But both substances are somewhat like water in fact is. Suppose also that
Cousin English has different (non-scientific) words for the two substances,
neither one of which is spelled or pronounced like "water," but that otherwise Cousin English is a lot like English. Now suppose my counterpart on
Cousin Earth believes that salt is soluble in water, but does not believe that
salt is soluble in the other stuff. Does his belief have the same narrow content as my belief that salt is soluble in water (and so the same narrow content as my twin's belief that salt is soluble in the other stuff)? Fodor's
abstract account, by itself, gives no guidance about how to answer this
question.[10]

There are several disanalogies between Kaplan's notion of character
and Fodor's proposed account of narrow content—disanalogies that suggest that Fodor's project is much more ambitious, and much more speculative. First, Kaplan's notion of context is not designed to include
everything external to the individual, and the character of an utterance is
not something determined by the purely internal properties of the speaker.
As a result, characters are not required to have the counterfactual power
that narrow contents must have. That the pronoun "I" has the character it
has is a fact about a social practice—the practice of speaking English. The
functions from context to content that Kaplan calls characters are not
intended to tell us what speakers would be saying if they were speaking
some other language. Kaplan's notion need not tell us this since the aim of
his theory is not to isolate the purely internal component of what determines the content of speech acts, but simply to explain how some languages in fact work. The practice of speech is more efficient if speakers can
exploit information about the environment—information available to all
the participants in a conversation—in communicating. So languages make
this possible by including rules that make what is said a function of that
kind of information. That a language contains such rules (rather than, say,
just lots of unsystematic ambiguity) is a substantive hypothesis, though in
this case an obviously correct one. That our minds contain much more

---

[10] The point of my Cousin Earth story is not just that narrow content may in some cases
be indeterminate. That I would argue and many would agree, is true of wide content as well.
The point is that once we go beyond the Twin Earth scenario, it becomes clear that we have
been told nothing at all about how to identify narrow content. That there is such a thing to
be identified is a substantive hypothesis.

general systematic procedures for determining content as a function of context in a more general sense is a much more ambitious and speculative hypothesis.

Second, because Kaplan's theory is a theory of speech rather than a theory of thought we can identify, more or less independently of theory, the objects that the theory is interpreting: the objects that *have* character and content. A speech act can be described in terms of its content (O'Leary said that salt is soluble in water), but it also may be described in more neutral ways (O'Leary uttered the sentence, or the sounds, "Salt is soluble in water"). But in the case of thought it is much less clear what it is that has a particular content, or narrow content. As with a speech act, we can describe a particular belief in terms of its content (O'Leary believes that salt is soluble in water), but in this case there is no easily identifiable mental state, describable independently of its content, that constitutes that person's having that belief. Of course a psychological theory might turn up such a mental state or object. It might be that what it is to believe that salt is soluble in water is to be storing in a certain location a mental sentence that says that salt is soluble in water. If this were true, then we could identify the thing that has the content independently of the content that it has. But it also might be that states of belief are more holistic. Suppose a total belief state were a complex cluster of dispositions to behave in various ways under various conditions. One might be able to use particular belief contents such as the belief that salt is soluble in water to describe such a state without it being possible to match up those contents with particular dispositions in the cluster. On this kind of account, the question "what makes it true (given the facts about the external context) that O'Leary believes that salt is soluble in water?" will be answered by describing how O'Leary is disposed to behave under various conditions. But the same behavioral dispositions that constitute O'Leary's total belief state will also make it true that he believes various other nonequivalent propositions. Compare: the question "what makes it true (given the facts about the external context) that O'Leary is three miles from a burning barn?" will be answered by describing O'Leary's location. But this same location will also make it true that O'Leary has various other nonequivalent relational properties (being more than two thousand miles from Los Angeles, being closer to Istanbul than to New Delhi, etc.). Even if we could find a narrow, purely internal characterization of the belief state as a whole, it wouldn't follow that we could find narrow analogues of the (relational) facts about the belief state that are expressed by ordinary attributions of belief.[11]

[11] The point is that it doesn't follow that one could find *interesting* purely internal analogues of the relational properties of belief states that are expressed by ordinary attributions of belief—internal properties that might be expected to play a role in an explanatory

Fodor's abstract account of narrow content is motivated by a particular picture of belief and other mental states, a picture that he has made explicit and vigorously defended. Beliefs are internal sentences stored in the mind. The particular contents of those sentences depend on the believer's environment, but the sentences themselves can be identified as sentences, and as *beliefs*, independently of the particular environmental conditions that determine their interpretation. The sentences are beliefs in virtue of their internal functional role—the way they are affected by sensory inputs, interact with other internal states, and determine behavioral outputs. Their semantic properties will depend in part on what is going on outside—beyond the periphery—but the way they depend on what is going on outside is determined by the purely internal state. This is a very attractive picture, but it is not inevitable; it has strong, highly speculative, empirical presuppositions. Fodor's abstract account of narrow content as a function from context (in a very broad sense) to truth-conditional content may seem plausible given this picture, but it does not contribute much to defending the picture, or to explaining how it is to be developed. It does not, by itself, tell us how to identify narrow contents, and it does not give us reason to believe that internal states determine functions of this kind that will do any explanatory work. No general a priori argument will show that this is the way that things must be.

Is there a way to define narrow content that does not depend on the language of thought picture? Daniel Dennett, after criticizing the sententialist approach, makes some suggestions about how we might isolate what he calls the "organismic contribution" to the content of belief in a way that is neutral as to how that contribution is represented in the believer.[12] He calls his approach "*notional attitude psychology*," and contrasts it both with *propositional attitude psychology*, which describes attitudes in terms of the ordinary wide conception of content, and *sentential attitude psychology*, which takes the contents of attitudes to be syntactic objects— sentences of an inner language. The contents of notional attitudes are explained in terms of a kind of possible world, which Dennett calls a "notional world." "A notional world should be viewed as a sort of *fictional* world devised by a theorist, a third-party observer, in order to character-

---

theory of behavior. One could always, by brute force, define some sort of internal property. Consider the location analogy: there is a set of absolute locations that are (in fact, at a certain moment) three miles from a burning barn. The property of being in one of those locations is (assuming, as we have been for purposes of the analogy, absolute space) independent of the external environment, and it is distinct from the property of being in one of the locations in the set that is in fact at least two thousand miles from Los Angeles. But such properties will have no interest; at other places, there will be no point in distinguishing the locations where, at this time and in this situation, a barn is burning three miles away.

[12] Dennett (1982).

ize the narrow-psychological states of a subject."[13] Notional worlds are supposed to be defined so that, "although my *Doppelganger* and I live in different real worlds—Twin Earth and Earth—we have the *same* notional world."[14] The set of notional worlds that define the narrow contents of a person's beliefs is something like the worlds that *are* the way that the person takes the real world to be.

Notional worlds, it seems, are just the possible worlds that have been used to characterize ordinary wide contents in *propositional* attitude psychology. Possible worlds—at least all but one of them—are also fictional worlds in the sense that they are not actual. So how are notional attitudes different from propositional attitudes, characterized in this way? What difference explains why the contents of notional attitudes are narrow, while the contents of propositional attitudes are wide? The difference will not be found in the nature of the worlds themselves, or in the nature of the contents, which in both cases are just sets of worlds. So far as I can see, narrow contents, on Dennett's account, are just propositions. The difference between notional and propositional content is to be found in the different answers that the two theories give to the question, "in virtue of what facts do a believer's beliefs have the (notional or propositional) contents that they have?" According to propositional attitude psychology, the contents of an organism's attitudes are picked out as a function of relations between the organism and its actual environment. Just what relations do the job is a difficult and controversial question, but the Twin Earth thought experiments show that the content of a belief, as ordinarily conceived, is not a function of purely internal properties of the believer. The task of narrow, notional attitude psychology is to explain how purely internal properties of an organism can be used to pick out a set of possible worlds—a perhaps different set that will characterize the organism's attitudes in a way that is different from the way it is characterized by an ordinary propositional attitude attribution. The idea is roughly this: O'Leary believes (correctly) that there is water in the basement. The proposition he believes is true in the actual world, but false in the counterfactual world where there is no water, but only XYZ in the basement. There is, however, a different proposition that does not distinguish the actual world from this counterfactual world— a proposition that we might roughly describe as the proposition that there is some water-like stuff in the basement. The first proposition is the wide content of O'Leary's belief; the aim of Dennett's project is to define narrow content so that the second of these propositions is the narrow content.

One can contrast Fodor's strategy with Dennett's in the following very abstract way: Fodor proposes to revise and narrow the folk concept of

[13] Ibid. 38.   [14] Ibid.

belief by changing the *kind* of thing that is the content of belief. Narrow contents are not propositions; they are functions from context to propositions. But for Dennett, in contrast, narrow contents are the same kind of thing as wide contents: both are propositions—functions from possible worlds (= notional worlds) into truth-values. What is changed in the move to narrow content is the relation between a believer and a proposition in virtue of which that proposition correctly describes the believer's beliefs. To accomplish that change, Dennett needs to tell us just how the purely internal properties of individuals determine the narrow propositional content of their beliefs.

Here is Dennett's strategy for answering this question: suppose we know about an organism everything there is to know about its capacities and dispositions, but nothing about how it got that way: nothing about its historical properties, or about the environment that it came from. The problem is to say how to go from this limited information about the organism to a characterization of its notional world. "Our task," Dennett says, "is like the problem posed when we are shown some novel or antique gadget, and asked: what is it for?" We can't know, Dennett supposes, what it was actually designed for, but we could try to figure out, from its internal properties, what functions it is ideally suited to perform. "*We try to imagine a setting* in which . . . it would *excellently* perform some imaginably useful function."[15] In the same way, to find an organism's notional world—the world according to it—we try to imagine "the environment (or a class of environments) for which the organism as currently constituted is best fitted."[16] Propositions true in those possible environments will be the narrow contents of the organism's beliefs.

On the face of it, this doesn't look like what we want at all. Possible worlds picked out in this way look more like worlds in which the organism's needs or wants are satisfied than like worlds in which its beliefs are true. The antelope, for example, is aware of lions in its environment, and equipped to detect and escape from them. But it is not clear that it is better fitted for a lion-filled environment than for one that is lion-free. The antelope would have some useless defense mechanisms in certain lion-free environments, but it might still do a better job of "surviving and flourishing and reproducing its kind"[17] in such an environment. But, Dennett says, we are not supposed to understand "ideal environments" in a straightforward way: "By 'ideal environment' I do not mean the best of all possible worlds for this organism. . . . It might be a downright nasty world, but at least the organism is prepared to cope with its nastiness."[18] So ideal environments, in the intended sense, are environments for which the

---

[15] Dennett (1982: 41).   [16] Ibid. 42.   [17] Ibid. 41.   [18] Ibid. 42.

organism is prepared to cope. This is better: we do try to cope with the world as we believe it to be, and so worlds that are that way are presumably among the ones that our behavior is best fitted to cope with. But something essential still seems to be left out. Many features of organisms that help them cope with their environments seem intuitively to have nothing to do with their beliefs, and the fact that we have some feature that *would* help us cope with some counterfactual environment is surely not sufficient to say that such a counterfactual possibility is compatible with the world as we take it to be.

Consider the porcupine whose quills protect it from predators. It is best fitted, in Dennett's sense, for an environment containing animals that would attack and eat it if it weren't for the quills, and this will be true even if the porcupine's *only* defense mechanism is this passive one that does not require the porcupine to perceive or respond in any way to the presence of such predators. If the porcupine goes through life oblivious to the potential predators that its quills protect it against, it would surely be unreasonable to populate its notional world—the world according to it—with them.

The dangers that the porcupine's quills protect it from are real ones. The problem gets even worse if one considers, as Dennett's procedure requires, merely possible dangers that some actual feature we have might help to guard against. For example, consider a possible world containing fierce and powerful beasts that would love to eat human beings if it weren't for the fact that these beasts are repelled by the distinctive smell that humans in fact give off. We humans, as we actually are, are ideally fitted to cope with such predators, but I don't think worlds containing them can be used to characterize our beliefs.

It seems to me right that states of belief are states that help the believer to cope with an environment, and that the contents of those states are essentially connected with the kind of environment they help the believer to cope with. But to be a belief state, a feature of an organism must contribute in a particular way to the fitness of the organism to cope with its environment. At the very least, a belief state must involve the reception of information from the environment, and a role for this information in the determination of the behavior of the organism. While Dennett's general account of his procedure for identifying narrow content is not restricted to this kind of case, the examples he uses focus on it, and we can consider how his strategy fares if we apply it only to states of an organism that help it cope by receiving and storing information in a form that makes it available to help determine the organism's behavior.

Understood in this way, Dennett's procedure is a variation of one kind of naturalistic account of wide content that has been proposed. According to this kind of account, a representational system is a system that is capable of being in a range of alternative internal states that tend to be causally dependent on the environment in a systematic way. Suppose that an organism is capable of being in internal states, $S_1, S_2, \ldots, S_n$, and that which of these states it is in normally depends on which of a corresponding range of alternative states the environment is in. Normally, for each i, the organism is in state S_i if (and because) the environment is in state E_i. Whenever a structure of causal dependencies of this kind obtains, it is appropriate to say that the organism *represents* the environment as being in state E_i in virtue of the fact that it is in state S_i, and that the organism's states contain *information* about the environment. Suppose further that the states of the organism are, or determine, behavioral dispositions, and that for each i, the behavior that state S_i disposes the organism to engage in is behavior that would be appropriate (given its needs or wants) in environment E_i. Then those representational states will be of the right general kind to be belief states.

This account of representation is like Dennett's account of narrow content in that it identifies content with a set of possible states of the environment. This account, like Dennett's, treats the descriptions of the relevant environments as the theorist's way of classifying internal states: the descriptions are not attributed to the organism. And like Dennett's, it does not distinguish information from misinformation. If the organism is in state S_i, then it represents the world as being in state E_i, whatever state the environment is actually in. But the notion of content that results from the causal account of representation will be a notion of *wide* content since the structure of causal relations in virtue of which the internal states are representational states will depend not just on the internal structure of the organism, but on general features of the environment. If the environment were radically different in certain ways, then the same states of the organism might tend to be sensitive to different features of the environment, or might not be sensitive to the environment al all. Content ascriptions, on this kind of account, are descriptions of internal states, but they describe them in terms of the organism's capacity to distinguish between a limited range of alternative possibilities, a range of possibilities that is constrained by certain facts about the organism's actual environment.

But even if our ordinary concept of content depends on facts about the actual environment in this way, might we apply this sort of procedure without relying on such facts? If we knew enough about the purely internal dispositional properties of a believer, might we be able to determine, from this information alone, a set of possible environments meeting this condition: if the believer were in such an environment it would tend to behave in ways that are appropriate (that tend to satisfy its needs better than alternative actions available in that environment), and it would do so *because* it is in such an environment? Dennett claims that if the believers were sophisticated enough we could, and that the resulting notion of content would be just the notion of narrow content we want.

Highly adaptive organisms like ourselves . . . have internal structure and dispositional traits so rich in information about the environment in which they grew up that we could in principle say: this organism is best fitted to an environment in which there is a city called Boston, in which the organism spent its youth, in the company of organisms named . . . and so forth. We would not be able to distinguish Boston from Twin-Earth Boston, of course, but except for such virtually indistinguishable variations on a theme, our exercise in notional world formation would end in a unique solution.[19]

I see no basis for this optimism. I suspect that the attempt to recover information about a virtual environment without making any assumptions at all about the actual environment is just too unconstrained to work. Imagine a purely internal description of the movements that I am disposed to make under various internal conditions, as I walk down the streets of Boston going places to satisfy my wants and needs, a description that makes no reference to what is going on either specifically or in general beyond my skin. How could anything about *Boston*, or about Boston-like cities, be recovered from such a description? With a little imagination, one should be able to tell all kinds of wild fairy tales about environments in which the movements I am disposed to make are appropriate, but that are not anything like the way the world seems to me. The world beyond myself *could* be wired up so that the actions whose actual appropriateness depends on facts about Boston instead depended for their appropriateness on some totally different set of facts, say facts about the social organization of termite colonies. If the organism's internal structure and dispositional traits are rich and complex, then we will have to tell a long fairy tale. The world described by such a tale will perhaps have to share an abstract structure of some kind with the worlds that define the ordinary wide content of the organism's beliefs, but I don't see why they would have to share any content.

In normal everyday ascriptions of content we usually ignore not only fairy tale possibilities, but all possibilities except those that differ from the actual world only in very limited ways. When I say that O'Leary believes there is water in his basement, I may be saying only that O'Leary's conception of the world distinguishes the possibility that there is water in the basement from the possibility that his basement is dry. What this means, on the causal-informational account of representation, is that O'Leary is

---

[19] Dennett (1982: 43).

in a state that he would normally be in only if there were water in his basement. Further, that state is one that would normally cause O'Leary to
behave in ways that would better serve his needs and wants if there were
water in his basement than if the basement were dry: it disposes him to get
out the mop, or call the plumber. But does O'Leary really believe that the
liquid on his basement floor is *water*? Well, he certainly knows, or assumes,
that it is not gasoline or olive oil. If it were any of a range of familiar alternative liquids, O'Leary's states and behavior would normally be different.
But what about the possibility that it is a substance just like water in its
superficial properties, but different from water in its underlying chemical
structure? Does O'Leary's internal state contain information that distinguishes the actual situation from this one? Is there anything about him
that would dispose him to behave differently (under normal conditions) if
that situation were actual? In the usual context, that possibility is not relevant. When we claim that O'Leary thinks there is water in the basement,
we are not claiming that he has ruled out the possibility that the stuff down
there is really not water, but XYZ. We can, however, raise the question,
and in this way change the range of relevant alternatives. The question will
then shift, focussing on O'Leary's knowledge and beliefs about the chemical composition of water. If O'Leary is innocent of even the most elementary knowledge of chemistry, then nothing in his mind or behavioral
dispositions will distinguish Earth from Twin Earth, but that won't make
it wrong to say, in a normal context in which Twin Earth possibilities are
ignored, that O'Leary believes that the stuff on his basement floor is water.
That ascription of content distinguishes, in the right way, the relevant
alternative possibilities that are compatible with O'Leary's conception of
the world from the relevant possibilities that are not.

   The revisionist may argue that it is this context-dependence of ordinary
wide content ascriptions that makes them inappropriate for the purposes
of theoretical explanation in cognitive science. Dennett's project might be
seen as an attempt to eliminate the context-dependence by defining content relative to an absolutely neutral context that is free of all presuppositions about the external environment. But on the causal-informational
account of representation, informational content is *essentially* relative to a
range of alternative possibilities that are determined by general facts
about the causal structure of the world in which the organism functions. It
is internal states of the representor, on this kind of account, that contain
information (or misinformation), but the system of causal relationships in
virtue of which those internal states contain information cannot itself be
something internal to the representor. The theorist, in describing the internal states of a representor in terms of informational content, has some
choice in the range of alternatives relative to which content is defined. It

may even be that for any possibility we can describe, there is a context in which we can ask whether the representor's beliefs distinguish that possibility from certain others. But this does not imply that there is an absolutely neutral context, a context free of all presuppositions about the environment, relative to which content ascriptions make sense.

In his attempt to characterize narrow content, Dennett has tied one hand behind his back. He proposes to extract a kind of content from facts about the believer while ignoring certain information that is available and that is used to determine ordinary wide content—information about the believer's historical properties and relation to the actual environment. I have argued that no reasonable notion of content will result from this procedure; one might also question the point of the exercise. Why bother? Why shouldn't an explanatory theory make use of historical and environmental information in defining content? To answer this we need to look at the other half of the revisionist's project: the arguments for the negative thesis.

The negative side of the revisionist doctrine has been formulated in various ways and given various labels: *methodological solipsism*,[20] *individualism*,[21] *the principle of autonomy*.[22] These different theses are sometimes distinguished from each other, but the general idea of all of them is that the states and properties that are described and expressed in an explanatory psychological theory should be intrinsic states and properties of the organism whose behavior is being explained. A number of similar arguments for this thesis have been advanced; they go roughly like this: an explanatory theory of human behavior, or of the behavior of anything else for that matter, should concern itself only with properties that are relevant to the causal powers of the thing whose behavior is being explained. Things that are intrinsically indistinguishable are indistinguishable with respect to causal powers, and so should not be distinguished by an explanatory theory. The Putnam–Burge thought experiments help to bring this point out: it is clear that people on Earth and their doppelganger on Twin Earth will behave in exactly the same ways when put into the same environments. No tenable theory will explain their behavior in different ways, and so no tenable theory needs concepts that distinguish them.[23]

[20] This term is used for this doctrine by Hilary Putnam in Putnam (1975) (see note 1). Jerry Fodor defends the doctrine in Fodor (1981a).

[21] This is Burge's term. Fodor distinguishes methodological solipsism from individualism in ch. 2 of Fodor (1987), though I think it is not clear that Fodor and Burge are using the term in the same sense.

[22] This is Stephen Stich's term. Stich distinguishes the principle of autonomy from methodological solipsism. See Stich (1983).

[23] See Fodor (1987: ch. 2) for a clear development of this argument. See also the replacement argument in Stich (1983: 165 ff.).

Before turning to this argument, we need to look more closely at the thesis it is intended to support. First, here is Fodor's formulation of what he calls *individualism*: "Methodological individualism is the doctrine that psychological states are individuated *with respect to their causal powers*."[24] This doctrine is, Fodor says, a special case of a completely general methodological principle that all scientific taxonomies should conform to, a principle that can be defended on a priori metaphysical grounds. He emphasizes that individualism, in his sense, does not by itself rule out the individuation of mental states by relational properties.

Relational properties can count taxonomically whenever they affect causal powers. Thus, "being a planet" is a relational property par excellence, but it's one that individualism permits to operate in astronomical taxonomy. For whether you are a planet affects your trajectory and your trajectory determines what you can bump into; so whether you're a planet affects your causal powers.[25]

There is a shift in this characterization of individualism from a stronger to a weaker claim: it is one thing to individuate by causal powers, another to individuate by what *affects* causal powers. The fact that a planet is a planet is a fact about the configuration of its environment. This configuration plays a role in causing the planet to have the causal powers it has, for example its velocity. But the environmental facts do not *constitute* causal powers. Does individualism really require only that mental states be individuated by what causally affects causal powers? If so, then individualism in Fodor's sense is a much weaker doctrine than the individualism that Burge has argued against. On this interpretation, individuation by ordinary wide content will be compatible with Fodor's individualism since, for example, the fact that it is *water* in O'Leary's basement—or at least the fact that there is water in his environment generally—surely plays a role in putting him into the internal state that disposes him to behave as he does. Of course as the Twin Earth story shows, there are alternative causal histories that could have put O'Leary into the same internal state, but an analogous claim will be true for the planets. Imagine a Twin Earth that is not a planet but is in a field of forces exactly like the one the Earth is in.

The defense of the negative thesis by Fodor and others trades on a conflation of the weaker and the stronger thesis. If the thesis is to have any bite—if it is to be a thesis that rules out the individuation of psychological states by ordinary wide content—it must be the stronger thesis. But the arguments and examples used to support individualism often count only against the weaker thesis. Fodor, for example, illustrates his version of individualism and defends its plausibility with an example of a causally irrelevant relational property: call a particle an h-particle if a certain coin

---

[24] Fodor (1987: 42). Fodor's emphasis.   [25] Ibid. 43.

is heads up, and a t-particle if the coin is tails up. No plausible theory, Fodor argues, will use this distinction to explain the behavior of particles. No one will disagree with this; it should be clear and uncontroversial that facts that are causally irrelevant to the internal states of a particle or an organism should play no role in characterizing its theoretically important physical or psychological states. But it does not follow from this that such states must be purely internal.

The same shift between a weaker and a stronger version of the negative thesis is evident in other discussions. Consider, for example Stephen Stich's principle of autonomy: "The basic idea of the principle is that the states and processes that ought to be of concern to the psychologist are those that supervene on the current, internal, physical states of the organism." This is clearly the strong thesis, restricting the psychologist to purely internal states. But causal language creeps into Stich's subsequent discussion of the principle: historical and environmental facts, he says, will be irrelevant to psychological theory except when they "make a difference" to the organism's internal state; such facts "will be psychologically relevant only when they *influence* an organism's current, internal, physical state." The facts about distant causal histories of a term that determine its reference are said to be psychologically irrelevant because they need not "leave their trace" on the current internal state of the subject using the term.[26]

Stich argues for his principle of autonomy with what he calls the *replacement argument*: "Suppose that someone were to succeed in building an exact physical replica of me—a living human body whose current internal physical states at a given moment were identical to mine at that moment. . . . The replica, being an exact physical copy, would behave just as I would in all circumstances. . . . But now, the argument continues, since psychology is the science which aspires to explain behavior, any states or processes or properties which are not shared by Stich and his identically behaving replica must surely be irrelevant to psychology."[27] Stich illustrates his point with an example of an industrial robot. Suppose we describe the robot by saying that it is successfully performing its millionth weld. This is, in Stich's terminology, a nonautonomous behavioral description. An exact physical replica behaving in a way that is, in a reasonable sense, exactly the same, might not satisfy it. The description is a "conceptual hybrid" of an autonomous description—"successfully performing a weld"[28]—and a purely historical description—"having

---

[26] Stich (1983: 164–5).   [27] Ibid. 167.

[28] Paul Teller has pointed out that "successfully performing a weld" is not really an autonomous description, since its application depends on a social and technological context. With a little imagination, one could tell a Twin Earth story in which what twin robot was doing did not count as performing a weld.

performed 999,999 other welds." "If we are seeking a set of generalizations to explain robot behavior, it would be perverse to expect them to explain the latter fact or the hybrid into which it enters."[29]

The argument and the example seem compelling, I think, only if we assume that the historical property is causally irrelevant to the current state of the robot. But if we keep in mind that those first 999,999 welds must surely have taken their toll, then it may not seem so perverse to look for generalizations that explain the fact that the robot satisfies the hybrid description. Suppose that, because of metal fatigue, robots of this kind almost always break down soon after about nine hundred thousand welds. If the robot failed to break down, we might ask for an explanation: how was this particular robot able to perform its millionth weld? We might call robots "old" after their nine hundred thousandth weld, and generalize about the behavior of old robots. We certainly generalize about the behavior of human beings on the basis of historical properties such as age and experience.

If we replace our robots with new ones after 900,000 welds, they won't break down as often, but, Stich might point out, this is because real replacements won't be the exact replicas required by the replacement argument. If the new robots were really physically exactly like the ones they replace, then of course they would be similarly unreliable. If an eighty-year-old woman were physically exactly like a seven-year-old child, then she would behave like a seven-year-old child, falsifying biological and psychological generalizations about eighty-year-old women. But this counterfactual possibility does not, by itself, threaten the truth, or even the explanatory power, of such generalizations.

There may be a sense in which certain nonautonomous properties are causally irrelevant. Consider a simple causal chain: A causes B, which in turn causes C. Suppose that B is sufficient, in the circumstances, for C: that is, B would have caused C even if it had been caused by something other than A. So this causal chain contrasts with a more complex one where A is doing some additional work, perhaps not only causing B but also causing other things that enable B to cause C. To rule out this contrasting case, we might say that A is causally irrelevant to the fact that B causes C. But in another sense, A is causally relevant to this fact, since without A, B would not have happened, and so would not have caused C. Suppose we have a pair of alternative causal chains: alternative inputs A_1 or A_2 will cause a device to be in one of two alternative internal states, B_1 or B_2, which in turn will cause the device to produce outputs C_1 or C_2. If we ask why the internal state B_1 produces output C_1, it is not relevant to mention A_1. But if we ask why the device produces output C_1, it would be correct

[29] Stich (1983: 168).

and informative to say, because it is in the B-state caused by A_1. It is one thing to explain why a particular internal state has the causal powers it has; it is another to explain why something is in an internal state that has those causal powers.

Does the internal state of the device contain *information* about how it came to be in that state? If there are alternative causes of B_1, then the fact that the device is in state B_1 does not distinguish them: the device does not "know" that A_1 causes B_1, as contrasted with a counterfactual possibility in which A_2 causes B_1. But since it is A_1 that in fact causes the device to be in state B_1, and since the device would not have been in that state if A_1 hadn't happened, it "knows", in virtue of being in state B_1, that A_1 happened.

In light of these distinctions, consider the following argument in defense of methodological solipsism from a paper by P. M. and P. S. Churchland:

> A neuron cannot know the distant causal ancestry . . . of its input. . . . An activated neuron causes a creature to withdraw into its shell not because such activation represents the presence of a predator—though it may indeed represent this—but because that neuron is connected to the withdrawal muscles, and because its activation is of the kind that causes them to contract. *The "semantic" content of the state, if any, is causally irrelevant.*[30]

One cannot explain why the neuron's being activated causes the creature to withdraw by citing the fact that the activation represents the presence of a predator. But this does not prevent us from explaining why the creature withdraws by citing the presence of a predator, or by citing the fact that the creature is in a state that represents the presence of a predator. The semantic content is causally relevant to the behavior of the creature since if the creature had not been in a state with that semantic content, it would not have withdrawn into its shell. Can a neuron know the distant causal ancestry of its input? It cannot distinguish the situation in which its activation is caused by the presence of a predator from the situation in which it is caused by something else. But if in fact the neuron was activated by the presence of a predator, and would not have been activated if a predator had not been present, then it "knows", in virtue of being activated, that a predator is present.

The critic of wide content might respond to these general considerations as follows: even if a theory *can* generalize about properties and states that are individuated by their causes, wouldn't it be better, methodologically, to try to find a theory that individuates them more narrowly? Won't generalizations in terms of the internal properties be deeper and more accurate? Generalizations about the causal powers or behavioral dispositions of old

---

[30] Churchland and Churchland (1983). Emphasis mine.

robots, creatures that are representing the presence of a predator, or footprints will inevitably have exceptions; to the extent that they are true, they
must hold in virtue of internal properties of those things, and we won't
understand why the generalizations hold until we are clear about the relevant internal properties.

It is right that *one* explanatory task is the task of characterizing the mechanisms that underlie certain causal regularities. We want to know how the
creature represents the presence of a predator, and how that representation
causes it to withdraw into its shell. But there are at least three reasons why
we may still want to generalize about causal and historical properties. First,
we need to refer to such properties, and to generalizations about them, in
order to pose the explanatory questions about the mechanisms. The creature
has certain capacities: it can recognize predators and protect itself from
them. The reason we are interested in the neurophysiological processes in the
creature is that they explain how it is able to do such things. Second, we may
not know enough to be able to generalize in terms of internal properties.
Suppose our device is a black box and that all we know about the states B_1
and B_2 is that they are the states caused (or normally caused) by A_1 and A_2,
respectively. Often we know something about the mechanisms that explain
why a device has certain capacities or incapacities, but not enough to
describe them in purely autonomous terms. We may have to wait for the
completion of science before we are able to describe things in purely internal
terms, if there are such terms. As Fodor said in another context, and in
defense of the opposite conclusion, "No doubt it's all right to have a research
strategy that says 'wait a while', but who wants to wait *forever*?"[31] Third,
there may be generalizations that can be stated only in terms of non-
individualistic states and properties. Different mechanisms explain how different creatures recognize predators, but we may still be able to generalize
about the recognition of predators. Suppose there are lots of black boxes that
take inputs A_1 and A_2 into outputs C_1 and C_2, but that they do it in different ways. It is, of course, the idea of functionalism that it is possible and useful to generalize about causal roles independently of the specific mechanisms
by which those causal roles are realized. Functional theories are theories that
characterize the internal states of individuals in nonautonomous terms in
order to generalize at a certain level of abstraction. It is not a mysterious
coincidence that such generalizations hold. There may be general causal
pressures, such as evolutionary pressures, that tend to favor situations in
which A causes C but that leave open the question of the means or interven-
ing process by which this is accomplished. In such a case there may be two
different questions about why A causes C. If the question is about the mech-

---

[31] Fodor (1981a: 248).

anism, one cites B. If it is about the general pattern, then one cites the general pressures. Why do chameleons change color to match their background? Because this provides camouflage and in this way helps them survive, or because certain chemical processes take place in the chameleon's skin.

Any psychological theory, folk or scientific, that understands mental states in terms of intentional states is a theory that sees a person or other organism as a receiver and user of information. The real lesson of Twin Earth is that the fact that we are receivers and users of information is a fact, not just about us, but about the way we relate to our environments. In different environments, the internal states that in fact carry certain information would carry different information, or would not carry information at all. Ironically, the Twin Earth stories that make this point so vividly also serve to obscure its significance in at least two ways: they make the dependence of intentional states on the environment seem, first, easier to avoid, and second, more mysterious, than it is. In the special case of Twin Earth, it is easy to match up O'Leary's beliefs with corresponding beliefs of his twin, and to identify the narrow content with what these corresponding beliefs have in common. It is less easy to say, in general, how to factor out the purely internal component of a belief. I have argued that it is a highly speculative substantive hypothesis that there is any narrow notion of content that can be used to individuate intentional states autonomously. The special case of Twin Earth also makes the dependence of intentional states on environment seem stranger than it is. Since the internal states of O'Leary's twin are exactly the same as O'Leary's, there is a sense in which the environmental differences between the two worlds make no difference to the internal states of the two twins, and so one is tempted to conclude that the environmental facts on which intentional states depend are therefore causally irrelevant. But the fact that a state might have had different causes does not show that the causes it does have are causally irrelevant.

Is O'Leary's belief that there is water in his basement an internal state of O'Leary? Is it in his head? Of course it is, in the same way that the mosquito bite on his nose is on his nose, and the footprint in the sand is in the sand. We can appeal to that belief to explain the fact that he is looking for the mop, just as we can appeal to the mosquito bite to explain why he is scratching his nose. We commonly individuate states and properties in terms of the way things interact with their environments, and use them to explain why things behave as they do. It is not easy to see how we could get along without doing this, or why we should try.[32]

[32] Many people provided me with helpful comments on an earlier version of this paper. I want to thank Kathleen Akins, Ned Block, Richard Boyd, Dan Dennett, Hartry Field, Sydney Shoemaker, Paul Teller, J. D. Trout and Paul Weirich.

10

Narrow Content

The narrow content of a mental state is supposed to be a kind of content that is wholly internal to the mind of the person in the mental state. A number of philosophers have argued that for purposes of the psychological explanation of behavior, and perhaps also for the purposes of explaining the authoritative access that we all seem to have to our own intentional mental states, we need a notion of narrow content. These philosophers acknowledge, in response to arguments and examples presented by Tyler Burge,[1] among others, that the ordinary contents referred to in ordinary attributions of occurrent thoughts and propositional attitudes are often not narrow in the required way, but they argue that we must, and we can, factor out the component of content that is internal to the person, that this component is what does the work in intentional explanation of behavior, and that this component is what explains the essential accessibility of our own thoughts and beliefs.

The internalist project—the project of explicating a conception of narrow content and applying it to the explanation of intentionality—is an appealing one since it seems intuitively obvious that our thoughts and beliefs are wholly our own. What we see and know is partly a matter of what we are looking at, and what is true, and we can get it wrong. But we can't be wrong about what we think, or think we think about. When I retreat from saying how things are to saying how they seem—how they are *according to me*—I retreat from a claim about the world to a claim about my own mind, and I can tell that the claim is true by introspection—by observing what is internal to my mind. Burge's anti-individualist arguments seem to conflict with these compelling intuitions; the internalist project tries to defuse these arguments by carving out a different notion of content—one that somehow can reconcile the intentionality of mental states with their apparent internality. But despite its intuitive appeal, I have some doubts about the project; I think it is less clear than is sometimes supposed what narrow content is, and what function it is supposed to play. And I am not convinced that there is a conflict between the con-

[1] See Burge (1979).

clusions that the anti-individualist reaches about intentional states and the intuitions that motivate the internalist. I will raise a number of questions about narrow content: first, just what kind of object is a narrow content supposed to be, and in what sense is this kind of content narrow or purely internal to the mind? Second, what role is narrow content supposed to play in the description and explanation of mental phenomena? How is the ascription of narrow content related to the ordinary ascription of wide content? Third, do we really need narrow content to explain the role of content in the explanation of behavior, and the access that we have to the contents of our own thoughts?

I will focus in my discussion on two recent papers[2] by Brian Loar in which a concept of narrow content is developed, motivated, and applied. Loar's papers contain some ingenious examples and challenging arguments, and I think they make explicit some of the deeper and more elusive reasons for the attraction of the internalist project, and for the intuitive resistance that most of us feel to the anti-individualist conclusions that Burge argues for. But as I will argue, I don't think his defense of internalism is entirely successful, or entirely clear. I do think that something like Loar's conception of narrow content will play a role in a satisfactory account of intentional explanations, but I will argue that it isn't really narrow content at all.

I. What is Narrow Content, and What is Narrow about It?

We might begin by asking about ordinary wide content.What kind of object is a wide content, and why is it wide, or "not wholly in the head"? There is little agreement about the details of an account of ordinary wide content, but it seems clear and uncontroversial that the content of a speech act, attitude, or thought is an abstract object that has (or perhaps just is) a set of truth-conditions. When I believe, hope, or predict that Dukakis will win in November, the content of my belief, hope, or prediction is something that is (or will be) true if and only if Dukakis wins in November. Everyone agrees that truth-conditions are essential to propositional content as ordinarily conceived: if there are conditions in which your belief will be true and mine false, that is sufficient to establish that our beliefs have different contents. On some accounts, a difference in truth-conditions is also necessary for a difference in content. The content of a belief, hope, or prediction on this kind of account is just the set of truth-conditions itself. We may represent content, on this conception, as a set of

---

[2] Loar (1987, 1988).

possible situations or possible worlds, since thoughts true under the same conditions are true in the same possible worlds.

Whether one adopts this simple coarse-grained conception of ordinary content or some more fine-grained notion that determines a content in this sense, it will be common ground that the contents of thoughts are abstract objects and not mental events or states. While there may be disagreements over the identity conditions for propositional contents, it is generally agreed that different people may sometimes believe the same thing, and that it can happen that what I hope is exactly what you fear. So there is a trivial sense in which the contents of thoughts and the meanings of expressions "ain't in the head": as abstract objects, they are not anywhere in space. But Burge and Putnam[3] had more in mind than this when they argued that meaning and content were not wholly internal. What the Twin Earth stories purport to establish is that the having of a particular thought or attitude is a non-intrinsic property. What fails to be internal if content is wide is not the content itself, but the property of having a thought with that content. It is not the proposition that copper is cheaper than gold that is external in the relevant sense; it is the property of believing (or thinking, wishing, etc.) that copper is cheaper than gold. The Putnam–Burge thought experiments show such properties to be non-internal by exhibiting cases of thinkers differing with respect to such a property while not differing with respect to any intrinsic property.

So what the internalist needs is not just a new notion of content, but a different account of the way we are related to those contents. Contents, wide or narrow, are abstract objects we use to pick out certain mental states. Narrow content must be a kind of content that can be used, together with a different account of the way we are related to that kind of content, to pick out mental states that are intrinsic. How does it do it? Loar's idea is that the narrow content of a belief should be identified, not with its *truth-conditions*, but with what Loar calls its *realization conditions*. Realization conditions, like ordinary truth-conditions, determine a set of possible worlds: the worlds associated with the realization conditions for Bert's belief will be, Loar tells us, "those in which Bert's thoughts are or would be true if they are or were not misconceptions." It is not entirely clear what this means, but on a straightforward interpretation, the idea might seem to be this: to see whether a certain belief is realized in a given possible world, we ask whether a certain possibly counterfactual conditional is true in that world. Suppose the belief in question is Bert's belief that copper is less expensive than gold. To see whether a given possible world w satisfies the realization conditions for that belief, we ask not

---

[3] See Burge (1979) and Putnam (1975).

whether it is true in w that copper is less expensive than gold, but rather whether it is true in w that if Bert's conceptions of gold, copper, etc., were not misconceptions then copper would be less expensive than gold. But this can't be what is meant. For whether Bert's conceptions are misconceptions or not in w, it is unlikely that the relative prices of gold and copper will depend on whether his conceptions are correct. Suppose that in w, Bert's conceptions of gold and copper are misconceptions. What will the truth-value be, in w, of the counterfactual, "if Bert's conceptions of gold and copper were correct, copper would be less expensive than gold"? Unless this is a bizarre world in which Bert's mental states have some kind of causal influence on the economic situation, this counterfactual will be true in w if and only if its consequent is. So, ignoring such bizarre worlds, the realization conditions will be the same as the truth-conditions on this interpretation, and they will not, in any case, be narrow in the required sense.

I think what was intended is instead something like this: Imagine a set of possible worlds, in all of which Bert exists and is thinking a certain thought. Now we can distinguish the following two questions: first, we may ask what the actual content of Bert's thought is, and then evaluate that content relative to each of the possible worlds in the set. Second, we may ask, for each of the worlds in the set, what the content of Bert's thought is in that world, and whether that content is true in that world. Question one asks, what is the content of Bert's thought in the actual world, and then, for each world w, what is the truth-value of that fixed content in w. Question two asks, for each w, what is the truth-value, in w, of the content that Bert's thought has in w. Each of these questions will yield a proposition—a set of possible worlds. But if the content of Bert's thought—what he is thinking, when this is understood in the ordinary wide sense—varies from world to world, then the two propositions will be different. And if Burge's thought experiments are to be believed, the content of Bert's thought will vary from world to world, even if Bert's subjective perspective remains the same. But while this wide content—the proposition determined by the answer to the first question—might vary with changes in social and other environmental conditions, the proposition yielded by the second question will be the same no matter which of the possible worlds in which Bert is thinking his thought is the actual world. So this proposition is a plausible candidate for the narrow content. To see more concretely how the procedure goes, consider a familiar Twin Earth example. Bert is thinking, "Water is the best drink for quenching thirst." We can evaluate the wide and narrow contents of this thought relative to four possible worlds: a is the actual world (in which, let us assume, water is indeed the best drink for quenching thirst); b is the usual Twin

Earth counterfactual situation: this world is just like the actual world, except that the stuff called "water" there is XYZ. In *b*, XYZ is the best drink for quenching thirst. *c* is a world with water, like the actual world, but in *c* there is another drink, called gatorade, that quenchs thirst better than water. Finally, *d* is the Twin Earth version of *c*, where twin gatorade quenches thirst better than XYZ, the stuff they call water there. Bert inhabits all of these possible worlds, and in each of them he is thinking a thought that he would put by saying, "Water is the best drink for quenching thirst." The actual wide content of Bert's thought is the proposition that is true in *a* and false in *b*, *c* and *d*. The wide content that Bert's thought has in world *c* is the same, since what they call "water" there is water. But in *b* and *d*, the content of Bert's thought is a different proposition, one that is true in *b* and false in the other three worlds. These facts about the actual and counterfactual wide contents of Bert's thought can be represented in a two-dimensional matrix that defines what I have elsewhere called a *propositional concept*—a function from possible worlds into propositions. We can extract from it a proposition—which I have called the *diagonal proposition* determined by the propositional concept: the proposition that is true at *w* if and only if the proposition that is the value of the function for argument *w* is true at *w*. In this example, the diagonal is the proposition that is true in worlds *a* and *b*, and false in worlds *c* and *d*. I think this is a plausible candidate for the realization conditions, or narrow content, of a thought, in the sense Loar had in mind.

Now I think, and have argued, that propositional concepts and diagonal propositions are useful devices for representing and explaining some facts about the *attribution* of belief, but I am not sure they will yield a notion of narrow content that will do all that the internalist wants such a notion to do. Let me point out a number of facts about it.

First, this explanation makes clear that the determination of narrow content presupposes that we can identify a thought independently of its content. The analogous presupposition about speech acts is unproblematic. If I *say* that water is the best drink for quenching thirst, I do it by uttering certain sounds, and we can describe the utterance event in a way that makes no commitment about its content. So there is no problem asking what the content of *that* utterance event would have been had *it* taken place on Twin Earth. Perhaps one can also identify occurrent thoughts independently of their contents, but it is not at all clear in the case of beliefs, intentions, and other states and attitudes that one can identify something that is the belief or intention in abstraction from its content, something about which we can ask, what would the content of *that* belief have been if *it* had been a belief I had on Twin Earth. If we assume that there is a language of thought, and that to have a belief or desire is to have a token of a mental sentence expressing the belief or desire stored in the appropriate place in the brain, then the presupposition would be unproblematic; but if we don't make this assumption, we have no obvious way to individuate the property of believing that P except by using the content, that P.

Even if we could individuate thoughts or beliefs independently of their contents, this would not necessarily suffice to yield a determinate narrow content for them by the procedure I have suggested. Suppose we identify mental thought tokens by their physical or syntactic properties. These properties surely will not be sufficient to determine even the narrow content of the thought token. Presumably, the same particular physical event or state that is a particular thought that water is the best drink for quenching thirst might, if the functional organization of the thinker were different enough, have not only a different wide content, but also a different narrow content. Consider again the analogy with sentences. Suppose that in a counterfactural situation more radically different from ours than Twin Earth we find the pattern of sounds identical to the one that in fact constitutes an utterance of "Water is the best drink for quenching thirst." But suppose that in this counterfactual world, these sounds occur in a language utterly unlike English, both in syntax and semantics. What they mean there might be roughly translated as "what time does the next bus leave for the zoo?" Presumably, the similarity in the acoustical pattern will not be sufficient to give this utterance the same meaning or content that it has in the actual world in any sense, wide or narrow, even though one could define a propositional concept, and a diagonal proposition representing realization conditions, for a sentence token individuated simply by its sound pattern or shape. For this procedure to yield a plausible notion of narrow content for tokens of either a public or a mental language, we need to assume the tokens have the same narrow content in each of the relevant possible worlds. But the procedure itself provides no basis for saying when narrow content differs, or changes, and when it remains the same. We do know that the narrow content of a mental state is an internal property of the person who is in that state, so we know that the narrow contents of the thoughts of internally indiscernible twins are the same. But presumably it is not only wholly indiscernible twins who can think the same thought—thoughts with the same narrow content. In what ways might two thinkers differ in their overall mental states while still remaining capable of thinking thoughts or having beliefs with the same narrow content? Suppose I continue to believe that water is the best drink for quenching thirst, but my other beliefs about water change: I learn that water is H_2O, and not XYZ as I previously thought, that it expands when it freezes, that salt dissolves in it, etc. The wide content of my belief that water is the best drink for quenching thirst remains the same, but what about the narrow content? I'm not sure how this question is supposed to be answered.

Even if these questions receive satisfactory answers, it will remain true that the narrow content or realization conditions of a thought, explained as I have explained them, will be defined only relative to a very limited set of possible worlds: specifically, only for possible worlds containing the thought token. The realization conditions for the thought are satisfied in a given possible world if and only if the proposition expressed by the thought *in that possible world* is true. Suppose the thought I am thinking could be naturally expressed as follows: "There is a hole in the ozone layer." If I focus on the wide content, then I can consider not only whether this thought is true in the actual world, where I am thinking it, but also whether it would be true if, say, human beings had never existed to pollute the atmosphere. But we can't evaluate the realization conditions for the thought in such a possible world, since the thought won't exist there. We might try to extend the procedure to apply to possible worlds not containing the thought by asking a counterfactual question about such a world: what *would* the content of the thought be if it were thought there. This may work in some cases, but it is likely to leave a large amount of indeterminacy in the narrow content of our thoughts. Consider a version of another one of the familiar stories: Bert, who is a little confused about arthritis, thinks his father has this disease in his thigh. In a counterfactual world, Bert's belief is internally the same, but the social semantic facts in this world are different: "arthritis" refers there to a wider class of diseases, including the one that Bert's father has in his thigh. The wide content of Bert's belief is false in all worlds, but the narrow content is false in the actual world and true in the counterfactual world. But now consider a possible world in which both the language and the state of medical knowledge are quite different. In this world there is no word like "arthritis," in Bert's language, and Bert has no thoughts about his father's health. Are the realization conditions for Bert's actual thought satisfied in this counterfactual world? Bert didn't have the belief there, but if he had, would it have been true or false? So far as I can see, there is no way to tell.

The source of all these problems with this procedure for defining narrow content is the fact that according to this account, narrow content is derivative from (actual and possible) wide content. The explanation of realization conditions takes for granted that somehow, the external and internal facts about a mental event or state that we have identified determine a content (in the ordinary sense) for that state. Then from the actual wide content, together with the facts about what the wide content would be under various counterfactual conditions, we extract the narrow content. Narrow content, as defined by this procedure, presupposes rather than explains wide content.

A number of narrow content theorists, including Loar, have pointed to an analogy between narrow content and what in David Kaplan's semantics for demonstratives is called *character*.[4] Character is the kind of meaning that context-dependent expressions have. The character of a sentence is a function from context into content. If one thinks of a possible world containing an utterance token as providing a context for that utterance, then a propositional concept will also be a function from contexts into contents. But even if characters and propositional concepts are similar abstract objects, their roles in the explanation of content are reversed. Kaplan's characters are a kind of meaning. They are part of a semantic theory explaining how utterances come to have the contents they have. The semantics for a context-sensitive language assigns characters to sentences; then these characters, together with facts about the contexts in which they are used, determine contents. But narrow content, or "context indeterminate realization conditions" are abstracted from the wide contents that mental acts and states acquire, by whatever means, from the way they are embedded in the world.

If narrow contents don't play a role in a semantics for the language of thought, what role do they play? What claim does the internalist want to make about narrow content? Loar appeals to two very different kinds of considerations to motivate his internalist account, two very different roles for narrow content in the explanation of intentionality. The first concerns the role of content in the explanation of behavior; the second concerns the accessibility of thinkers' thoughts to themselves.

II. Narrow Content and the Explanation of Behavior

In "Social Content and Psychological Content" Loar develops ingenious variations on some of the examples that echo through the literature on intentionality in order to raise some problems for the externalist about the role of content in the explanation of behavior. The general point is that content of the ordinary wide, socially infected kind does not individuate intentional mental states in the way that is optimal for the explanation of rational behavior. On the one hand, it fails to distinguish psychologically distinct intentional states; on the other, it distinguishes cases that are the same in all relevant respects, and so misses generalizations. Let me sketch briefly one of Loar's examples, and then look at the conclusions he draws from this example, and others like it. The story is a variation on both Kripke's story of Pierre and Burge's arthritis example: Paul, when living in

---

[4] Kaplan (1989: 505).

France, learns of a disease that is called, in French, "arthrite," and comes to believe that he has this ailment in both his thigh and his ankle. But he does not realize that this is the same disease as the one that, in English, he has learned to call "arthritis." He knows that arthritis—the disease he calls "arthritis"—is a disease of the joints only. Now suppose that Paul comes to believe that he has two problems with his ankles, one that he calls "arthrite", and another that he calls "arthritis." "It seems," Loar says, "that 'believes that he has arthritis in his ankles' is doubly but univocally true of Paul, by virtue of beliefs with distinct psychological contents."[5] It seems intuitively obvious that Paul has two distinct beliefs that play distinct roles in the explanation of his actions. One of these beliefs might lead him to call the doctor, while the other motivates him to take aspirin. He might change his mind about one, while continuing to believe the other. So we need a kind of content that can distinguish the two beliefs, as (Loar alleges) ordinary wide content does not.

Loar does not take examples like this one to support a revision of our commonsense psychological explanations; instead, he takes them to show that commonsense psychological explanations, as they are, appeal to narrow content even though the "that"-clauses that occur in such explanations refer to wide or socially infected content. "I shall argue," he says, "that psychological content is not in general identical with what is captured by oblique 'that'-clauses, that commonsense constraints on individuation induce only a loose fit between contents and 'that'-clauses."[6] Loar identifies two principles relating content to the ascription of content that he takes the examples to show to be mistaken. First, "sameness of *de dicto* or oblique ascription implies sameness of psychological content." Second, "differences in *de dicto* or oblique ascription imply differences in psychological content."[7] Loar suggests that Burge's arguments that the kind of content we appeal to in ordinary explanations of action is wide content assumes these principles, and we can avoid or defuse his conclusions if we deny them.

Now I agree that Loar's examples present a puzzle and a challenge, but I am not at all clear what his response to them is. I do not understand the two principles that he questions, and I do not see how one can distinguish the content we appeal to in ordinary belief attributions from the referents of the "that"-clauses that occur in such attributions.

I see two ways to interpret the principles about the relation between oblique ascription and psychological content, the difference depending on what sameness or difference of oblique ascription is taken to be. On the one hand it might mean that the *expressions* (the "that"-clauses) that ascribe the content are the same or different; on the other hand, it might

[5] Loar (1988: 104).   [6] Ibid. 102.   [7] Ibid.

mean that the *referents* of the "that"-clauses are the same or different. But on the first interpretation, neither principle has any plausibility, and neither need be assumed by Burge's arguments. The first principle—that sameness of the ascription clause requires sameness of content—will be false of "that"-clauses that are context-dependent. Loar does restrict this principle so that it does not apply to ascriptions containing indexical pronouns and demonstratives, but if there are general terms that are context-dependent, then the principle will be false even if the contents referred to are ordinary wide contents. The second principle implies, on this interpretation, that there cannot be two different expressions referring to the same content; this can't be what was intended.

On the second interpretation, what the principles say is simply that the referents of the "that"-clauses in ordinary belief ascriptions are psychological contents. So to deny the principles is to say that the kind of content referred to in the belief ascriptions that occur in commonsense psychological explanations are not psychological contents. But this can't be right, since psychological content is *defined* by Loar as the kind of content referred to in such belief ascriptions: "By *psychological content*," he says, "I shall mean whatever individuates beliefs and other propositional attitudes in commonsense psychological explanations."[8] The *thesis* is that psychological contents, defined this way, are narrow contents. The way the thesis is supposed to be reconciled with Burge's arguments is by denying these principles about the relation between ascription clauses and contents. But interpreted the second way, the principles look to be true by definition—by Loar's definition of psychological content.

At one point Loar puts his point in terms of "a loose fit between contents and 'that'-clauses." We have no reason to think "that psychological states are captured by a neat set of content-specifications." The suggestion seems to be that there is a determinate "way things are from the thinker's point of view," and that the fact that things seem the way they do is a purely internal property of the thinker. But our language, being "shot through with social and causal presuppositions," can capture that internal content only imperfectly. I think this is partly right: I agree that there is a kind of looseness of fit in some cases between states of belief and the words we use to describe them. But I don't think the belief states themselves—the ways the world is according to the thinker—are any less causally and socially infected than the language in which beliefs are ascribed. Let's look at some of the examples.

In the world as Paul thinks it is, there are two distinct diseases both of which he suffers from in his ankle. One is called "arthritis" (in English),

---

[8] Ibid. 99.

and the other is called "arthrite" (in French). The first is a rheumatoid ailment that is limited to the joints, while the second is one that can reside in one's thigh. Paul (in the world as he believes it to be) has the second disease in his thigh as well as in his ankle. Now the problem of looseness of fit comes when we try to say what belief attributions are made true by these facts about what the world according to Paul is like, and which facts about the world according to Paul are the ones that make certain belief attributions true. As Loar says, our description of the world according to Paul seems to make it true twice over that Paul believes he has arthritis in his ankle. When he says "I have arthritis in my ankle," he is expressing a different belief from the one he expresses when he says "j'ai l'arthrite dans ma cheville." But which of these beliefs are we ascribing when we say "Paul believes that he has arthritis in his ankle"? This is, I agree, a puzzle—about belief *attribution*—but I don't think it supports internalism. Suppose we set aside questions about belief attributions and look directly at the world according to Paul: what facts make it true that the world as Paul takes it to be is the way it is? Are the relevant facts purely internal facts about Paul, or are facts about the environment Paul is embedded in—for example about the way he came to be in the internal state he is in, and the way words are used by people in Paul's linguistic communities—also part of what makes it true that we can describe Paul's mental state in terms of the set of possible worlds conforming to the description I have given? To answer this question we need an account of what makes content attributions true. The strategy for providing such an account that seems to me most promising—the causal-information theoretic strategy—will explain content in terms of counterfactural dependencies that tend to hold, under normal conditions, between thinkers' internal states and their environments. I don't see how an account of this general kind could be an internalist one, and I don't know of any promising alternative.

Suppose an externalist, information-theoretic account of belief were a correct account of what relates a thinker to the kind of situation that is the way the world seems to him. Suppose that what makes it correct that the world according to Paul is as described is that under certain normal conditions Paul would be in the internal state he is in only if, and because, the world were actually that way. This would be a non-internalist account of what Loar calls psychological content, since the correctness of the content description would depend on certain general causal regularities external to Paul. But the same problems about belief ascription that Loar's examples bring out will still arise. So I don't think those problems tend to support an internalist account of psychological content.

According to Loar's picture, there are two dimensions of content associated with a particular mental state, a purely internal content—the way the world seems from the point of view of the thinker—and a social content, which is what content ascriptions refer to. The former kind of content is what really explains behavior. I am not sure what, on Loar's account, the role of the latter kind is supposed to be. But it seems to me that to talk of the way the world seems from the point of view of the believer is just to talk about what the believer believes. If there is a divergence between the way the world seems to the thinker and the way the world must be to make a content clause in a belief ascription true, then the belief ascription is false. What the puzzle cases bring out is that in some situations, when one's picture of the way things are diverges from the way they actually are in certain ways—it is difficult, without some circumlocution, to describe that picture. But when we describe it correctly, psychological content and so-called social content will coincide.

I have been trying to argue that Loar's examples and arguments raise genuine problems for an account of belief and belief attribution, but they don't show that psychological content—the kind of content relevant to psychological explanation—is narrow. But Loar has phenomenological reasons for thinking that the way the world seems from the thinker's point of view, must be an internal property of the thinker. I will conclude by looking at some of these reasons.

III. Narrow Content and Subjective Intentionality

The basis of Loar's phenomenological argument for internalism is the intuition that we have privileged access to our own thoughts—specifically to their intentional or semantic properties. It seems to be essential to thought that one know what one's thought is about, and this, Loar suggests, is incompatible with the anti-individualist conclusions. "A natural view of one's own thoughts," he says, "stands in sharp contrast with the conclusion of the externalist argument. From a pre-critical perspective, knowledge of the references of my own thoughts is privileged in a certain way, and that perspective involves no apparent conceptions of external reference relations."[9] The idea is that it is essential to having a thought that, in some sense, the thinker knows what the content of the thought is, and what the thought is about. I can't think about my thought about x without at the same time thinking about x, and recognizing that my thought is indeed a thought about x. Loar makes this point with the following example; "I am now attending to my thought that Freud lived in Vienna. I register what the thought is about—Freud, Vienna, the one

[9] Loar (1987: 96).

inhabiting the other. I note the thought's references and truth conditions.
I may be wrong about the non-semantic question whether Freud actually
exists (timeless). But it is difficult to see how I might be wrong in my purely
semantic judgment that this thought is about Freud if Freud exists."[10]
Most of this seems right, but why does it contrast or conflict with the
externalist's conclusion? Loar's argument for a conflict between externalism and privileged access focusses on a number of externalist analyses of
the reference relation. The general form of the argument is like this: in
judging that my thought is about x, I do not judge that I stand in relation
R to x [where what goes in for "R" is some possible externalist analysis of
reference or aboutness]. Therefore, R cannot be a correct analysis of the
aboutness relation to which I have privileged access. For example, Loar
says "It is implausible that in judging that my thought is about Freud I
judge that it has a given causal-historical relation to Freud—a relation no
one has yet managed to characterize."[11] There are two things wrong with
this argument: first, a philosophical analysis of some concept might be
correct, even if someone competent in using the concept does not know
the analysis. In general, one cannot refute an analysis (for example, of
knowledge as justified true belief + . . .) simply by noting that a person may
judge that he knows something without judging that the various conditions of the analysis hold. There may be a problem explaining how an
analysis can be correct if a competent speaker doesn't know it—a paradox
of analysis—but this is a general problem. Unless all philosophical analyses are either trivial or false, the argument Loar gives cannot be sound. But
second, in any case, the externalist is not committed to the claim that relations of reference and aboutness are analyzable. Burge, in defending an
externalist account of intentionality, proposes no analysis of aboutness
and does not suggest that there is one to be found. Kripke, in his defense
of a causal account of reference, explicitly disclaims any reductive ambi-
tions. One may characterize or categorize aboutness without defining or
analyzing it.

    Is it right, as Loar claims, that "from a pre-critical perspective," my
thought that my thoughts about Freud are about Freud "involves no
apparent conceptions of external reference relations"? I don't think so.
Even if our pre-critical perspective is committed to no detailed analysis of
reference—no *articulated* conception of an external reference relation—I
think the intuition that reference and aboutness are causal, external relations lies close to the surface. Look, for instance, at the arguments and
examples developed by Saul Kripke[12] in defense of a causal account of
reference. The arguments appeal, not to philosophical theory, but to

---

[10] Loar (1987: 96).   [11] Ibid. 97.   [12] See Kripke (1972).

intuitions about our ordinary "pre-critical" conception of reference. It will be readily agreed, independently of philosophical theory, that we could not possibly refer to or think about Feud if the man had no influence or effect at all on our minds. If we had never heard of him, our thoughts could not be about him. *That* is surely not an esoteric philosophical conclusion.

If we set aside questions of the reduction or analysis of intentional relations, is there a conflict between the thesis that we have privileged access to what our thoughts are about and the thesis that the aboutness relation is external? I don't think so. One way to see at least the prima facie compatibility of these theses is to construct a simple model of something with analogues of intentional states about which the analogues of the two theses are uncontroversially true. Suppose we have an electronic device capable of registering some limited information about its environment. Suppose it is equipped with a sensor that observes blocks passing by on a conveyor belt and records their shape (sphere, cube or pyramid) and color (red, yellow or blue). It records this information in a simple code: "Rs" means red sphere, "Yp" means yellow pyramid, etc. As new blocks appear, the old information is passed on through a succession of memories. So at any time, the machine stores information about what the current object is, and what the preceding objects were. A "Bc" in the first memory means (or tends to carry the information) that the previous object was a blue cube. The reason this internal state has that content is that under normal conditions, it will be in that state only if the previous object was a blue cube. The "normal conditions" qualification is there because our device is not perfect. If lighting is abnormal, if a non-standard object is put on the conveyor belt, or if a chip is defective, the device's main register might contain the inscription "Bc" when there is no blue cube before it. But in this case, the inscription still has the content, *blue cube there* because this is the information that *would* be carried if conditions were normal.

Our device is very simple—it does not have beliefs or other full-blooded intentional states—but it does have states that can be described in terms of propositional content, and it is clear that its contentful states are relational, and not intrinsic, states. Its states have the content they have—they tend to carry the information that they tend to carry—in part because of facts about the environment in which the machine functions.

Now let us add a reflective capacity to our device—the capacity to have second-order informational states, or to carry information about its own representational states. We will do this by giving our device an internal sensor that can observe its own memories. (Maybe this is part of a system for introducing redundancy to correct for errors.) If the first memory contains a "Bc," the internal sensor, when it observes it, records a "Bc_1," registering that its first memory is of a blue cube. This state has this content because under normal conditions the internal sensor's register will be in this state only when the first memory registers a blue cube. Since this is a different sensor, its normal conditions may be different—for example, external lighting conditions will be irrelevant. Its conditions may be normal (correctly observing that the first memory has the content, *blue cube*), even if the content of the memory itself is misinformation.

Now this is about as simple a case of second-order informational states as one could have; it is a long way from self-consciousness or thought, but it is a case in which content can be used to characterize internal states, and in which there are states with content that other states with content are about. And while I don't think such a machine would have a rich inner life—I suspect there isn't much it is like to be it—it does, I think, illustrate the kind of privileged access, or "self-interpretation," that Loar finds in more full-blooded cases of thinkers reflecting on their thoughts. As Loar says, a thought about a Freud thought is itself a Freud thought. In the same way, the registering of a registering of a blue cube is itself a registering of information about blue cubes. This is because the content of the second-order state is derivative from the content of the first. There is nothing very mysterious here, and nothing incompatible with the externalist account I have given of the role of content in the description of the internal states of our device.

Still, there does seem to be a conflict between the intuition that we know what we are thinking about and the externalist's Twin Earth stories. The externalist taught us that the content of the thought that Bert would express by saying "water is the best drink for quenching thirst" is different from the content of the thought he has on counterfactual Twin Earth that he would express there the same way. But nothing internal to Bert distinguishes the two worlds, so he doesn't know which one he is in. But then doesn't it follow that he doesn't know what the content of his belief is? He does know that his statement, "my 'water' thoughts are about water" is true, but it seems that he doesn't know what the content of *that* is.

The first thing to note about this argument is that if it works it will support a much more general conclusion. There is nothing special about reflective thoughts about content here: if Bert does not know which of these two worlds he is in, then he doesn't know that there is water in the bathtub he is sitting in. The Twin Earth argument that we don't know the contents of our own thoughts (as the externalist understands content) is just a version of a familiar general skeptical argument.

This is not the place to develop a general response to skepticism, but the strategy that seems to me most promising (defended by Alvin Goldman and Fred Dretske[13] among others) recognizes that claims to knowledge are essentially contrastive and context-dependent. Bert knows that there is water in the bathtub because he can distinguish the actual world, in which there is water in the bathtub, from certain relevant alternative worlds, in which water is not there: for example, worlds in which the bathtub is dry, or filled with gasoline, or mashed potatoes. Similarly, Bert knows that his "water" thoughts are about water because he can distinguish the actual world, where they are about water, from relevant alternative situations in which he is thinking about other things such as gasoline or mashed potatoes.

We do not need narrow or purely internal content to explain privileged access to the content of one's thoughts. The explanation is simpler: the external facts in virtue of which my Freud thoughts are about Freud are the same external facts in virtue of which my thoughts about my Freud thoughts are about Freud. The external environment in which I think my thoughts is the same environment as the one in which I reflect on those thoughts.

I have argued that the externalist can account both for the role of content in psychological explanation and for privileged access and the transparency or self-interpreting character of thought, without invoking a notion of narrow content—content that picks out mental events and states in terms of purely intrinsic properties of the thinker. But Loar's examples and arguments do force us to recognize the context-dependence of ascriptions of content, and I think something like Loar's conception of narrow content will help to describe and explain the ways in which our uses of content to characterize the states of mind of ourselves and others are context-dependent. I think Loar is right that we can describe psychological content in terms of what he calls realization conditions—conditions that must be satisfied in a thinker's world for that world to answer to the thoughts he has there. But I have argued that he is wrong to think that realization conditions can give us a way to get at purely internal psychological properties of thinkers. Content, whether psychological or social, is a way to connect ourselves to others, and to the environments in which we and they are embedded.

[13] See Goldman (1976) and Dretske (1981).

11

Twin Earth Revisited

Twin Earth and its variants have been around for a couple of decades now. Most philosophers find the intuitions evoked by these fables to be compelling, but it remains controversial what to do with them. My aim in this paper is to put the Twin Earth thought experiments and arguments in a context, and provide a sketch of a theoretical account that I think makes sense of them. I will start by reviewing some familiar facts about the philosophical discussion that set the stage for Twin Earth.

Our story begins in the late 1960s with attacks, by Keith Donnellan and Saul Kripke, on the description theory of proper names.[1] According to these attacks, the received view, deriving originally from Russell, was that reference to particular concrete individuals was always mediated by a purely general concept, something that might be expressed in a definite description. In the unreconstructed version of the received view, proper names are abbreviations for specific definite descriptions. In later more liberal modifications of the received view, names were associated with open-ended clusters of descriptive information, and the association might be less a matter of meaning and more a matter of a pragmatic presupposition for the successful use of a name. But what was essential to the received view was the assumption that the explanation for the relation between a name or other referring expression and its referent was necessarily factorable into two parts: first, a relation between the expression and a purely general concept or cluster of concepts that could be "grasped by the mind," second, a relation of "fit" between the purely general concept and the individual referent. The speaker's semantic competence was entirely a matter of the first factor: to use a name competently is to associate it with the right descriptive concept. The question of which individual, if any, falls under the concept is a non-semantic question—a question not about what a speaker means, but about what the world he is talking about is really like.

The critics challenged this internalist picture with a battery of examples: cases of apparently successful reference despite the fact that the speaker

Meeting of the Aristotelian Society, held in the Senior Common Room, Birkbeck College London, on Monday, 21 June 1993 at 8.15 p.m.

[1] Kripke (1972) and Donnellan (1971).

was unable to provide any description of the referent that was sufficient to identify it, and cases where the identifying descriptions the speaker would provide were true of something other than the referent. The picture suggested by these examples was an externalist one: the semantic mechanisms that explain how names hook onto their referents are not internal to the mind, but involve causal chains that might be beyond the epistemic reach of the speaker. One's ability to refer, the examples suggested, is a function, not just of one's conceptual competence, but of the way one is situated in the world.

The critique of the description theory of names began with proper names of individuals, but the alternative externalist picture was extended to general terms as well. One's ability to refer to kinds as well as to instances of kinds was dependent on facts about the environment in which the referring took place. It was to nail down this point that Twin Earth made its first appearance in Hilary Putnam's "The Meaning of 'Meaning.' "[2] The Twin Earth thought experiment showed that two possible speakers might be indistinguishable with respect to all internal mental and physical properties, but differ with respect to what they meant in using a certain term. The difference in meaning was explained by a difference in the external environment in which the two speakers found themselves. Twin Earth is exactly like earth in all superficial respects. The difference is that on Twin Earth the stuff that flows through plumbing pipes and falls from the sky on rainy days is a different kind of stuff: not H_2O, but a substance Putnam abbreviated as "XYZ." Our actual speaker—call him O'Leary—has a twin on Twin Earth—someone who is internally exactly like O'Leary (save for the distracting but irrelevant fact that water plays a significant role in O'Leary's body chemistry). But despite their internal mental and physical similarities, O'Leary and his twin mean different things by their indistinguishable utterances. When O'Leary says, "there is water in the bathtub," he says something true on Earth, but false on Twin Earth, where there is no water. But when his twin utters these sounds, he refers not to water, but to the other stuff, and so his statement is true on Twin Earth, but false on Earth.[3]

[2] The Twin Earth example and argument were presented by Putnam in lectures at the University of Washington and the University of Minnesota in the summer of 1968. The full paper was not published until Putnam (1975). A shortened version of it was published as Putnam (1973).

[3] Putnam's fable is a story of a distant planet in our universe. In other versions of the story, what corresponds to Twin Earth is an alternative possible world, and the "twin" might be O'Leary himself in counterfactual circumstances. I don't think this makes much difference to the point of the stories, although, it may matter for exactly how the point is expressed. When I speak of O'Leary's statement being true on Earth and false on Twin Earth, I am treating Twin Earth as a counterfactual possibility. But on either understanding of what Twin Earth is, it remains clear that the propositions expressed by O'Leary and his twin are different.

Putnam's point was a point about semantics: about the source of the semantic values of the names and words speakers use. Some took the moral of the story to be that meaning was less closely connected with thought than we had tended to suppose. What you mean, according to this interpretation of the examples, is not a matter of your mental state, but is a matter of social convention and causal connection. Your words do their semantic work without your necessarily knowing what is going on. This moral conflicted with the compelling intuition that when I am sincere, and mean what I say, then what I say is what I believe.

That this was not quite the right moral was brought out by Tyler Burge's developments of the Twin Earth argument.[4] Burge pointed out that the Twin Earth stories showed not only that meaning and reference were partly external phenomena, but also that intentional mental states such as belief and intention were external. O'Leary's twin on Twin Earth not only means something different from what O'Leary means when he uses the word "water," he also expresses a different belief—a belief with a different content—when he says "there is water in the bathtub," and he acts on a different intention when he turns on the tap with the intention of filling the tub with the substance that he calls "water." The lesson is not that there is a gap between speakers' linguistic practices and their mental states, but that mental states themselves have to be understood partly in terms of the way a person interacts with his or her environment.

This point was implicit in the original critique of the description theory of names. The rejection of the internalist picture was not a rejection of the idea that reference was determined by the speaker's intentions and beliefs: rather it was the rejection of the assumption that intentions and beliefs need to be explained in terms of the grasping of purely general concepts. In the sketches by direct reference theorists of an alternative account of reference, intentions played a prominent role, but it was assumed that intentions could be directed to particular individuals, and need not be explained in terms of a purely conceptual content. A causal theory of reference was not a theory that explained reference independently of intentions, but a theory that explained intentions in causal terms.

The externalist insistence that mental as well as linguistic content was not wholly internal made it possible to reconcile the lessons of Twin Earth with an explanation of speech in terms of thought—with an intentionalist theory of meaning—but it conflicted with persistent internalist intuitions. Perhaps the externalist need not deny that what I say is what I think, when I am sincere, but it is hard to avoid the suspicion that if an externalist theory of speech and thought is right then we don't *really* know what we

---

[4] Burge (1979).

are either saying or thinking. The internalist will concede that what I know and what I see are in part a matter of my external environment, but will insist that what I *think* I know or see—and more generally the way the world is *according to me*—ought to be wholly a matter of my internal state of mind. The whole idea of talking about the way things *seem*, as contrasted with the way they are, about what I *believe* rather than what I know, or what is true—is to abstract away from the external environment, to focus on the internal contents of my mind. But the externalist insists that this intuition rests on a false conception of mind—the Cartesian conception that continues to bewitch us despite the widespread criticism to which it has been subjected.

The issue is a highly theoretical one concerning the nature of mind, and the nature of intentionality. But the externalist case, both the case for a direct reference theory of proper names and the more general case for an externalist theory of intentional mental states, was made with examples and thought experiments, examples and arguments that focussed attention on a range of phenomena. The case is not based on any theoretical explanation for the phenomena, or on any general theory of mind or of intentionality. It is thus open to the internalists, who have general theoretical reasons to resist the externalist picture, to accept the phenomena—the intuitive judgments about the examples—but argue that they rest on superficial facts about the way we happen to talk, and the way we happen to describe our mental states. On the surface, say the internalists, is broad content, a kind of content that individuates mental states in part in terms of the thinker's social and physical environment. But beneath the surface, they argue, is the *narrow content* of the mental states, a kind of content that characterizes the purely internal properties of a mental state. It is these properties, the internalists contend, that are relevant to the explanation of behavior, and to the description of the way the world seems, from the inside, to the thinker. Just as the description theorists separated the factors determining reference into two components—a purely internal and conceptual component representing what the speaker means, and an external component that was independent of what the speaker means—so the internalists about mental content postulate a purely internal component—the thinker's contribution to the content of her thought—which determines a function that takes the external environment into the kind of content to which the externalist's examples and arguments apply.

To answer this revisionist strategy, the externalist needs a theoretical account of intentionality that explains the externalist phenomena, and that justifies the claim that the phenomena show something about the nature of intentionality, and do not just reflect an accidental fact about the way we happen to talk about speech and thought. What I want to do here is to sketch a familiar theoretical strategy for explaining mental content and to connect this strategy with the phenomena that Putnam, Burge and the direct reference theorists have focussed our attention on. I should emphasize that my aim here is not to give a direct argument for this theoretical strategy, but only to use the strategy to try to clarify the externalist phenomena. So since the strategy is a frankly externalist one, I am not here giving a direct argument against the internalist.

The theoretical account I have in mind is the information-theoretic account of intentional content.[5] The rough idea is this: states of mind *carry information* when there exists a pattern of counterfactual dependencies between those states and corresponding states of the environment. If x is in a state caused by the fact that P, and would not have been in that state if it had not been that P, then that state of x carries the information that P. If x is capable of being in a range of alternative states that tend to vary systematically with variations in the environment, then those states will be information-carrying states. Representational states and systems can carry misinformation as well as information in the strict sense, but according to the information-theoretic picture, misrepresentation must be understood as a deviation from a norm. It is reasonable to assume that representational states are *normally* correct—that they are states that *tend* to represent things as they are.[6] Given an appropriate conception of normal conditions, we can explain representation generally in terms of information: a state represents the world as being such that P, and so is a state with informational content P, if and only if under normal conditions it would carry the information that P. Normal conditions will include both conditions on the environment and conditions on the internal functioning of the representational mechanisms.

For an information-bearing state to be a belief state it must do more than tend to carry information. The information it carries must be available to play a role in determining how the believer acts to satisfy its wants and needs. If there are systematic dependencies between the state of an organism's environment and the way it is disposed to act, then the behavioral dispositions themselves will be representational states—states that tend to carry information about the environment. Beliefs, whatever else they must be, are presumably states of this kind.

States like belief, purporting to represent how things are, are the primary focus of the information-theoretic story. Intentions and desires,

[5] Developments and applications of this strategy are found in Dretske (1981, 1988). See also Stampe (1977) for an early statement of the idea.
[6] In the sense I intended, normal conditions need have nothing to do with statistical regularities. What is normal may rarely happen. The same goes for the relevant sense of "tendency." Something may tend to carry information even if it rarely or never actually carries it.

hopes and fears, do not carry information, or tend to carry information, in the way that beliefs do. But the content of desires and other motivational states is explained, according to the information-theoretic story, in terms of the way these states interact with beliefs in the determination of rational behavior. If my *beliefs* about water have an external component because of the causal role of water, under normal conditions, in the determination of those beliefs, then my *desire* for water will have an external component as well, in virtue of the fact that my desire is a disposition to do things that I *believe* will get me water. Intentions, hopes and fears are more complex states involving both beliefs and motivational states, or "pro-attitudes," and presumably deriving their content from the content of those states.

The information-theoretic story is controversial, but the controversies mainly concern two issues that we can set aside. First, it is controversial whether the information-theoretic story can provide a reductive analysis of intentionality—an analysis of belief and other intentional mental states in physicalistic or naturalistic terms. Carrying out such a reduction would require, first, a way of distinguishing belief from other more primitive information-carrying states such as the states of thermostats, and second a non-circular naturalistic account of the normal or ideal conditions relative to which informational content is defined. But even if no reductive account is possible, it seems reasonable to say that it is a necessary condition for a state's being a belief state that it tend to carry information in this sense, and that the content of a belief should be explained in terms of the information that it tends to carry, and perhaps also in terms of the way it carries that information.

The second controversy concerns the identity conditions for propositional contents. The information-theoretic story appeals only to a coarse-grained notion of content—content individuated according to truth-conditions. According to this way of individuating content, necessarily equivalent contents are identical. But the facts about belief and other propositional attitudes suggest, at least prima facie, that our ordinary notion of content is individuated more finely—that one may believe that P while not believing that Q even when P and Q are necessarily equivalent, and so have the same content in the sense defined by the information-theoretic story. But for our purposes, we need not assume that the information-theoretic story is the whole story about content, and so need not assume that the coarse-grained notion of content is sufficient for a complete story of the propositional attitudes. If the contents needed for a complete story of the attitudes are more fine-grained, it must still be true that the fine-grained content of a belief determines a truth-conditional or informational content. All we need to assume is that it is a necessary condition for a belief to be a belief that P that it tend to carry the information that P.

How does this theoretical account fit the Twin Earth examples? Content, according to the account, is determined relative to a conception of normal conditions, some of which are conditions constraining the external environment. Certain of my internal states are beliefs about water because they are normally sensitive to facts about water. Normally, I would not be in the state I describe as believing that there is water in the vodka bottle if there weren't water in the vodka bottle. Among the facts that make it the case that those internal states tend to depend on facts about water is the fact that water normally has certain superficial observable properties, and (normally) is the only stuff around that has those properties. These facts do not obtain (or normally obtain) on Twin Earth, and that is why the same internal states fail to carry, or tend to carry, information about water. Different but corresponding facts make it the case that those same states tend to carry information about the other kind of stuff.

A similar account can be given for the very different kind of Twin Earth story first told by Tyler Burge—the kind of story that brings out the relevance to the determination of content of social facts, in particular facts about the linguistic practices of the members of the speech community that a person identifies with. Among the conditions that make it the case that certain of my internal states carry information about arthritis are facts about the way the word "arthritis" is normally used in my community. If normal usage were different—if, for example, the word "arthritis" referred to a wider class of diseases, the very same internal states would tend to carry different information even if the actual causal interactions between me and members of my linguistic community were all the same.

If something like this information-theoretic story is the right way to account for the content that intentional mental states have, then we can see why, in general, the having of mental states with particular contents *must* be a property that depends on the external environment. But on the other hand, we can also explain why there is something puzzling or problematic about this fact. On the first point: the story explains content in terms of causal regularities and counterfactual dependencies that hold, or hold under normal or ideal conditions. Such regularities are inevitably contingent, and in the case where the content concerns the world outside of the person, are inevitably at least partly external. Internal states that carry information, or tend to carry information, carry it, or tend to carry it, in virtue of facts about the way the world affects, or tends to affect, those internal states. If the world were different in such a way that other things caused, and normally caused, the very same internal states, then those states would not carry the same information.

The general, abstract, information-theoretic story does not provide a criterion for identifying the particular external regularities and dependencies relative to which content is defined. For this we rely on the intuitions about content brought out by the thought experiments. So within the context of the information-theoretic account, there is room for argument about any particular Twin Earth story. One might argue, for example, that if I am ignorant of the chemical composition of water, then I don't really believe that it is *water* in the bathtub, but only that there is, in the bathtub, some substance that has the superficial properties that water in fact has. But while such a move, if it could be made intuitively plausible, might defuse a particular Twin Earth argument, it could not free us from the general externalist conclusion that the Twin Earth arguments are used to support. Whether the content of my belief involves water itself or just a general description of a substance meeting certain conditions, if my belief is to be understood as a belief about the world outside of me, and not just about my sensations and experiences, then (according to the information-theoretic story) my having a belief with that content will depend on the existence of *some* regularities and dependencies that relate me to my environment. Phenomenalism would be a way—the only way—to avoid the moral of the Twin Earth arguments; we can avoid an externalist account of content only by moving the external world itself into the mind.

The information-theoretic account also helps to bring out what is problematic about the Twin Earth stories, and the externalist conclusion they support. It is an essential part of the information-theoretic story that a state can carry information that P only if there is some feature of the state that bears the mark of the fact that P. The reason that O'Leary's internal cognitive state, as he steps into the bathtub, carries the information that there is water in the tub is that if there weren't water in the tub he would not be in the internal state that he is in. But the Twin Earth story suggests that this requirement is not really met. What if it were twater—XYZ—the stuff that is superficially like water but chemically different from it—in the bathtub? O'Leary would be in exactly the same internal state. Thus, one might think, O'Leary's mental state does not really tend to carry the information that there is water in the bathtub, but only the information that there is some kind of stuff that has the superficial properties that water in fact has. And once one grants this, then wilder and more fanciful Twin Earth stories will show that O'Leary's mental state does not carry, or tend to carry, even this information, since O'Leary *might* be situated in a world in which the particular state O'Leary is in fact in was caused, and was normally caused, in some completely different way—by the phases of the moon or the political situation in Bulgaria.

The information-theoretic story says that O'Leary's internal state tends to carry the information that P just in case *under normal conditions*, O'Leary would be in that state only if P. We can grant that Twin Earth shows that O'Leary could be in the same internal state even if there were no water in the bathtub, but still say that his internal state tends to carry the information that there is water in the bathtub if we say that normal or ideal conditions fail to obtain on Twin Earth. The problem is that Twin Earth is designed to be a case not only in which the twin's mental state is in fact caused by something other than water, but also a case in which the state is *normally* caused by something other than water. This is an essential part of the story, since otherwise it would not show what it was designed to show: that the contents of twin O'Leary's "water" speech acts and thoughts are different, on Twin Earth, from the contents of O'Leary's corresponding speech acts and thoughts on Earth.

As Twin Earth situations illustrate, it is a contingent matter what conditions count as normal conditions: what is normal in one possible situation may be abnormal in another. But the notion of normal conditions is a modal notion: a given set of normal conditions determines a set of possible situations—all the situations in which those conditions obtain. In asking whether conditions are normal in a given counterfactual situation (such as a Twin Earth situation) we might be asking either of two different questions: (1) is the counterfactual situation a member of the set of possible situations determined by conditions that are normal in the *actual* world? or (2) is the counterfactual situation a member of the set of possible situations that are normal relative to that counterfactual situation itself. Twin Earth counterfactual situations are designed to be situations about which these two questions get different answers, and the questions must get different answers if the thought experiment is to make its point. The situation must be abnormal from the point of view of the actual world so that O'Leary's actual belief (that there is water in the bathtub) will be false there, but normal from its own point of view so that the content of twin O'Leary's belief will be different.

This distinction provides a way of reconciling the claim that O'Leary's internal state tends to carry the information that there is water in the bathtub, and so tends to carry a mark of the fact that there is, with the fact that O'Leary's mental state would not be different if he were on Twin Earth, where the lakes and bathtubs are filled with XYZ rather than H_2O. I think this is the right response, but it does slide by the following problem: It was part of Putnam's original Twin Earth story that the agent, in the actual world, is ignorant of chemistry—that he neither knows nor believes that water is H_2O. So we are supposed to assume that for all O'Leary knows or believes, water might be XYZ. But if we explain this attribution of ignorance in terms of the information-theoretic story, it seems that we must say that O'Leary does not know whether he is on Earth or on the counterfactual Twin Earth. Twin Earth, it seems, is not just a wild science fiction tale; it is a genuine epistemic possibility for O'Leary, or for anyone who is ignorant of chemistry. On Twin Earth, there is no water in the bathtub, so if Twin Earth is an epistemic and doxastic possibility for O'Leary, it follows that he does not know or believe that there is water in the bathtub. And since the word "water" means something different on Twin Earth, it seems that O'Leary does not know what "water" means, or even have the belief that this word refers to water.

Obviously there has got to be something wrong with these conclusions. What the argument forces us to recognize is that attribution of content is sensitive to context. The normal conditions relative to which content is determined are context-dependent as well as contingent; they vary not only from possible world to possible world, but within the actual world from context of attribution to context of attribution. And here too, the information-theoretic account helps to explain why this should be so. According to this account, the attribution of content is essentially contrastive, distinguishing between relevant alternative possibilities that are all compatible with the normal conditions for the transmission of information that define the context. On the one hand, according to this account, the attribution of content makes sense only against a background of contingent regularities and dependencies. But on the other hand, questions can always be raised about the believer's attitudes toward any contingent proposition. About the regularities relative to which an attribution of belief to O'Leary is understood, we can ask whether O'Leary believes that those regularities obtain, and making sense of that question requires a shift to a context of alternative possibilities that the propositions about those regularities distinguish between. The examples make clear that when we are talking about the absence or presence of water in ordinary situations—when we ask whether someone thinks there is water in the bathtub, or in the vodka bottle, or whether someone wants a glass of water, we (the attributors of content) presuppose that the stuff we are talking about is water, which is to say that in attributing content we are distinguishing only between situations in which the stuff that is normally in lakes and that normally comes out of faucets is the same stuff as what is actually in lakes and what actually comes out of ordinary faucets. It is only if our discussion shifts to one about what people know or believe about the nature of the stuff that ordinarily fills lakes and comes out of faucets, that we shift to a broader range of relevant normal alternative possibilities, one that includes some possible situations that look a lot like Twin Earth.

If something like the information-theoretic story is right, then this kind of context-dependence is an inevitable feature of the attribution of attitudes. Any attribution of content must be made relative to presumed facts about the background normal conditions, but any such facts can themselves be called into question: we can ask, does the agent know or believe what we presupposed in attributing an attitude to her? Answering that question requires a shift in content. Given that there is no presupposition free context in which content attributions can be made, such context shifts would be avoidable only if there were contingent facts that were beyond question—that were necessary presuppositions of any attribution of attitude.

A look at examples suggests that this kind of context-dependence is intuitively plausible, as well as theoretically motivated. Suppose I see a dog that I have never seen before. His name is Fido, though I don't know it. Fido is covered with mud, and I see that he is. Do I believe that Fido is covered with mud? Of course. But do I really believe that it is *Fido* that is covered with mud? What if it had been some other dog that looked just like him who had wandered by? What if Fido had been clean and I had seen his twin brother? Suppose later I learn that there are two similar dogs in the neighbourhood, one named "Fido" and one named "Rover", both fitting the description that I would give of the dog I saw. Fido is lost, I am told. Have I seen him? I don't know. I did see a dog that might have been Fido, covered with mud, that went that way. But I don't know, or have a belief about, whether it was Fido or Rover. And if it was Rover that I saw, then maybe Fido is not covered with mud. So I don't believe that Fido was covered with mud. But I haven't changed my mind, or stopped believing anything that I previously believed. (I didn't previously believe that it was Fido, rather than Rover, that I saw, covered with mud.) What changed was the context of attribution—the context that defines the relevant alternative possibilities relative to which the content of my belief is defined.

Let me conclude with an example that takes us back to one of the early critiques, by Keith Donnellan, of the description theory of reference.[7] This example is not, like Kripke's notorious story of Pierre, a case of one thing represented in two ways, but of two persons represented as one. At a party, a man is introduced to a student as the famous philosopher, J. L. Aston-Martin. The student had heard of Aston-Martin, and knew, before being introduced to this man, something of his work. He talks at length with the man at the party, and they become long-term acquaintances. The student continues to believe that the man he was introduced to is the famous philosopher, but in fact he is a different person with, we may suppose, the same

---

[7] Donnellan (1971).

name. Donnellan suggests that when the student says, on the day after the party, "Last night I met J. L. Aston-Martin and talked to him for almost an hour" he refers unambiguously to the famous philosopher, and so says something false. But in other contexts, for example in a narration of events at the party (". . . and then Robinson tripped over Aston-Martin's feet and fell flat on his face") he refers unambiguously to the man he was introduced to, and so says something true. Donnellan is discussing reference rather than attitudes, or attribution of attitude. But reference depends on intentions. In this example the student intends to refer both to the man at the party and to the famous philosopher, who are, in the world as the student takes it to be, one person. The student's representation of that person is the way it is because of facts about two different people: the famous philosopher and the man at the party. If the relevant facts about either were different, the student's representation would be different in corresponding ways. But one might take one or the other of these dependencies to be a deviation from the norm. Initially, before the student met Aston-Martin at the party, his representation was unambiguously a representation of the famous philosopher, and any change in that representation that derived from facts about someone else are cases of misrepresentation of that person. But later, as the student's representation comes to be more richly dependent on facts about the man at the party, it becomes possible to shift to a context in which these dependencies are the normal ones, and the information that derived from the philosopher are the distortions. Which context is relevant to the interpretation of the student's utterances of the name "Aston-Martin" will, as Donnellan says, depend on the point of the utterance, the relevant alternatives that the student is trying to distinguish between.

In either kind of context, the primary intention that determines the student's reference is the intention that he might express by saying "I was intending to refer to Aston-Martin." The content of this intention determines the referent of the names, pronouns and possibly some definite descriptions, that the student uses with this intention. And this content is determined by the answer to the question, which of the two candidates is the student's Aston-Martin representation a representation of? Thus, according to this story, the relation between the uses of a name or other referring expression and its referent is not direct, but is mediated by a mental representation whose content determines the content of the relevant intention. This may look suspiciously like a throwback to a version of the description theory, but the story remains an externalist one. The referring expressions and the mental representations both have the referents and contents they have only because of the causal interactions that take place in the environment that the speaker-thinker shares with those referents.

PART IV

Form and Content

12

Mental Content and Linguistic Form

Many philosophers have argued or assumed that language is, in some way or other, essential to thought. Philosophical explanations of the nature of intentional mental states, psychological explanations of the mechanisms of mental representation and semantic explanations of the attribution of content frequently rely in various ways on an analogy between linguistic and mental representation. Some of these philosophers explains thought as an internalization of speech, or as a disposition to speak, with the content of the thought being derived from the content of the speech act that is internalized, or in which the disposition is displayed. Some describe the internal states that constitute thoughts in terms of the compositional structure with which semantic theory interprets complex expressions. In previous work I have resisted projects of this kind, arguing for a conception of content that has no semantic structure, and for an explanation of the intentionality of thought that makes no reference to language or speech.[1] But it must be granted that linguistic structure and linguistic practice are intimately involved in our mental life. Even if there can be thinkers who are not speakers or interpreters of speech, thinkers who do not in any sense talk to themselves or store their thoughts in words, it is clear that such thinkers would be very different, both in what they think about and how they do it, from us. In this paper I want to try to come to terms with what I have called the linguistic picture—the cluster of metaphors, analogies and strategies that use language in some way to help account for thought. I will try to separate out some of the different ways that mental content may be related to linguistic form, and some of the different ways that linguistic practices and objects may be involved in thought. Although I will make some concessions to the linguistic picture, I will continue to defend the course-grained conception of informational content, arguing that it is adequate to explain the various intimate relations between language and thought, and that it in fact helps to clarify those relations.

I am going to begin with an abstract semantical problem about belief attribution, although my main concern will be to use this problem to raise

---

[1] In Stalnaker (1984).

and sharpen some more substantive questions about belief: both philosophical questions about the nature of representational states and
psychological questions about how such states are in fact realized. The
semantical problem is to explain how the meaning or content of a statement attributing a belief is determined as a function of the meanings or
other semantical values of its parts. The basic semantic structure of a
statement of the form *x believes that P* is straightforward: it says that a
relation (expressed by "believes") holds between the individual denoted by
the subject term and whatever it is that is denoted by the sentential clause.
The problem is to say, first what sort of thing it is that is denoted by the
clause, and second, how a thing of this sort is determined as a function of
the constituents of the clause. The semantical problem is concerned solely
with the compositional structure of such sentences. All that needs to be
said about the meaning of the simple expression "believe" is that it
expresses a relation between a believer and an object of belief. But while a
solution to the semantical problem can be stated without making any
claim about the nature of this relation, the evaluation of competing
hypotheses about what the object of belief is will require us to consider
more substantive questions about belief.

It might seem that if our general semantic theory—our theory of constructions other than those involving discourse—is sound, then belief constructions—at least simple sentences of the form *x believes that P*—ought
to raise no new problems. For if our semantic theory is compositional, it
must be that the semantic value of a sentential clause is a function of the
semantic value of the sentence from which it is derived. It seems natural to
assume that the clause "that alligators are irritable" *denotes* what the sentence "alligators are irritable" *expresses*. So if our semantic theory tells us
what "alligators are irritable" says (or at least how what it says is a function of the meanings of its parts), then without any further work it will tell
us what is is that someone believes when she believes that alligators are
irritable. I think this is roughly right, but what it implies is not that belief
constructions are unproblematic, but rather that any problems with belief
constructions are symptoms of a much more general problem in the foundation of semantics. And it is clear that there are problems with belief
constructions—prima facie conflicts between what the phenomena
suggest about how objects of belief must be individuated and what a truth-
conditional semantic theory standardly says about the semantic values of
sentences. Truth-conditional semantics (whether developed in the possible
worlds framework or in some other way) takes the primary task of semantics to be to explain how the truth-conditions of a statement are determined. According to such a theory, statements with the same
truth-conditions—sentences that are true and false together under all the

same conditions—say the same thing, although they may do it in different ways. But sentential clauses made from sentences that the semantics says are necessarily equivalent (and thus have the same truth-conditions) often seem clearly to denote different objects of belief. It seems clear, for example, that one may believe that seventeen is a prime number without believing that the sum of the angles of a Euclidean triangle is equal to a straight angle. But these two propositions are both necessarily true, and so true under the same conditions.

This, then, is the semantic problem: to find an object of belief finely enough individuated to account for the phenomena of belief attribution, and to explain how such objects are determined as a function of the constituents of the sentential clauses that refer to them.

One might respond to the problem by holding to the thesis that objects of belief are individuated by truth-conditions and changing one's account of the truth-conditions of the problematic examples. Or one might deny that the referent of a *that* clause is a function of the meaning of the constituent parts.[2] But the strategy I want to explore is the most straightforward one: it takes at face value what the examples of belief attribution seem to show—that the object of belief is an entity individuated more finely than by its truth-conditions, and it accepts the apparent consequence of this—that our semantics must attribute more fine-grained semantic values to sentences generally. The task then is to say just what sort of fine-grained objects are the right ones, and to see that one's semantic theory explains how such values are determined. There are many ways to carry out this strategy,[3] but the most promising way is to build some kind of semantic structure into the object of speech and thought. According to the standard truth-conditional semantic theory, the semantic structure of a sentence or sentential clause is a part of the means by which the semantic value of the sentence or clause is determined, but not part of the value itself. The structure provides a recipe for determining content as a function of the values of the parts of the sentences, but the values of the parts are not constituents of content. The same content might be determined in quite different ways, as the value of different functions applied to different arguments. But while this is the way semantic theories standardly treat content, such theories do have the resources to define abstract objects that reflect the semantic structure of sentences—objects that represent the recipes themselves rather than the end results of

---

[2] Davidson's paratactic account, and any quotational account of belief attribution is an instance of this strategy. See Davidson (1984b) and Hill (1976).

[3] For an abstract and unconstrained theory of fine-grained objects of attitude, see Thomason (1980). For an account of objects of belief as sets of situations, see Barwise and Perry (1983). For some criticisms of Barwise and Perry's account, see Soames (1985).

following them. One might take the values of sentences and sentential clauses to be the structured meanings by which the truth-conditions, or informational content, of those sentences or clauses are determined. According to this approach, these structures will be the senses of sentences, and the referents of sentential clauses. They will thus be the objects of both speech and thought.[4]

There are questions about the details of the development of this kind of theory. Should the structured meanings include Russellian propositions with individuals as constituents, or should they be structures containing only intensional objects such as senses or modes or presentation? At what level of abstraction should structure be analyzed? Might sentences with different superficial structures have the same structured meaning? There are some technical problems to be overcome—for example, avoiding the threat of semantic paradox—and there will remain some prima facie conflicts between a structured meaning account of the objects of belief and the phenomena of belief attribution. Sentences with the same structures and synonymous constituents may in some contexts seem to express different objects of belief. ("All woodchucks are groundhogs" and "All groundhogs are groundhogs," to take a familiar example). But I will assume that a theory of this kind that is formally adequate and more or less true to the phenomena can be developed. The question I want to consider takes us beyond the semantic problem—the problem of the structure of sentences attributing belief—to the substantive problem about the nature of the belief relation: what are the facts about the believer and his relation to his environment that make a belief attribution correct? If semantic structure is essential to the abstract object the believer is said to be related to, how must that structure be involved in the state of the believer that constitutes his having the belief in order for the attribution to be correct?

However a fine-grained content is defined, it will be something that determines truth-conditional content, or what I will call *informational content*. Belief states, whatever they are, *could* be described simply in terms of their informational content. If x believes that P, then x is in a state that has the informational content determined by the referent of "that P." But according to the fine-grained strategy, a belief attribution says more than this, since even when P and Q determine the same informational content, it may be true that x believes that P, and false that she believes that Q. The question is, what is it about the believer's state—a state that has the informational content determined by Q (as well as by the equivalent P)—that makes it a belief that P, rather than a belief that Q.

---

[4] For developments of this strategy, see Cresswell (1985), Bigelow (1978) and Salmon (1986).

To help sharpen and clarify this question, I will review a familiar, and I think plausible, answer to the prior question, what is it about a belief state that accounts for its informational content? States of organisms, according to this answer, carry information when there exists a pattern of counterfactual dependencies between those states and corresponding states of the environment. If x is in a state caused by the fact that P, and would not have been in that state if it had not been that P, then that state of x carries the information that P. If x is capable of being in a range of alternative states that tend to vary systematically with variations in the environment, then those states will be information-carrying states. While it may be controversial whether one can explain the content of intentional states entirely in such terms, it seems reasonable to assume that it is at least a necessary condition for a state's being a belief state that it tend to carry information in this sense. Further, it seems reasonable to assume that if a person believes that P, then the relevant belief state tends to carry the information that P (even if carrying the information that P is not sufficient to make it a belief that P).

Representational states and systems can carry misinformation as well as information in the strict sense. We need an account of informational content that is neutral as to whether the world is as it is represented to be. But misrepresentation must be understood as a deviation from a norm. It is reasonable to assume that representational states are *normally* correct— that they are states that *tend* to represent things as they are. Given an appropriate conception of normal conditions, we can explain representation generally in terms of information: a state represents the world as being such that P, and so is a state with informational content P, if and only if under normal conditions it would carry the information that P. Normal conditions will include both conditions on the environment and conditions on the internal functioning of the representational mechanisms. The question of what the specific relevant normal conditions are is an empirical question, and answering it is part of the task of explaining the capacities and limitations of believers and other organisms that represent.

Information and representation in this sense are necessary for belief, but obviously not sufficient. For an information-bearing state to be a belief state, the information must be available to play a role in determining how the believer acts to satisfy its wants and needs. If there are systematic dependencies between the state of an organism's environment and the way it is disposed to act, then the behavioral dispositions themselves will be representational states—states that tend to carry information about the environment. Beliefs, whatever else they must be, are presumably states of this kind.

Now let me return to the question about what kind of claim a belief attribution is making. The semantical hypothesis we are considering is that a belief attribution of the form *x believes that P* relates a believer to an object that has semantic form as well as informational content. The question is, what does such a belief attribution say about the believer's state beyond the claim that it has the informational content determined by the object of belief. Here is one kind of answer: just as a sentential clause has both informational content and semantic form, so an internal representational state of a believer will have both content and form. The information carried by such a state will be carried in some particular form, and, according to this answer, it is plausible to suppose that the form in which the information is stored is a linguistic form. Suppose that the way we represent the world is by storing sentences or sentence-like structures of a mental language—mentalese, or the Language of Thought. Then these representations will have the kind of structure that is represented by a structured meaning or a Russellian proposition. The claim that a belief attribution *x believes that P* makes, according to this suggestion, is that the way the believer internally represents the informational content expressed by *that P* is the same (at the appropriate level of abstraction) as the way it is represented in the clause *that P*.

It is important to recognize that the suggestion being made is not just a claim about what is going on in the believer; it is a claim about what a belief attribution says about what is going on in the believer. That is, the claim is not just that belief states take the form of internal linguistic representations; it is the claim that when we attribute specific beliefs, we say something about the specific semantic structure of the sentences of the internal language that encode those beliefs. According to this suggestion, if I say that *x* believes that *P*, my claim will be false if the form in which the informational content of *that P* is stored is relevantly different from the form of the clause "that *P*." I think this suggestion makes a belief attribution carry more theoretical weight than it is plausible to assume that it carries. If it were correct, belief attributions would be far more speculative, and believers would be far less authoritative about their beliefs, than they seem to be. While theoretical and experimental developments in cognitive psychology may someday convince me that I store my beliefs in a form that is structurally similar to the form in which they are expressed and described in English, I don't think that my ordinary belief attributions commit me to thinking that they will. Consider an example: Angus believes that Edinburgh is closer to Liverpool than it is to London, or so it seems. He acts as if he believes this; for example, when he wanted to go from Edinburgh either to London or to Liverpool, he didn't care which, and wanted to go as few miles as possible, he went to Liverpool. Furthermore, his linguistic behavior seems to support the hypothesis that he has this belief: he says, sincerely, and without hesitation, "yes" when asked, "do you believe that Edinburgh is closer to Liverpool than it is to London?" Angus thinks he has this belief. But does he, or do we, have reason to believe that the form in which this geographical information is stored in Angus is appropriately similar to the semantic structure of the sentence "Edinburgh is closer to Liverpool than it is to London"? Suppose the information is represented in Angus in a mental map. When planning his trips, or answering questions, he consults his map, visualizes it perhaps, and sees that London is farther from Edinburgh than Edinburgh is from Liverpool. Or suppose the information is stored in a quite different linguistic form—in a mental machine language whose semantic structure is quite different from English, although capable of representing the same information. Would this mean that Angus, despite what he thinks, does not really believe that Edinburgh is closer to Liverpool than it is to London? Surely not.

Those who want to explain beliefs as stored sentences of a mental language usually distinguish implicit beliefs from explicit or core beliefs. It is acknowledged that there is lots of information implicit in the believer and accessible if needed, that it is not plausible to assume is written down: unconsidered instantiations of universal generalizations believed, or propositions too trivial to notice such as, for example, that 4652 is an even number, or that no aardvark weighs more than an aircraft carrier. Such implicit beliefs are explained as dispositions to form explicit representations upon considering them.[5] Exploiting this distinction, we might say that even if Angus's representation of the informational content that Edinburgh is closer to Liverpool than to London does not *initially* have the right form, perhaps he would come to represent it in this form if it were presented to him in this way, and so perhaps he at least implicitly believes this all along. But this too is speculation. Even when Angus is asked the question, in English, and gives his answer, there is no reason to think a sentence of the language of thought with just this structure needs to be stored. Angus does need to process the English sentence, to represent the fact that it has the semantic structure that it has. But this metalinguistic information is different from the geographical information that Angus may continue to store only in some quite different way.

There may be good empirical reason to believe that we store at least some information as sentences of an internal language. If one assumes a conception of language that is sufficiently broad and flexible, one might argue that anyone with the kind of sophisticated representational capacities that human beings have *must* store information in linguistic form. But

[5] See Lycan (1986) and Cummins (1986).

I don't think it is plausible to believe that our ordinary belief attributions make claims about the specific structure of these representations. If belief is a relation to a fine-grained structured meaning, it is still not the structure of internal representations that makes them true.

I want now to consider a contrasting alternative account of what a belief attribution is saying about the semantic structure of the informational content of a belief. Perhaps the claim is not about how the information is stored or represented internally, but about how the believer is disposed to express the belief. Whatever is going on inside the head of the believer, if he is disposed to assert or assent to a sentence with a certain semantic structure, then it will be correct, according to this suggestion, to attribute to him a belief with this structure. If a person has a belief with the informational content *that P*, but sincerely dissents from sentences with the semantic structure of the sentence *P*, then, according to this suggestion, it will be false that she believes that *P*.

I think this suggestion about the role of semantic structure in the attribution of belief is more promising but it does require a closer conceptual connection between speech and thought than some will find plausible. The suggestion implies that there cannot be thinkers who are not speakers, at least not believers who are not speakers. For if someone or something is not disposed to express or communicate the information it represents in any form at all, then this proposal will imply that all attributions of belief to it will be false.

Not everyone will find this consequence unpalatable, Donald Davidson, for example, has defended a conception of belief that connects it essentially to speech. He makes such claims as that "making detailed sense of a person's intentions and beliefs cannot be independent of making sense of his utterances,"[6] and that "we have the concept of belief only from the role of belief in the interpretation of language, for as a private attitude it is not intelligible except as an adjustment to the public norm provided by language."[7] Part of Davidson's motivation seems to be verificationist: he says, "we have no good idea how to set about authenticating the existence of such attitudes when communication is not possible."[8] But he also seems to be concerned with our problem: he suggests that we need speech and the interpretation of speech to make the kind of fine discriminations between intentions and beliefs that we seem to make.

While the conception of belief required by this response to the problem does have some independent support, it also has some facts to explain away. We do attribute beliefs to nonhuman animals and prelinguistic children, and it does not seem difficult to imagine cases of highly sophisticated

[6] Davidson (1984a: 144).   [7] Davidson (1986: 170).
[8] Davidson (1984a: 144).

but totally uncommunicative agents and inquirers. Suppose there were a species of solitary martians who go through life never seeing another creature of their kind. (They hatch from eggs long after their single parents have died.) Suppose that although these creatures have no need or opportunity to communicate, they are highly intelligent creatures who observe, calculate, experiment, and formulate hypotheses about their environment, history and nature, and about their own thought. Perhaps they think in an internal mental language, but because of their prodigious memories and great powers of concentration, they have no need to externalize their thought—they make no pencil and paper calculations and keep no written records. If all of the alleged thoughts of such creatures remain internal, must we say that they have no beliefs? If we did attribute beliefs to them, would we have to understand our attributions in a highly counterfactual way—as claims about what they would be disposed to say if they had the resources and motivation to communicate? But of course how they expressed their beliefs if they did would depend on the particular means of expression that they are counterfactually assumed to acquire.

Even if we forget such counterfactual martians and restrict ourselves to the actual paradigms of thinkers—thinkers who are also speakers—we have to recognize some mental states that thinkers are not in a position to express. We make tacit presuppositions, have unconscious beliefs, and take things for granted without noticing that we are doing so. The correctness of the attribution of attitudes of this kind cannot be dependent on the means that we would use to express the information that those attitudes are carrying. Of course it might be that only certain attitude attributions make a claim about form as well as informational content. One might hold that attributions of conscious belief are correct only if the believer is disposed to assert or assent to a statement of the same form as the attribution clause, while also holding that the correctness of attributions of tacit presupposition depend only on the informational content of the attribution clause. But this would be plausible only if the original problem—the problem that motivated us to look for a more fine-grained object of belief—was a problem only for conscious belief. Our original semantic problem was that there seemed to be clear cases of belief that P without belief that Q, where P and Q had the same informational content. But just as one can *believe* that seventeen is prime without *believing* that the sum of the angles of a Euclidean triangle is equal to a straight angle, one might also take the first for granted, or presuppose it in one's mathematical practice, without presupposing or taking for granted the second. This seems to imply that the root of the problem—the apparent fact that it is possible to believe something without believing everything equivalent to it—is not to be found in the fact that we are disposed to express our beliefs. This should be clear from the case of the solitary martian. Whether we say that it has beliefs or not, it is difficult to deny that it has some kind of intentional, information-bearing states. Call them schmeliefs instead of beliefs. The fact that our martian is deeply uncommunicative will not render it logically omniscient. We assumed that our martian calculates and reasons; it may have done the calculation that gave it the schmelief that seventeen is prime without yet having constructed the proof that would lead it to schmelieve that the sum of the angles of a Euclidean triangle is equal to a straight angle. If linguistic structure plays a role in the explanation of the fact that there can be equivalent but distinct objects of schmelief, we will have to explain that role in a way that does not involve the structure of outward expressions. Perhaps the same explanation will work for belief as well.

I have considered two ways in which semantic structure might be involved in belief. First, the informational content of a belief may be stored in a form that has a semantic structure. Second, beliefs may be expressed in a form that has semantic structure. These two ways in which semantic structure is involved are different: information might be stored in one form and expressed in a different one, or it might be stored in a linguistic form and not expressed at all. Even if one assumes that all beliefs are represented internally in linguistic form, it is not plausible, I have argued, to take belief attributions to be making a claim about this form. And while it might be plausible on some conceptions of belief to take belief attributions to be making a claim about the form in which beliefs are expressed, this won't provide a general solution to the problem of the ignorance of necessary equivalence. The real problem is that in cases where an agent believes that P but fails to realize that Q where P and Q are necessarily equivalent, it seems that this failure is a fact about the information available to the agent, and not just a fact about how he represents, either internally or externally, the information that he has. If this is right, then the question is, what information does an agent have, and what information does he lack, when he believes or presupposes one thing while not believing or presupposing something equivalent. This question is deflected, rather than answered, when we shift our attention to the means used to represent the information, and away from the information itself. In the remainder of this paper, I will consider two ways that semantic structure may be involved in the informational content of belief, and not just in the means of representing that content.

First, and most simply, beliefs may be *about* semantic structure, or about either internal or external representations that have semantic structure. One may have beliefs about the informational content of a representation, or about its truth-value. One can believe that a certain statement has a certain content, or a certain semantic structure, without having an opinion about the truth-value of the statement, and one can believe that a certain statement is true without having an opinion about what the statement says, or what information it conveys. Beliefs can be about sentences and speech acts in a public language, and they can be about internal representations, linguistic or otherwise. Some of our internal representations may be about other of our internal representations—about what they mean, and whether they are right.

How is semantic knowledge, ignorance and error relevant to the general problem of the object of belief? It is clear that some kind of semantic ignorance or error will be present in any prima facie case of failure to believe things with the same informational content. Suppose M and N are fine-grained objects of belief of some kind with the same informational content. Suppose x believes M, but not N. Then obviously, x will have to be ignorant of the fact that M and N have the same informational content, since he does not know that they are even materially equivalent. But then he must be ignorant, either of what content M has, or of what content N has, and this is purely semantic information.

So it seems clear that in the kind of case that motivates us to look for a more fine-grained object of belief—cases where it seems that an agent believes something without believing something necessarily equivalent to it—there is always a difference in the information available to the agent, and not just a difference in the way the agent packages the information. Might it be that when we attribute belief that P and deny belief that Q in case where semantic theory tells us that P and Q are necessarily equivalent, the beliefs being attributed and denied are beliefs that are at least in part about semantic relations? Might the information that distinguishes between necessary truths (which on a straightforward interpretation all have the same informational content) be semantic information—information about the expressions and structures used to state those truths?

In some simple case, it should be uncontroversial that this is right: if O'Leary fails to believe that all woodchucks are groundhogs, or that a fortnight is a period of fourteen days, then it is clear that the information O'Leary lacks, and the information that we are saying he lacks when we deny that he has those beliefs, is information about the semantic values of certain words. But in most cases, the information in question does not seem, intuitively, to be information about expressions. Plausible semantic theories tell us, for example, that it is necessarily true that Hesperus is Phosphorus, and that measles is caused by a virus. If I point at Oliver North and say "*That* is Oliver North," the proposition I express is necessarily true. And of course all mathematical statements are necessarily true or necessarily false. But none of these statements seems to be about language; the information they convey seems to be about astronomical and

medical facts, facts about who is being pointed at, or, in the case of arithmetical and geometric statements, facts about numbers and the abstract
structure of certain spaces. One does not need to know any names to
know, or be ignorant of, the fact that Hesperus is Phosphorus, and we may
share mathematical beliefs with those who do not share our language. The
ancient Greeks, for example, believed that the square root of two was
irrational, and so do we. How can these facts and intuitions be reconciled
with the hypothesis that the information relevant to distinguishing necessarily equivalent beliefs, and beliefs in necessary truths, is information
about semantic values and structures?

First, it may help to keep in mind that questions about semantic values
and structures may be mixed with questions about the world. If I have certain partial information about the content of a statement, then learning
that the statement is true may tell me something about the world without
giving me the information that the statement itself conveys. Suppose you
say to me, "John is under the bed," and I know that you are referring either
to John Jones or John Smith, but I don't know which. I accept that what
you tell me is true, but I don't know what you have told me. I do, however,
learn something about who is under the bed from what you told me. And
I am now in a position to infer something that has nothing to do with language from a piece of purely semantic information: if I learn who you were
referring to, I can infer from what I already know who it is that is under
the bed.

Sometimes semantic values are determined as a function of certain
extra-linguistic facts. According to causal theories of reference, who I am
referring to with a proper name, and what I am saying when I use the
name, may depend on facts about causal chains of which I am ignorant.
Anyone who accepts such a theory of reference must agree that the fact
that Hesperus is Phosphorus is a semantic fact in the following sense: one
who learns that Hesperus is Phosphorus learns a fact on which the semantic value of the names "Hesperus" and "Phosphorus" depends; no one
who is ignorant of the fact that Hesperus is Phosphorus can be fully
informed about the informational content of statements containing the
names "Hesperus" and "Phosphorus." But while this information is in this
sense semantic, it is also astronomical. One who learns that Hesperus is
Phosphorus learns something about the way the solar system is arranged.

Beliefs about semantics can be beliefs about specific expressions, speech
acts, or representational tokens, but they can also be about more abstract
structures shared by specific tokens. Suppose I know of a set of sentences—sentences that all have the same structure at some level of abstraction—that they have the same structure and semantic value. Suppose there
is a different set of sentences that share a different structure but the same

semantic value, as those in the first set. Suppose I also know of these sentences that they are equivalent to each other, but I do not know that these sentences are equivalent to those in the first set. We might describe this cognitive situation in terms of the structures shared by the sentences rather than in terms of the specific sentences that share the structure. Now suppose there is a different person who speaks a different language, but who is in a parallel cognitive situation. The sentences she has beliefs about will be different, but the structures they share may be the same. There is a common piece of semantic information that these speakers of different languages lack: the information that representations with *this* structure have the same informational content as representations with *that* structure.[9] Even though the ancient Greeks shared no beliefs with us about the specific words, numerals and other notion that I would use to say that the square root of two is irrational, it may be this kind of cognitive parallel that explains why we can correctly attribute this belief to them.

People who speak different languages and who use different notations may have the same mathematical beliefs when there are relevant similarities between the semantic and notational structures of the different languages, but it is sometimes difficult to separate the content of a mathematical belief from the means used to express it. Suppose there were a community of English speakers that grew up doing its arithmetic in a base eight notation. The words "eight" and "nine" don't exist in its dialect; the words "ten" and "eleven," like the numerals "10" and "11" denote the numbers eight and nine. Now suppose that some child in this community has a belief that he would express by saying "twenty-six times one hundred equals twenty-six hundred." Would it be correct to say that this child believes that twenty-two times sixty-four equals fourteen hundred eight? This does not seem to capture accurately his cognitive state. His belief, like our simple arithmetical beliefs, is not really a belief about the numbers themselves, independently of how they are represented.

Mathematical information is most often received in linguistic form, and the behavior that mathematical beliefs dispose us to engage in is primarily behavior that involves linguistic and other representations: calculation, symbolic construction, and proof. It is not implausible, I think, to take representations and representational structures to be the subject matter of mathematics, and to be involved in the subject matter in other prima facie cases of necessarily equivalent but distinct objects of belief. If we do

---

[9] There are some ambiguities one has to be careful about here. The relevant belief is not about the structure itself, but about certain sentences that in fact share the structure. The proposition that a certain structured meaning determines a certain informational content will be a necessary truth, and so we cannot use the informational content of this proposition to distinguish different mathematical beliefs.

assume this, then we can distinguish between different mathematical
truths and other equivalent statements and clauses, and we can explain
how semantic structure is essential to some objects of belief, without giving up the idea that belief attributions relate a believer to a coarse-grained
informational content.

Before concluding, I want to mention briefly a fourth way that language
may be involved in belief, a way that is independent both of the subject
matter of the belief and of the way the believer represents or expresses his
belief. Linguistic practices and institutions are essential to the medium
through which a lot of information is transmitted. The point is not just
that linguistic communication may be part of the means by which someone comes to be in a belief state; rather, the point is that facts about linguistic communication may be essential to the fact that certain belief states
have the informational content that they have. Suppose I am told, and
accept as true, something about a place I have never heard of before. To
borrow an example discussed in several places by Daniel Dennett, suppose
I am told that Balzac was married in Berdichev. Now one thing I acquire
from this communication is the partly metalinguistic information the
Balzac was married in a place called "Berdichev," but it seems plausible to
say that I also come to believe something about Berdichev itself—that
Balzac was married there. By the mere fact that I assent to and remember
this sentence, I am in a state that tends, under normal conditions, to carry
the information that Balzac was married in Berdichev. Under normal conditions, I would not assent to that statement unless it were true, since I
would not have assented to the statement if someone hadn't made it, and
under normal conditions what people say is true. We must assume that
statements are normally true if we are to explain how information can be
transmitted by linguistic communication.[10]

If this is right, then the representational state that constitutes my believing that Balzac was married in Berdichev will be a state that has *that* informational content only because of facts about the semantics of the public
language. If "Berdichev," as used by my informant, had referred to
Novokuznetsk then the same internal state would have been the belief that
Balzac was married in Novokuznetsk.

This kind of case is different from each of the other three kinds of lan-
guage-dependence that I have discussed. First, while a belief that is language-dependent in this way *might* be represented internally in a
linguistic form—for example the English sentence itself might be the

[10] Of course being in a state that tends to carry the information that *P* is not sufficient
for believing that *P*. Other conditions, including the condition that the information be
accessible to guide action, need to be met. So we need not say that every case of accepting
that a statement one hears or reads is true is a case of believing what that statement says.

form that the representation took—this is not essential. Information received in linguistic form might instead be used to construct or modify a mental map. Second, people need not be disposed to express beliefs that are language-dependent in this way: they may be unconscious or tacit. Third, the content of such beliefs need not involve language. Even if my belief that Balzac was married in Berdichev is language-dependent in this way, someone else—Balzac's wife, for example—might have believed the same thing without her belief having any dependence on linguistic facts at all.

Dennett, in one context where he discusses the Berdichev example, suggests that we should distinguish sharply a primitive, language-independent kind of intentional state—belief—whose objects are informational contents, from a more sophisticated state—*assent* or *opinion*—whose objects are sentences "collected as true."[11] But I think we can better understand the phenomenon Dennett is pointing to, and get clearer about the way that assent and opinion interact with belief in general, if we see language-dependent opinion as a special case of the general kind of belief that applies to nonspeaking animals as well as to ourselves.

Whatever else it is to have a belief, I have suggested, it is at least to be in a state that tends to carry information, where information is understood in terms of a pattern of counterfactual dependencies of internal states on states of that part of the world that determines the subject matter of the beliefs. For such information-carrying states to be belief states it is at least necessary that their informational content be accessible, that the state tend to dispose the believer to behave in ways that are systematically related to its content. One can characterize systems and states of this general kind independently of linguistic structure and linguistic practice, and one can explain many of the puzzling features of intentional states in terms of the fact that they are states of systems of this kind. But while there can be systems of this kind that don't involve linguistic representation, language is obviously involved in the case of the paradigms of believers—ourselves—and perhaps in the case of anything capable of being in intentional states that are rich and powerful enough to be called beliefs. My main point has been that language can play many different roles, and that the languages and linguistic representations involved at different points in such a system need not be the same. It helps to get clearer about the different roles that language can play in belief—the different ways that beliefs and belief attributions can be language-dependent—to see believers as information-carrying and information-using systems of this kind And if we can get

---

[11] Dennett (1978). Dennett is endorsing a suggestion made by Ronald de Sousa in (1971).

clear about the different roles that language plays in the beliefs of sophisticated believers, I think we will see how to reconcile the simple conception of content as informational content with the subtle distinctions that can be made between objects of beliefs.

13

The Problem of Logical Omniscience, I

From their beginning,[1] epistemic and doxastic logics—the logics of knowledge and belief have been modeled on modal logic—the logic of necessity and possibility. Knowledge and belief, in such logics, are analogous to necessity. There is a wide variety of modal logics, but all of the normal ones contain certain distribution or deductive closure principles; for example, if "$\phi \to \psi$" is valid, then so is "$\Box \phi \to \Box \psi$." Most versions of epistemic logic are normal in this sense, accepting analogous principles for knowledge and belief. Developers of such logics invariably remark that the principles of deductive closure are unrealistic, since it is obviously false that knowers in general know all of the deductive consequences of anything that they know. The assumption that knowers do, as a matter of logic, have such knowledge—that they are deductively omniscient—is defended as an idealization. Sometimes the divergence between the assumptions of the ideal theory and the facts about the domain of its intended application is described as a problem for epistemic logic—the problem of logical omniscience. My aim in this paper is to try to get clear about just what kind of idealization such normal epistemic and doxastic logics are making, and what the motivation is for idealizing in this way. If there is a problem of logical omniscience, I want to try to see if I can say what the problem is. My broader aim is to try to get clearer about the concepts of knowledge and belief, and about what work we should expect a logic of these concepts to do.

I shall begin by contrasting two different ways that the divergence between idealization and reality might be explained, and considering several different kinds of reasons that one might have for idealizing in one or the other of the two ways. Then I shall look at the problem of logical omniscience from the perspective of a certain conception of the nature of belief, the sentence storage model. I have little sympathy with this influential conception of belief; I think the problem of logical omniscience helps to bring out its limitations, and to point the way to a more adequate conception. But the problem of logical omniscience is not solved by giving up

---

[1] See Hintikka (1962).

the sentence storage model. I shall suggest, in conclusion, that it is a symptom of a tension in our ordinary conceptions of knowledge and belief.[2]

I. Idealization

There are two ways that one might try to reconcile the fact that people do not believe all the logical consequences of their beliefs with a theory that seems to say that they do. On the one hand, one might interpret one's logic to be a logic of belief in the ordinary sense, but restrict its domain of literal application to imaginary believers of a special idealized kind—perhaps to agents who have unlimited memory capacity and infinite computational power and speed. Ordinary people, and even extraordinary real people, can't think of everything, but ideal believers can, and if there were such believers they would believe, in the ordinary sense of "believe," all the logical consequences of everything that they believe. On the other hand, one might take the domain of literal application of one's logic of belief to be unrestricted, including ordinary agents who have no special computational powers, but interpret the concept of belief that the theory models to be belief in a special sense. The divergence between ideal and real is explained as a difference between belief in the ordinary sense and belief in some special technical sense. For example, one might distinguish belief in the ordinary sense from *implicit* belief: one's implicit beliefs include, by definition, all of the deductive consequences of one's beliefs, whether or not they are or could be recognized as such by the agent. To be logically omniscient with respect to implicit belief is no great feat; not even the most ignorant and unreflective of us can avoid being logically omniscient in this sense.

Both of these stories begin by conceding that ordinary agents do not believe, in the ordinary sense of "believe," all of the logical consequences of their beliefs. Why, one might ask, should one idealize in either of these ways? Why shouldn't one's logic of belief be a logic of belief in the ordinary sense and at the same time a logic that applies to ordinary believers—to anyone who has beliefs in the ordinary sense? In such a realistic logic a proposition of the form *x believes that P* should entail a proposition *x believes that Q* only if it is impossible, as a matter of logic, for anyone to be correctly described as believing that *P* unless that person also believes that

---

[2] Throughout my discussion, I shall talk sometimes about knowledge and sometimes about belief. Different conceptions of knowledge and belief will say different things about the relations between them, but I am assuming that the problem of understanding how and why we do not know all the consequences of our knowledge is essentially the same as the problem of how and why we do not believe all the logical consequences of our belief.

Q. Is the problem that a logic of real belief is too hard to find, and so we have to settle for the simpler logic of a simplified concept, or a simpler domain of application? Or, is there a more positive reason for idealizing: perhaps the concept of real, explicit belief is a concept that picks out uninteresting surface phenomena, while belief in an idealized sense, or the belief we *would* have if we were free of certain limitations we all have, is deeper or more basic or more interesting in some way. I shall look at four different motivations for populating one's theories with idealizations which might provide reasons for idealizing in one or the other of the two ways I have contrasted.

First, one may idealize to get at underlying mechanisms. The complicated behavior of some system may be explained by the interaction of a number of different components, components that can be best understood by seeing how they would work in isolation even if they are, in a realistic context, never found in isolation. A theory may focus on one component, seeing the action of the others as external, interfering factors. In the ideal system these external factors are not there at all. The frictionless planes and weightless pulleys of elementary physics problems are familiar examples of idealization justified in this way. Another is Chomsky's use of the competence–performance distinction to isolate a psychological capacity that is specific to language. Performance is the surface phenomena: what speakers do and don't say, and what expressions they do and don't find odd. But, it is hypothesized, the surface phenomena have different kinds of explanations. Some things are not said, or seem unintelligible to speakers, because they are ungrammatical; others are just too complicated, just too hard to process or remember. One abstracts away from memory and processing limitations by describing the performance of an ideal speaker-listener who has our grammatical competence, but no such limitations. One idealizes in this way in order to better explain the performance of ordinary speakers.

Some theories that idealize for this reason hypothesize that the system the theory is about tends towards some equilibrium state. Various external forces may divert it from its natural state, but when they do its internal dynamics tend to move it back toward the equilibrium. One part of the articulation of such a theory is the description of the equilibrium state— the state that the system *would* be in if it were free from external forces. Even if real systems of the kind one is studying never reach equilibrium, the description of the ideal, equilibrium state may help to explain their behavior. Economic theories are familiar examples of theories that idealize in this way.

The assumption of deductive omniscience is sometimes conceived, at least implicitly, as an idealization motivated in this way. Failures to know

or believe all the consequences of one's knowledge or beliefs are to be
accounted for by a kind of cognitive friction impeding a natural process of
drawing consequences. It is natural to think of belief sets that are inconsistent or not deductively closed as unstable, tending toward an equilibrium at which they satisfy conditions of perfect rationality, an equilibrium
that is never reached because our belief state is constantly perturbed by the
receiving of new information from outside. This is an attractive picture,
but I shall argue below that it rests on an implausible conception of what
belief and knowledge are.

A second reason to idealize is to simplify. Some features of a system that
greatly complicate its accurate description and explanation may nevertheless, for some purposes and in some contexts, be negligible. The cost of the
distortion that comes from ignoring such features may be less than the
benefit of simplification. For example, despite the fact that we know that
these things are strictly false, we may, in some contexts, be justified in
assuming that mass is concentrated at a point, that the gravitational force
between two bodies remains constant as they approach each other, that air
offers no resistance, that light always travels in straight lines. It has been
suggested that the assumption of deductive omniscience implicit in normal epistemic logics is a simplification of this kind. Robert Moore, for
example, writes that logics of knowledge that imply deductive omniscience

represent idealizations that are reasonable approximations to the truth for many
purposes. While no rational agent's knowledge is closed under logical consequence, outside of mathematics there seem to be few cases where this significantly
affects an agent's behavior.[3]

But I think this underestimates the extent of the distortion. It is not only
mathematicians who need to worry about their failure to know all the consequences of their knowledge. Any context where an agent engages in reasoning is a context that is distorted by the assumption of deductive
omniscience, since reasoning (at least deductive reasoning) is an activity
that deductively omniscient agents have no use for. Deliberation, to the
extent that it is thought of as a rational process of figuring out what one
should do given one's priorities and expectations is an activity that is
unnecessary for the deductively omniscient. In fact any kind of information processing or computation is unintelligible as an activity of a deductively omniscient agent. It is hard to see what a logic of knowledge could
be for if it were a harmless simplification for it to ignore these activities
that are so essential to rationality and cognition.

A third kind of justification for idealization is normative: whatever the
inner dynamics of our states of knowledge and belief, and whatever the

---

[3] Moore (1988: 363).

extent of our divergence from the ideal of deductive omniscience, isn't this ideal at least something that rational agents ought to strive to approximate? Isn't a divergence from deductive omniscience a defect in one's state of knowledge, even if a defect that is unavoidable? This suggestion seems plausible, but a number of philosophers have resisted it suggesting that one may have good reasons to avoid accepting all the consequences of one's beliefs, even for having beliefs that are inconsistent with each other, and which are recognized to be so. It has been argued, for example, that rationality requires us to recognize our fallibility. Rational people should believe that at least some of their many beliefs are false; if they do, then they will disbelieve some conjunctions of propositions each one of which they believe. A different reason for rationally withholding belief—at least explicit belief—from some consequences of one's beliefs is given by Gilbert Harman: "Many trivial things are implied by one's view which it would be worse than pointless to add to what one believes." Harman proposes a principle of reasoning he calls *clutter avoidance*: "One should not clutter one's mind with trivialities."[4] I don't find either of these reasons for deliberately refraining from believing the consequences of one's beliefs persuasive since I think they presuppose implausible accounts of what belief is,[5] but even if deductive omniscience is a normative ideal, it is not clear that that is a reason to build it into a logic of knowledge.

A fourth motivation for idealizing is more pessimistic. Perhaps the best we can do is to get a logic of the knowledge of an idealized knower, or of knowledge in some special idealized sense. Perhaps we know how to give a clear account of a concept of knowledge from which it follows that the knowers to which it applies are logically omniscient, but that there are insurmountable problems with any account of knowledge we know how to give that lacks this consequence. I shall argue that this fourth kind of motivation comes closest to the reason why we make this idealization about knowledge. Once we see why this is so, we can be clearer about just what the problem of deductive omniscience is, and how we might solve it.

I have suggested that the nature of the idealization, and the motivation for it, depend on what one takes knowledge and belief to be. I want to look now at a popular picture or model of what belief is, and at the problem of logical omniscience from the perspective of this model. I call it a model rather than a theory because it is not always clear how literally its proponents want it to be taken, but whether meant literally or as a metaphor, it has had a profound influence on the way philosophers and cognitive scientists think about belief, and the logic of belief.

---

[4] Harman (1986: 12).
[5] The first kind of consideration is discussed in Stalnaker (1984: ch. 5). I shall discuss Harman's principle of clutter avoidance below.

II. The Sentence Storage Model of Belief

The *sentence storage model* is perhaps common enough to be called the received view.[6] According to this model, one's beliefs[7] are determined by a set of sentences, perhaps of a mental language, perhaps of one's natural language, that one stores in memory. To a first approximation, the idea is that to believe that P is to have a sentence that says that P stored (to use the fashionable idiom) in one's belief box. This is only a first approximation, since no one thinks that *everything* one believes, in the ordinary sense, is explicitly stored. The sentence storage model distinguishes explicit from implicit belief. The explicit beliefs are those in the set of sentences stored in the belief box; other things one believes, for example certain obvious consequences of the sentences one stores, are believed only implicitly. Different proponents of the sentence storage model have different accounts of what implicit belief is, but what is essential to the model is that implicit belief, and belief in general, is determined by the explicitly stored beliefs.

If this is how belief is to be explained, then what should the logic of belief be? First, what kind of logic should belief have if it is given a realistic semantics—one that is intended to apply to the actual beliefs of ordinary believers? Second, what kind of idealization of this model of belief would yield the standard logic of belief, according to which believers are logically omniscient, and what might motivate the idealization? Third, is there a *problem* of logical omniscience on this account? If so, what is it?

One might ask these questions about either explicit or implicit belief. I shall start with explicit belief, with the logic of the belief set: the set of sentences that is stored in the agent's belief box. One might think that a realistic logic of belief would impose no conditions at all on the contents of belief boxes. How can it be a matter of logic that if some sentence is stored in a belief box, then so is some distinct sentence? And so, one might expect that a realistic logic of explicit belief would have no logical principles at all that depend on the internal structure of belief attributions. But there are two possible sources of principles for a logic of explicit belief, sources that are distinct and important to distinguish. First, even if there are no constraints whatsoever on the sets of mental sentences that may constitute a person's explicit beliefs, there may be some logical relations between different sentences attributing beliefs for the following reason: while it is

---

[6] See e.g. Harman (1973); Fodor (1981b); Cherniak (1986).

[7] In discussing this account, I shall focus on belief rather than knowledge. If one's beliefs are the sentences stored in one's belief box, then presumably one's knowledge will be explained in terms of a subset of the set of beliefs—beliefs meeting some additional, partly external conditions.

sentences that are the explicit beliefs, according to the sentence storage model, it is what the sentences say, rather than the sentences themselves, that belief attributions refer to. In a sentence of the form "*x* believes that *P*," or its formalization in the language of doxastic logic, "B_xP," the sentence that goes in for "*P*" is *used*, and not mentioned. A semantics for the language should tell us what "B_xP" says—what semantic value it has—in terms of the semantic value of what goes in for "*P*." The semantic value of a sentence, it seems reasonable to assume, is what the sentence says; sentences with the same value are those that say the same thing. Even if to believe (explicitly) is to store a sentence, the sentence stored is not identified in a belief attribution. When we say that *x* explicitly believes that *P*, we say (on the storage model) that *x* stores *some* sentence that says that *P*. So a sentence of the form "*x* believes that *P*" make an existential claim about *x*'s beliefs: that there exists a sentence in *x*'s belief box that says that *P*. Now suppose there are distinct sentences of the language of belief attribution (not the believer's language, but the language in which his beliefs are being described) that, as a matter of logic, say the same thing. Suppose, for example, that a sentence of the form "*P & Q*" says the same thing as the corresponding sentence, "*Q & P*." Then, "B_x *(P & Q)*" will be logically equivalent, on the storage model, to "B_x *(Q & P)*." Any set of sentences at all, and so any belief set, will contain a sentence that says that *P & Q* if and only if it contains a sentence that says that *Q & P*, on the assumption that any sentence that says the one also says the other.

Just which principles of the logic of belief are validated by this kind of consideration will depend entirely on what is assumed about the contents of sentences—about the nature of what it is that sentences say. If we individuate contents very finely, then there will be fewer such equivalence principles, while, if we choose a coarse-grained conception, there will be more. Suppose we followed the simplest course, individuating contents by their truth-conditions. Then, our semantics for explicit belief will validate the equivalence principle:

$$\text{if} \vdash \phi \leftrightarrow \psi \text{ then } \vdash B_x \phi \leftrightarrow B_x \psi.$$

This, by itself, is not quite deductive omniscience, but it is a very strong principle, one that would not be plausible for a realistic semantics of belief. It implies, for example, that anyone who believes any necessary truth—for example any trivial tautology—therefore believes all necessary truths. And if ψ is a consequence of something *x* believes, say ϕ, then while *x* may not believe ψ, it will follow from the equivalence principle that *x* believes the conjunction of ϕ and ψ. Nothing, however, is implied or assumed about the powers of believers to recognize logical equivalences. The choice of a coarse-grained conception of content is a decision about how to describe the sentences that one might find in a belief box, not an assumption about what sets of sentences might be found in one. The decision is, thus, not a decision to idealize but, rather, to describe belief sets only in a very abstract and imprecise way. The decision does bring a problem, since there is a sharp divergence between the way beliefs are ordinarily described and the way the language of doxastic logic, interpreted this way, would describe them. But, assuming the sentence storage model were correct, this would not be a very deep or serious problem. All we need to do to avoid it is to choose a more fine-grained conception of content, one that categorizes sentences in a more revealing way. We don't want contents to be *too* fine-grained, since we want belief attributions to be capable of bringing out similarities between different sentences stored in different belief boxes—sentences that play the same roles in the respective cognitive economies of the agents storing them. But they should be individuated finely enough so that a belief attribution will reveal what is important about the stored sentence that makes the belief attribution true. This decision will to a large extent determine the logic of belief, but it will not have anything directly to say about the nature of the sets of sentences that, according to the sentence storage model, define our beliefs.

The second possible source of principles of a logic of explicit belief does concern the relations between the sentences that may be found in the belief box. Some proponents of the sentence storage model argue that a belief set must meet certain minimal standards of logical coherence in order to count as a set of beliefs at all. Christopher Cherniak, for example, notes that, "[a] collection of mynah bird utterances or snippets from the *New York Times* are chaos, and so (at most) just a sentence set, not a belief set."[8] The suggestion is that if an alleged belief box were filled with a random collection of sentences, it would not count as a belief box, and the owner of the box would not count as an agent. So, perhaps, a sentence storage theory of belief—even nonidealized belief—should impose some conditions on the relations between the sentences in the set of beliefs that is stored and, perhaps, those conditions will have consequences for the logic of explicit belief.

It is not clear, however, what constraints would be plausible. A conception of minimal rationality could at best justify some consistency requirements—perhaps a requirement that belief boxes not contain sentences that are blatantly contradictory—but it would not justify any closure or inference conditions on explicit belief. Minimal rationality may require that one *believe* certain obvious consequences of the sentences one stores in the belief box, but it cannot justify a requirement that one *store* sen-

---

[8] Cherniak (1986: 6).

tences that are obvious consequences of sentences one stores. The obvious consequences of sentences one stores are just the kind of thing that one does not need to store, since they can always be inferred when needed. Cherniak points out that it may sometimes be unreasonable to make sound inferences from one's beliefs because one's limited time and cognitive resources are better spent on other things, and Harman's principle of clutter avoidance enjoins one not to clutter one's belief box with trivial consequences. It is hard to see why even an idealized conception of explicit belief should have any deductive closure conditions. Would an agent with unlimited memory and computational power and speed have any reason to store the obvious consequences of its beliefs? Such an ideal believer might have less need to avoid clutter in its belief box, but it would also have less positive reason to add any deductive consequences to its store of explicitly represented sentences, since consequences can always be inferred when needed, cost free. Deductive closure, as a constraint on the sentence storage model's notion of *explicit* belief, is plausible neither as a normative ideal nor as an equilibrium state toward which belief sets tend.

A logic of explicit belief motivated by the storage model would reveal nothing about the inferential powers, either real or ideal, of believers, since it would be a logic of the base from which believers infer, not of the conclusions they draw from this base. Any nontrivial principles of such a logic would derive from decisions about how to describe the sentences stored, and would say nothing about the relations between the sentences themselves. The storage model would provide no motivation to idealize the concept of explicit belief and, so far as I can see, it would give rise to no problem of logical omniscience. Nothing could be easier than to design a realistic logic of explicit belief appropriate to the storage model, but such a logic would have little interest. It would not be a logic of belief in the ordinary sense since, for both real believers and logically perfect ones, most of what is believed in the ordinary sense is believed only implicitly. So let us look at the storage model's concept of implicit belief.

There are at least two different notions of implicit belief, a broad notion and a narrow notion. On the broad notion, the implicit beliefs of a believer include everything the believer is committed to in virtue of having the explicit beliefs he has—all the information that is implicit in what is explicitly stored. This will include all the deductive consequences of the explicit beliefs and, perhaps, also beliefs about what the believer does and does not (implicitly) believe. On the broad notion, implicit beliefs are by definition deductively closed, for ordinary believers as well as for those with extraordinary computational powers. The claim that something is implicitly believed says nothing about whether the believer has access to that belief—whether the believer will assert or assent to it, or act as if he thinks it is true. No one thinks that implicit belief in this broad sense is an analysis of belief in the ordinary sense; all that is claimed for it is that it is a notion of some interest. The logic of implicit belief, in this sense, is simple and unproblematic: it is a normal modal logic, with an assumption of logical omniscience. But implicit belief in this sense tells us no more than explicit belief about the inferential powers of the believer.

Something is an implicit belief in the narrower sense only if it "is *easily* inferable from one's explicit beliefs."[9] Easy inferences will include both inductive and deductive consequences of explicit beliefs that obviously follow from them, and also things that can be easily inferred from the fact that something is explicitly believed. The task of clarifying implicit belief in this sense is the task of characterizing the easy inferences.

Suppose that the storage model were correct—that all of our beliefs were derivative from a set of sentences in some mental language stored in the belief box—and suppose also that we had a clear explanation of the notion of an easy inference. Would implicit belief in the narrow sense then capture the ordinary notion of belief? Not necessarily. The problem is that there is no reason to assume that even explicit beliefs will be accessible to consciousness. Harman is clear about this: "A belief," he says, "can be explicitly represented in one's mind, written down in Mentalese as it were, without necessarily being available to consciousness."[10] Harman's example of inaccessibility is a Freudian one where the inaccessibility is explained by repression. But explicit beliefs, just like beliefs that are only implicit in the broad sense, may be inaccessible because of the computational limitations of the believer. Search is a kind of computation, and if the belief box is large and full enough, the search may be a long and hard computation. But if an explicit belief is inaccessible because of the computational limitations of the believer, then the fact that something is an easy inference from it will not render it a belief, in the ordinary sense. If a belief is present to consciousness—if the agent is currently judging that it is true—then it will be reasonable to infer that the agent also believes whatever may be easily inferred by that agent from that belief. But being present in a conscious act of judgment is neither necessary nor sufficient for explicitly stored belief. Not only may explicit beliefs be tacit and inaccessible, occurrent judgments—beliefs that are neither tacit nor inaccessible—may also fail to be explicit in the storage model's sense. A belief I am actively entertaining may be something that I inferred from the contents of my belief box, and that I do not, perhaps for reasons of clutter avoidance, add to what is explicitly stored there. The problem is that the distinction between implicit and explicit belief is being used to do two

---

[9] Harman (1973: 13); my emphasis.   [10] Ibid. 14.

different jobs that one distinction is not suited to do. The manifest fact that we are not logically omniscient is a fact about our computational limitations—the fact that some of the information that is implicit in what we know or believe is, because of computational limitations, not accessible to us. To get at belief and knowledge in the ordinary sense we need a distinction between what is accessible and what is implicit but inaccessible. The explicit–implicit distinction is sometimes tacitly assumed to be this distinction. But, if it is, then it is a completely different distinction from the one that the storage model makes between two different forms in which information is represented, the distinction between propositions expressed by sentences written down in the belief box and propositions not written down there but somehow implicit in the ones that are. Now I don't see the slightest reason to take seriously this belief box myth as anything more than a highly misleading metaphor; but, even if it were literally correct as a theoretical account of the mechanism by which human beings store the information they use to guide their behavior, it would still not give us the resources to explain the distinction between accessible and inaccessible stored information, and this is the distinction we need in order to give a realistic account of belief and knowledge in the ordinary sense.

Ordinary knowledge is a *capacity*, and ordinary belief a *disposition*. Because of our computational limitations, we may have the capacity constituted by the knowledge that P, or the disposition constituted by the belief that P, while at the same time lacking the capacity or disposition that we would have if we knew or believed some deductive consequence of P. But what is the capacity or disposition a capacity or disposition to do? The storage model has nothing to say about this, and so has little promise of clarifying the problem of logical omniscience. Let me sketch a slightly different picture, one that brings in the uses to which knowledge and belief are put. This will be a very simplified and idealized model that considers only one use to which knowledge and belief are put, but it is a model that helps to bring out some of the obstacles that make it difficult to give a realistic account of knowledge and belief.

III. The Question-Answer Machine

Suppose that an agent is a question and answer machine. Its belief and knowledge are to be understood as capacities and dispositions to answer questions. Such a machine will need some mechanism or mechanisms for storing information, and some way of using that information to generate answers to the questions it receives. How it stores the information is not directly relevant to what it knows or believes. It might, for example, have lists of question-answer pairs, pictures or maps and procedural rules for reading them, vast look-up tables, or a small number of axioms and some powerful deductive rules. Or, information might be implicit in the command structure of its programs. Presumably, a necessary condition for the machine to know or believe that P will be that the information (or misinformation) that P be implicit in what is stored or represented in whatever way the machine stores information. But more will be required: the information must be available—the agent must be able to access the information in order to give answers that express the proposition that P when such an answer is appropriate. Propositions that meet the first necessary condition will be implicitly known or believed in a sense that corresponds to the storage model's broad sense of implicit belief—a sense that unproblematically satisfies the logical omniscience condition. But the set of propositions that also meets an appropriate accessibility condition need not be closed under logical consequence.

But how will the accessibility condition be spelled out? There are at least three problems. First, accessibility is clearly a matter of degree. There are questions I can answer quickly with a moment's thought or a minor calculation, and questions that I have the computational resources to answer eventually, but only after a lot of time and effort. For some questions of the latter kind, I may be able to say outright that I have the capacity to produce the answer eventually; for others, I may in fact be able to produce an answer, if I choose the right computational strategy, but may be unable to say whether I can until I actually produce the answer. How easy must the search or computation be in order for the answer to count as something the agent already knows or believes, and not just something it has the capacity to come to know or believe? I assume you know your multiplication tables—you know, for example, that 6 times 4 equals 24. And no doubt you also know certain simple arithmetic truths that it is not plausible to assume are memorized, for example, that 47 times 100 equals 4,700, and that 385 is not a prime number. It is equally clear that you do not know the prime factors of 75,563, even though you know that you could figure it out and might even be able to put a limit on how long it would take you. But there are intermediate cases that are not so clear. There is obviously a continuum here, and no very natural place to draw a line between information that is easily accessible and information that is not. I don't think this is a serious problem. Attribution of knowledge and belief are obviously highly context-dependent, and the line between what we already know and what we could come to know if we made the effort may be one thing determined somewhat arbitrarily in different ways in different situations. A more serious problem is this: on this model, information is accessed in response to a question, and the ease of access will depend on the question. The same proposition may be an answer to different questions, and whatever one's standards for easy access, the proposition may be easy to access in response to one question, but not to another. For example, it will take you much longer to answer the question, "What are the prime factors of 1591?," than it will the question, "Is it the case that 43 and 37 are the prime factors of 1591?" But the answers to the two questions have the same content, even on a very fine-grained notion of content. Suppose that we fix the threshold of accessibility so that the information that 43 and 37 are the prime factors of 1591 is accessible in response to the second question, but not accessible in response to the first. Do you know what the prime factors of 1591 are or not? The problem is not that the two different questions will affect your knowledge differently—that the second question, but not the first, will bring it about that you know (not just implicitly) what the prime factors of 1591 are. It seems to be a fact, not a problem, that questions—even nonleading questions without presuppositions—can change what we know and believe by bringing out what was previously merely implicit in what we believed. This is the familiar lesson of the Socratic method, made explicit in the *Meno*.[11] Our problem is that we are not just trying to say what an agent would know upon being asked certain questions; rather, we are trying to use the facts about an agent's question-answering capacities in order to get at what the agent knows, even if the questions are not asked. But attributions of knowledge and belief are not tied to any particular questions that the knowledge or beliefs might be used to answer. More generally, the problem is that we need to understand knowledge and belief as capacities and dispositions—states that involve the capacity to access information, and not just its storage— in order to distinguish what we actually know and believe, in the ordinary sense, from what we know and believe only implicitly. We can do this only by bringing the uses to which knowledge and belief are put into the concepts of knowledge and belief themselves, but, on the face of it, it does not seem that when we attribute knowledge or belief to someone we are making any claims about what the agent plans to do with that information.

Finally, even if we had a satisfactory account of accessibility for the question and answer model, it would not be clear how to generalize it to an account of knowledge and belief in terms of capacities and dispositions to use information (or misinformation) to guide not just one's question-answering behavior, but one's rational actions generally. For we want an account of knowledge and belief, not just for expert systems and people who staff information booths, but for all kinds of agents. We want a notion

---

[11] Cf. Powers (1978).

that helps to explain why people do what they do, in their nonlinguistic as well as their linguistic behavior. Very roughly, I know whether P if I have the capacity to make my actions depend on whether P. But, I may have this capacity for some actions, and not for others. Consider, for example, a shrewd but inarticulate chess player who may be able to access information for the purpose of choosing a move even if she is unable to access that same information for the purpose of answering a question, or giving an explanation of why she moved as she did. In the general case, it is even clearer that the accessibility of knowledge and belief can be understood only relative to the actions they are being used to guide.

The problem of logical omniscience, I am suggesting, is the problem of accessibility. The reason we idealize in our logics of knowledge and belief is because we have a much clearer conception of implicit knowledge and belief—the information or informational content that we store—than we do of accessible knowledge and belief—the information and belief that is available to guide behavior. The storage model may yield a logic of explicit belief that avoids logical omniscience, but it does it by avoiding the real problem. We won't have a clear understanding of knowledge and belief, and of an important part of cognition, until we address this question.

14

The Problem of Logical Omniscience, II

Logics of belief and knowledge tend to assume principles that imply that an agent believes or knows all logical truths, and all logical consequences of whatever he believes or knows. It has been widely recognized since logics of knowledge were first proposed more than thirty years ago that they have these consequences, and it is of course obvious that they are false of actual knowers and believers, so why do theorists continue to give formal representations of knowledge and belief that diverge in this way from what is obviously true? This divergence is thought to raise a problem: the problem of logical omniscience. But what is the problem? Why is the divergence not simply a reason to reject the logical principles that have these false consequences?

I will argue that there is a problem, and make some attempt to get a little clearer about what it is. I will suggest that it is a problem that reveals a tension in a familiar conception of rationality, in assumptions that our folk theories share with attempts at more scientific theories of cognition and rationality.

In an earlier discussion of this problem,[1] I considered a conception of knowledge and belief that does not face a problem of logical omniscience. This was the sentence storage, or "belief box" conception according to which an agent's beliefs are determined by a set of sentences (perhaps of a language of thought) stored in memory. To believe (explicitly) that P is to store a sentence that expresses the proposition that P. I argued that this conception of belief fails to address the real problem, which concerns the distinction between information that is *available* to the agent and information that is merely implicit, a distinction that fails to coincide, even in the context of the belief box model, with the distinction between information that is explicitly represented and information that is implicit in what is explicitly represented. In this paper I will consider a different theoretical account of knowledge—an account that explains knowledge independently of language and linguistic structure. The "knowers" in the theoretical model I will discuss are far simpler and more well behaved,

---

[1] "The Problem of Logical Omniscience, I," reprinted in Ch. 13 of the present volume.

in some cases, than the human agents that are our main concern, and the conception of knowledge is abstract and highly idealized. But the simplicity and transparency of this conception of knowledge helps to reveal the shape of the problem of logical omniscience that it faces, and I think the problem as it arises in this simple context is similar enough to our problem to be revealing.

I will begin by sketching the theoretical account, an account that has been developed and used by theoretical computer scientists for the purpose of giving abstract descriptions of distributed computer systems and the programs and protocols that they run.[2] Then I will say why there is a problem of logical omniscience in the context of this account, and consider some ways that the account might be elaborated to solve it. Most of the constructive suggestions that I will explore are not successful, but I think they help to bring out some of the different dimensions of the problem.

A distributed system, abstractly characterized, consists of a set of interconnected processors—finite state machines. They might be components of a parallel processing computer, or microcomputers that are connected in an office network, or parts of an electronic mail system. Or they might be interacting human beings. One participant in the system might be a null processor—"nature," whose states represent information about the world outside of the system. Each of the participants in the system is capable of being in a range of states, and for the purposes of the theory's abstract description, all that matters about the participant is the set of states it is capable of being in, and the relations between the states of the different participants. To specify the state of the system as a whole—its *global state*—is to specify the local states of each of the components of the system. But not every sequence of local states will be an admissible global state. The system is governed by rules that constrain the possible global states, and the transitions between states, rules that will be realized by the connections between the processors and the programs they are running. These constraints might be specified by giving a set of global states that are candidates to be the initial states of the system, and a binary transition relation that says which global states can follow which. An admissible global state can then be defined recursively as either an initial state, or a state that can be reached by the transition rules from an admissible state. For understanding how such a system works, it is obviously important to know what the different processors "know" about what is going on in other parts of the system. In designing programs for such systems, the programmers may want to make some action of a processor depend on

---

[2] See Fagin and Halpern (1995) for a survey of the theoretical developments and applications.

whether some proposition is true of the system as a whole, but they can do so only if the processor in question has the capacity to make its actions depend on whether that proportion is true. This capacity, it seems reasonable to suggest, is what knowledge is: to know whether P is to have the capacity to make one's actions depend on whether P. So the programmers need to know what the processors know, under various conditions, and the theorists need, in their abstract description of such systems, a characterization of what the processors know, including what they know about what other processors know. A distributed system is like a community of rational agents interacting, cooperating, and possibly competing. Like such a community, the participants in the system may need to coordinate their actions, which requires knowing about the knowledge and expectations of others.

The propositions that are the contents of the knowledge of processors in such a system are represented by sets of possible global states (or, in some cases, by possible global histories, since we may be interested in what a processor knows about how the system came to be in the global state it is currently in).[3] A processor knows that P if it knows that the global state or history of the system is a member of the set of global states or histories in which P is true. What is required for the processor to know this is that the global fact that P be reflected in the current local state of that processor. If the processor is in a local state that (according to the rules governing the system) it can be in only when the system as a whole is in one of the global states in the set determined by P, then it knows that P. If a processor's local state depends on whether P, then it knows whether P. This account of knowledge is a special case of the standard possible worlds semantics for interpreting epistemic logic. This standard semantics defines knowledge in terms of a set of possible worlds, and a relation of *epistemic accessibility*, which determines for each possible world the set of possible worlds that are compatible with what the knower knows in that world. The knower knows that P in possible world α if and only if P is true in all possible worlds that are accessible to α. In the more abstract semantics, possible worlds and the epistemic accessibility relations are unanalyzed

---

[3] If the "possible worlds" are taken to be global histories rather than global states, then propositions about what participants know will be time-dependent. In one and the same possible world (global history) a processor may know that P at one time, but not at another. Furthermore, the contents of knowledge claims will have to include a temporal dimension. One might (at a certain time) know what world one is in, but be ignorant of one's temporal location in the world. (Suppose there is only one admissible global history in which i can be in local state s, but in that history, i is in that state more than once.) There are interesting problems here that parallel familiar problems about indexical knowledge and belief, but for present purposes, I will ignore the temporal complications by staying with the simpler static models in which the propositions are all about the current global state.

primitives, but in the distributed systems theory, a possible world—a possible global state or history—is a complex object made up of a collection of local states, or by a sequence of such collections. The relations of epistemic accessibility are not additional primitives, but are defined in terms of the internal structure of the possible worlds. Epistemic accessibility is quite simple: global state g is epistemically accessible to global state h for processor i if and only if $g_i = h_i$, where g_i and h_i are the local states of i that are the components of g and h, respectively. This is an equivalence relation, so the logic of knowledge it yields is an S5 logic.[4] And, of course, like all the standard modal logics of knowledge, it implies a principle of logical omniscience.

As distributed systems theorists have emphasized, their conception of knowledge is an externalist one in the sense that the content of a knowledge claim is characterized from the point of view of the theorist, and not of the knower. The language of the epistemic logic talks about what processors know, but it is not intended to model the knower's way of expressing or representing what it knows. The content clause in a knowledge attribution in this language is the attributor's way of expressing the information about the system that, according to the attribution, is reflected in the local state of the knower. Nothing is said or implied about either the form in which the processor represents its knowledge, or how it would express it, or whether the knower has the capacity to express its knowledge at all. The participants in a distributed system might be language users: their actions might include the sending and receiving of messages, and the capacity to read and interpret messages—but they need not be. Their local states might include the storage of data in linguistic form, but they need not include this. And whether the processors are users of

---

[4] Both theoretical computer scientists and game theorists standardly assume, in theorizing about knowledge, that it has an S5 structure, which is appropriate only if one blurs the distinction between knowledge and belief by ignoring the possibility of error. As Jaakko Hintikka noted in the earliest work on epistemic logic, the S5 "negative introspection" principle, $\sim K\phi \rightarrow K \sim K\phi$, has no plausibility, since it implies that if one falsely believes that one knows that ϕ, then one both believes that one knows ϕ, and knows that one does not know ϕ (see Hintikka 1962). But if one makes the idealizing assumption that there is no error (in any possible world compatible with any agent's beliefs) then the assumption becomes more reasonable, since under that assumption, knowledge will coincide with belief.

This idealization (which is independent of the kind of idealization that is required for logical omniscience) may be appropriate for some purposes, but the possibility of error is important for computer science and economic applications, and not only for epistemology. Computers can break down, and theoretical computer scientists are concerned with fault detection, and with the consequences of breakdowns of various kinds. Game theorists must take account of counterfactual reasoning, including reasoning about what a player would believe and do if she were to discover that what she in fact knows were false. If doxastic and epistemic models are to be applied to such problems, they will have to go beyond the simple S5 models.

language or not, it cannot be assumed that the structure of the clause used to attribute knowledge is reflected in the local state of the processor that constitutes its knowledge. Let me illustrate this kind of externalism with an abstract example of a simple distributed systems model. Suppose there are three participants in the system, NATURE, ALICE and BOB. There are two possible states of NATURE; call them p and q. ALICE has three possible local states, a, b and c, and BOB has just two possible local states, d and e. There are just four admissible global states: w=pad, x=pbd, y=pde and z=qce. So the system can be represented by the following diagram:

Let ϕ express the proposition that NATURE is in state p—the proposition {w,x,y}. Suppose that the actual global state is in fact w. As one can check by routine calculation, the following conclusions can be drawn: Both ALICE and BOB know that ϕ, and each knows that each knows that ϕ. But BOB does not know whether ALICE knows that Bob knows that ϕ, and furthermore, ALICE knows that BOB does not know this. This very complex knowledge attribution is true of ALICE even though that component of the system is capable of being in only three local states. According to the semantics, the sentence, "BOB does not know whether ALICE knows that BOB knows that ϕ" expresses, in this model, the proposition {w,x}, and since the local state of ALICE in w is a, and since this local state reflects the fact that the system is in one of these two global states, ALICE knows this proposition, even though she does not have anything like the concept of knowledge, or a representation of BOB, or of the proposition ϕ. The concepts are the theorist's concepts: they describe, but are not attributed to the participants of the system.

The model is of course an absurdly simple one, and any concept of knowledge that is broad enough to apply to it is highly artificial. One-bit memories such as BOB do not really know things in the sense that we do. One might think that the uncompromising externalism that I have been illustrating is one of the features that distinguishes the simplified, perhaps metaphorical, conception of knowledge used in distributed systems theory from a realistic conception: knowledge in the ordinary sense applied to

ordinary knowers, and that perhaps this feature explains why, in the distributed systems sense of "know," even simple processors with no computational capacities at all know all the logical consequences of their
knowledge, while in the sense of "know" we ordinarily use, even the most
brilliant logician does not. But I don't think this is the root of the problem,
since I think our ordinary concept of knowledge is an externalist one in
the same sense. Real knowledge must be available in some sense, but the
knower need not be able to say what he knows; much of what we know is
manifested in action, but not in speech, and so it cannot be required by
our concept of knowledge that we describe knowledge the way the knower
would express it. Nor is it reasonable to take a knowledge attribution to
make a claim about the form in which the knowledge is stored. The form
in which information is stored—the structure of the local states of knowers in virtue of which they are correctly described as knowing things—will
have an effect on the availability of the knowledge, but it is the notion of
availability itself, and not what may influence it, that we need to get clear
about to understand the problem of logical omniscience. There is a problem of logical omniscience for the concept of knowledge defined in distributed systems theory, in fact a problem with some urgency. I think it is
essentially the same problem as the one that infects our ordinary concepts
of knowledge and belief, and that getting clear about how the problem
arises in this simpler setting will help us understand how it arises for us.

So why is there a problem of logical omniscience for distributed systems
theory? It is no part of that project to give an account of knowledge in our
ordinary sense, and so the fact that their concept has features not shared by
the ordinary one is not a problem. And this concept of knowledge does not
involve the kind of idealization that assumes that the knowers it applies to
have unrealistic computational capacities. The simplest real processors
really do know, in the intended sense of "know," all the logical consequences
of their knowledge. So why should distributed systems theorists be concerned that their concept of knowledge commits them to the logical omniscience of knowers? If we look back at what the theory wants from its
concept, we can see why there is a problem. The role of this theory's concept
of knowledge is to provide a way to characterize the location in a distributed system of various pieces of information about the state of the system.
Theorists and programmers want this kind of characterization for the purpose of identifying the places where the actions of the components of the
system can be made dependent on information about the system. Suppose
that progress on the computational task at hand calls for a certain processor to do, at a certain point in the execution of the task, one thing if ϕ,
another if $\sim\phi$. To know whether this is feasible, we need to know whether
the processor will know whether ϕ at the appropriate time, or how to

arrange the flow of information so that it does. But for this purpose, we need to know not just what information is implicit in the local state of a processor, but what information is available or usable for the purpose of making a decision. Any deductive consequence of information implicit in a local state will also be implicit in that state, and so will be known according to this concept of knowledge even if there is no way for the information to make a difference to the decisions of the processor that is in that state. What the theory needs is a concept that characterizes the available information. But this is the same problem that underlies the problem of logical omniscience as a problem about our ordinary concept of knowledge.

Here is a simple illustration: Suppose we have a processor with a twenty-bit memory, and so with just over a million possible local states. The input to the machine is an integer between one and a million. The processor has two possible actions, "yes" and "no," and we want it to output a "yes" when and only when the input integer is prime. Suppose the integer is 1591, so the processor goes into local state #1591. Does it now know whether the number is prime? Yes, since the processor is in state #1591 only when the input integer is composite. There is an internal property of the processor—a feature of its local state—that corresponds to the input integer being prime. But the problem is, there may be no way to make an action depend on that feature of the state. The information is there, but it may not be available. Even in such a simple case it is not easy to say just what it is for information to be usable without saying more about the decision-making capacities of the processor, but it is not hard to illustrate the difference between the case where it is plausible to say that the information is available and the case where it is not. Assuming that our integers are represented in the usual binary notion, it seems plausible to say that the processor knows, and has available, the information that the integer is, or is not, even. The property of the local state that reflects this property of the input integer is a *simple* feature of the local state, one that could easily be used to determine an output. One might adopt a notational system in which the information whether the number was prime was reflected in the same simple way. (I have invented this fantastically fast machine that will tell you in a few nanoseconds, for any positive integer, no matter how large, whether or not it is prime. In fact, you don't even have to input the whole number—just the last digit. But you do have to use the machine's notational system, which uses the usual binary numerals in the following non-standard way: for each positive integer n, the $(2n-1)$th numeral denotes the nth prime, and the $(2n)$th numeral denotes the nth nonprime.)

On the unreconstructed distributed system conception of knowledge, a processor knows that ϕ just in case the processor has some internal property F that it has only if ф, where an internal property is a property that depends only on the local state of the processor. We might try to get at the usable or available knowledge by selecting some subset of these internal properties—the ones that were simple enough to have the capacity to control action. A property of a local state F would be one of the selected ones just in case it would be feasible to program the processor to do something (send some output signal or go into some designated internal state) if and only if it had property F. According to this suggestion, a processor's knowledge that ф would be said to be available if and only if an internal property in virtue of which it knows that ф is one of the *selected* internal properties. But whatever the criteria for selection, this change, by itself, would have no effect on the logic of knowledge. If x's knowledge that ф is available in this sense, then x has a selected internal property that it has only if ф; if ф entails ψ, then it will have that same property only if ψ, so its knowledge that ψ will also be *available* knowledge that ψ. The abstract account of available knowledge is the same as the original account of knowledge: all we have done is to give a coarser characterization of the set of local states. To avoid the consequence of logical omniscience, we need to strengthen the definition of available knowledge by requiring that x's knowledge that ф be available only if ф is *sufficient*, as well as necessary, for the processor to have the selected internal property: x's knowledge that ф is available if and only if x has a selected internal property that it has *if*, as well as only if ф. Or equivalently, we need to require that for some selected internal property of x, ф is the strongest piece of information carried by the fact that x has that property.[5]

This conception of available knowledge would avoid logical omniscience, and it would avoid this consequence by taking account of at least one of the sources of the problem—the fact that some information that a

---

[5] This suggestion might be compared with proposals made by Fred Dretske in the course of trying to give an information theoretic account of semantic content and belief. Dretske (using familiar terminology in an idiosyncratic way) distinguished what he called digital and analogue ways of carrying information. "I will say that a signal (structure, event, state) carries the information that *s* is *F* in *digital* form if and only if the signal carries no additional information about *s* that is *not* nested in *s*'s being F" (Dretske 1981: 137). Dretske then identifies the semantic content of a structure with the information that the structure carries in digital form. Dretske's proposal differs from the suggestion we are considering in at least two ways: first, for Dretske, a structure may carry the information that *s* is *F* in digital form even if it carries additional information not entailed by this information, so long as the additional information is not information *about s*. But Dretske says little about the notoriously problematic notion of aboutness. Second, for Dretske, as I understand him, it is concrete signals, structures and events that must carry no additional information about *s*, if the information is to be carried in digital form. But our suggestion is that knowledge that *P* requires only that there be some selected feature of the local state such that *P* is the strongest information carried by the fact that the local state has that feature.

knower has is unavailable because that information is embedded in stronger information from which it cannot easily be extracted. But this kind of analysis introduces an element of relativity into our conception of knowledge—relativity to the actions that knowledge is used to guide. For what knowledge is available, on this account, depends on the properties or features of the local state of the knower that can be used to control action. But the feasibility of making action depend on a feature of a local state depends on the action. Information-carrying features of a knower that are too complex to be accessed for some purposes may be just right for others. An action may itself be complex: consider, for example, a complex physical movement performed by an animal or a robot, requiring a coordinated sequence of individual muscle contractions or other physical changes: A snake strikes at its prey, or retreats from a predator; a robot picks up a block, or moves around an obstacle; an outfielder chases down a fly ball, or ducks to avoids a beer bottle thrown by a fan. Whether, when, and exactly how such actions are performed will depend on subtle details of the agent's representation of the world, but for the relevant information implicit in the agent's representation to be available for the purpose of guiding such actions, there won't necessarily have to be some simple local state that carries the information. It may in fact help for the information-carrying state to be complex in ways that correspond to the complexity of the task that the information is being used to guide. Does the experienced outfielder know just when and where the ball is going to come down? Not for the purpose of answering the question, "Exactly when and where is the ball going to come down?" but for the purpose of getting to the right place at the right time to catch the ball, he does. If we are to define a kind of knowledge that requires availability, we need a notion that is relative to the uses to which the knowledge might be put.

This kind of relativity may be an inevitable feature of a conception of knowledge that is restricted to available or accessible knowledge, but even if we take for granted the distinction between features of local states that are available to control action and those that are not, there are at least two serious problems with the kind of analysis that I have sketched, problems that I think show that there are additional dimensions to the problem of logical omniscience. The account is too strong in some ways, and too weak in others, to capture the intuitive notion of available knowledge. First, by requiring that knowers have a completely general procedure for determining the truth of a proposition under all conditions in order to know whether it is true, the analysis rules out cases that seem, intuitively, to be cases of available knowledge. Second, while the analysis avoids full logical omniscience, the equivalence principle still holds for this conception of knowledge, which means that it implies that we know more of the

consequences of our knowledge than we should know according to a realistic account of available knowledge.

On the first problem: it is too demanding to require, for available knowledge, a selected feature of the internal state that is, or even tends to be,
both necessary and sufficient for the truth of what is known. Consider
again our prime number example. Suppose I am given the integers 3,232
and 13. Do I know whether these integers are prime? Yes: the first is not,
but the second is. This information seems to be available to me even
though I have no general procedure for telling, quickly, whether any given
integer is prime; there is no accessible feature of my internal epistemic
state that is both necessary and sufficient for the integer I am given being
prime. The knowledge that the number is not prime is, in the first case,
embedded in the stronger information that the number is an *even* non-
prime, and I can reliably identify that property in all cases. The knowledge
that the number is prime, in the second case, is embedded in the stronger
information that the number is on a list of small primes that I have perhaps stored in memory. More generally, a knower's epistemic state might
be capable of having any of three alternative available features that tend to
carry information about some proposition ϕ: one that the knower is in
only if ϕ is true, one that it is in only if ϕ is false, and one that it is in sometimes when ϕ is true, sometimes when ϕ is false. The states might be
labeled "yes," "no" and "maybe." The "yes" state carries the information
that ϕ, by carrying more information: ϕ is not only true, it is verifiably
true. Although the "yes" state is sufficient for ϕ, it is not necessary, and so
it does not give the agent available knowledge according to the kind of
analysis we are considering. But almost all cases of knowledge in the
ordinary sense will be like this. So long as it is possible (which means, in
the distributed systems model, compatible with the rules of the system)
that ϕ be true without the knower having even implicit knowledge of it,
there can be no internal property, selected or not, of a local state that is
both necessary and sufficient for ϕ, and so no available knowledge that ϕ
in the sense defined.[6]

It is not easy to see how to modify the account of available knowledge
to avoid this problem. Suppose, generalizing from our example, we tried

---

[6] I think this point shows that Dretske's notion of digital information will have far less
application than he suggests, and cannot, without modification, do the work he uses it to
do in *Knowledge and the Flow of Information*. For suppose it is possible for s to be F without x knowing it (even implicitly). Then any state of x that carries the information that s is
F will carry more information about s: that s is (implicitly) known by x to be F. Perhaps the
account of aboutness will say that this is not really information *about* s. But however aboutness is explained, if there are facts about s that are nomically or conceptually necessary for
knowledge that s is F, but not necessary for s to be F, then knowledge that s is F in digital
form, in Dretske's sense, will not be possible.

saying that x's knowledge whether φ is available provided x's local state has one of two alternative selected features: one (a "yes" feature) sufficient for φ and the other (a "no" feature) sufficient for ~φ. This is much too weak; according to this suggestion, our machine will know, without doing any computation, that 1591 is non-prime, since being in state #1591 is sufficient for the input integer being non-prime, and there are alternative states—for example state #1571—that are sufficient for being prime. This proposed weakening of our account of available knowledge would take us back to something very close to full logical omniscience.[7]

The notion of availability that we are trying to capture is availability for the purpose of determining action. Intuitively, the information φ is available to an agent provided the agent has the capacity to make its actions depend on whether φ. The problem is that it is too much to ask that the agent have the capacity to make its actions depend on whether φ in all cases in order for it to know whether φ in some particular case. Suppose I can make my actions depend on whether φ only under condition ψ. Then provided that condition ψ obtains, won't this be enough to make available my knowledge whether φ? But the problem is to distinguish the case for which this description seems appropriate from the general case in which one's knowledge that φ is implicit in one's knowledge of something that entails it. Suppose I can make my action depend on whether the input integer is 1571 (which entails that the input integer is prime), and I can also make my action depend on whether the input integer is 1591 (which entails that it is not prime). Then I have the capacity to make my action depend on whether the input integer is prime under condition *the input integer is either 1571 or 1591*. But as we have seen, this can happen when, intuitively, I don't *know* that 1571 is prime, or at least don't have this knowledge available, and so don't know that I am making my action depend on whether the number is prime. It seems that the distinction we need to explain the availability of knowledge presupposes that notion.

The distinction we need (the distinction between *knowledge, under condition ψ, that φ* and *knowledge that φ&ψ*) could be made if we could legitimately appeal to the content of the *motivational* states of our agent. The following seems intuitively plausible: An agent's knowledge that φ is available under condition ψ, provided that the agent has the capacity to make its action depend on φ under that condition, *and is disposed, under that condition, to make its action depend on whether φ whenever it wants its action to depend on whether φ*. In the prime number case, the reason it was not plausible to say that our agent knows that the input integer is prime

---

[7] More specifically, the proposal implies that if *x* has available knowledge that φ, and φ entails ψ, then provided it is possible for *x* to have available knowledge that χ for some χ that entails ~ψ, *x* has available knowledge that ψ.

when it is 1571 is that if the agent's decision rule was: "say 'yes' when and only when the number is prime," it would not be in a position to say "yes" in response to receiving the number 1571. But the problem is that we have no independent way to assign content to the motivational states. If we are talking just about machines and systems that we build and program to serve our needs, then it will be easy to see how to interpret the content of the "wants" of the processors, but we want our theory to apply also to organisms and systems that we find, and want to understand as autonomous agents. In our externalist account of knowledge, the information-bearing states of participants in the system have the (implicit) content they do because of the structure of the system—the constraints imposed by that structure on the relation between the internal states of the participant and the global states of the system of which it is a part. If our theory is to contribute to an explanation of intentionality, then the decision rules and motivational states should also get their content from the structure of the system, and not be imposed from outside by the intentions and desires of the users. Motivational states should derive their content from the dispositions of the participant to make its actions depend on the information it has. But it will be the dispositions to use the *available* knowledge, not the implicit knowledge, that will determine the content of decision rules and motivational states.

What our machine succeeds in doing, let us suppose, is to perform a certain action (which we may interpret as answering "yes" to the question, "is the number prime?" but that is our interpretation) only, but not always, when the input integer is prime. That is, it says "yes" when and only when the input integer is prime, and also meets some condition ϕ. The number 1571 fails to meet condition ϕ, so the machine does not perform this action when it is in state #1571. If the disposition to behave in this way is interpreted as a "desire" to say "yes" when and only when the number is prime, then the information implicit in state #1571 that the number is prime will be interpreted as unavailable information, while in a case—say the number 13—where the number meets the additional condition, the information that the number is prime will be interpreted as available. But if that same disposition is interpreted as the desire to say "yes" when and only when the number is prime and meets condition ϕ, then the information that the number is prime is not available in either case. What on one interpretation is partial success at identifying prime numbers is on another interpretation complete success at identifying a property that is sufficient but not necessary for being a prime number.[8]

---

[8] One can see here echoes of two themes that often arise in discussions of the problem of intentionality. First, there is the familiar potential for indeterminacy in the dispositional account of rationality. If belief and desire are correlative dispositional states, then any

Even if what knowledge a participant in a system has available will depend on how we interpret the way it is using its knowledge—on what we take it to be trying to do—if the system is sufficiently complex, there will be lots of constraints that reduce the indeterminacy of interpretation. The point is not that the distinction between available and merely implicit knowledge is arbitrary, but that it is not an isolable feature of the cognitive capacities of the knower, but is essentially connected to its motivations and actions.

The problem we have been discussing began with the observation that a proposal for characterizing available knowledge was too demanding. The second problem shows that the proposal is not demanding enough. The problem is that, while this proposal avoids full logical omniscience, it still gives us the equivalence property for available knowledge: If ϕ is necessarily equivalent to ψ, then x has available knowledge that ϕ if and only if x has available knowledge that ψ. But from an intuitive point of view, this is almost as bad as logical omniscience. It seems that our attempts to build availability into our conception of knowledge have bought us very little.

To get clear about this problem, in the context of the kind of theory we have been discussing, consider again our machine whose input is a representation of an integer between one and a million. According to the original proposal, the reason the knowledge that the input number, 1571, is prime was unavailable was that the internal property that is necessary and sufficient for carrying this information is a complex one that could not, without solving a hard computational problem, be used to control the processor's output. In contrast, the knowledge that the number is odd did seem available, since the state of just one of its binary digits is necessary and sufficient for the processor to be carrying this information, and it would be easy to use this property to control the output. But now consider, not the proposition that the input integer is prime, but the proposition that it is the sum of two odd primes. Suppose the input integer is 1572. Is the information that this number is the sum of two odd primes available? It seems that according to the proposal we are considering, it is since all the

hypothesis about the content of beliefs can be defended by manipulating the content of the desires, and vice versa. I and others have argued that the assumption that belief states are information-bearing states whose content is constrained by their counterfactual dependency on facts about the environment helps to resolve some of the indeterminacy, but here we see that a version of the problem recurs in the attempt to distinguish available from merely implicit information. Second, there is the familiar problem of misrepresentation: the disjunction problem. If a person is disposed to think "horse" when he sees either horses or, under certain unusual conditions, cows, why do we say that the content is HORSE, and the latter cases are misrepresentations, rather than that the content is HORSE OR COW UNDER CERTAIN UNUSUAL CONDITIONS? Here we see that a version of this problem can arise in the attempt to distinguish available from implicit information, even if we ignore error, assuming that (implicit) belief and knowledge coincide.

processor has to do is to consult the last digit, and then check that the integer is greater than four—an easy computational task. But suppose our processor hasn't heard of Goldbach's conjecture, or isn't sure whether it is true, even for the first million integers? (Suppose that our poor processor, on receiving this input, painstakingly checks for primeness each member of each pair of positive integers whose sum is 1572 until it finds a pair of odd primes. But it hasn't found one yet.) According to the conception of available knowledge we are considering, the knower's ignorance of this mathematical fact is not relevant. The information that the number is the sum of two odd primes is the same as the information that the number is even and greater than four; it is just differently described. The processor has that information, and it is available.

In the case of distributed systems, we might distinguish two problems of logical omniscience—one for the processor, and one for the programmer. In some cases, while there is an internal property of the processor that it has if and only if ϕ, the information that ϕ is inaccessible to the processor because the property is a complex one that cannot be used to control the output. In other cases, there is a simple internal property, available to control output, that the processor has if and only if ϕ, but it is a hard computational problem to figure out that this internal property is one that the machine has if and only if ϕ. The first problem is the processor's problem. It can be programmed to make use of the information that ϕ, only if it has the capacity to do the computation that puts it into a simple and accessible state that carries the information that ϕ. But the second problem is the programmer's problem. If the programmer in our example knows or assumes that Goldbach's conjecture is true, and wants a decision of the machine to turn on whether an input integer is the sum of two odd primes or not, then she will have no difficulty writing a program that does this. The second problem—the equivalence problem—looks like a problem about how it is appropriate to describe the knower's capacities, and not a problem about the knower's capacities themselves.

This characterization of the different problems may be appropriate when we are asking about what a programmer may do with a system that has information distributed in it in a certain way, but when we turn from simple machines to the knowers we are most concerned about—ourselves—the situation is less clear. We are interested, not in how others might use the information that is in us, but in how we might use it: we like to think of ourselves as our own programmers. If I want to perform some action if and only if a certain integer I have just been given—1572 say—is the sum of two odd primes, but I don't know about or believe Goldbach's conjecture, then I don't have the capacity to make my action depend on the relevant information. The information seems, intuitively, to be unavailable to me. But on the conception of informational content implicit in the distributed systems model, the information that the input integer is the sum of two odd primes is the same as the information that the input integer is an even number greater than 4, and this information is available. It seems that we need a finer-grained notion of content, and a different account of availability.

This second kind of unavailability and the need for a finer-grained notion of content to describe it, may apply to simple distributed systems as well as to ordinary knowers, and I think it will help to get clear about the general form of the problem to see how it might arise for a participant in such a system. Suppose our processor is capable of being in two different information-bearing states (or of having two different selected internal properties) each of which would tend to carry the information that ϕ. But suppose the two states play a different role in the cognitive economy of the machine: they are differently linked with the motivational states—the states that determine the machine's output as a function of its information-bearing states. Using just our coarse-grained notion of informational content, we might say that the machine may know that ϕ in either of two different ways, and that these ways correspond to different ways in which it is disposed to make its actions depend on whether ϕ. In describing this knower—in attributing knowledge to it—it would be nice to be able to distinguish the two states in terms of their content, but "x knows that ϕ" won't do the job. The need for a more fine-grained notion of content is the need for some way of making such distinctions. But it is not clear what sort of finer grain is, in the general case, appropriate. Just as with other dimensions of the problem of logical omniscience, it depends on the use to which the knowledge is to be put—in this case, on the way in which the different information-bearing states relate to different motivational states.

Consider a special case: the question and answer machine. Suppose there are two sentences, S_1 and S_2, in the language used by our question and answer machine that are logically equivalent, but not obviously so. Both have the informational content ϕ, but it is a hard computational problem to see that they have the same content. Suppose further that there are two different internal states of the machine, I_1 and I_2, each carrying the information that ϕ. State I_1 disposes the machine to give a "yes" answer when asked whether S_1; state I_2 on the other hand, is the state that disposes it to give a "yes" answer when asked whether S_2. Suppose this machine is in state I_1, but not in state I_2; what should we say about what the machine knows and does not know? If *our* language—the language in which we are describing the machine—is the same as the language the machine uses, then it would be natural to say that it knows that S_1, but does not know that S_2. If our language is different, but similar, with sentences whose structures parallel the structures of the machine's sentences, then it will be natural to use that-clauses made from those sentences to say what the machine knows and does not know. But it is not so clear how to generalize beyond the question and answer context. The usual way of getting more fine-grained content is to appeal to the semantic structure of sentences that have the content, and such structure is clearly relevant when the behavior that the agent's knowledge is being used to guide is the production of structured representations of what is known. But how does this apply when the relevant behavior is non-linguistic? The general problem affects not only expert systems, theorem provers, and people who staff information booths, but also animals and robots who act, but do not speak. They may have different information-bearing states that tend to carry the same information, but that play a different role in guiding rational behavior. We need a finer-grained notion of content to give perspicuous descriptions of what they know, and what knowledge they have available, but it is not clear that the semantic structure of sentences that might be used to express their knowledge will necessarily provide the relevant distinctions. Even where the knowers are language users who can express their knowledge, we may have a problem finding an appropriate way to distinguish different knowledge states that carry the same information. The standard puzzle cases in the literature about belief—Kripke's puzzling Pierre, for example—are cases that fit this pattern. But it is not the structure of Pierre's internal representations, or of the sentences he is disposed to assent to and dissent from, that distinguishes the internal state in virtue of which he believes that London is pretty from the internal state in virtue of which he disbelieves it.

The root of our second problem is the same as that of the first: to be available or usable, the information we store in our representation of the world must be appropriately calibrated to the desires or other motivational states that determine how the information is to be used. So if we want our concepts of belief and knowledge to be concepts of *available* belief and knowledge, we need concepts that are relativized to what the agent wants or seeks, and to the way that representations of how things are and representations of how one wants things to interact. We think of our ordinary concepts of knowledge and belief as concepts of available knowledge and belief—implicit knowledge and belief seem to be highly idealized and unrealistic concepts—but we are also inclined to think of knowledge and belief as states that at least ought to be independent of what we want or are inclined to try to get. There is, I think, a tension between these two assumptions about knowledge and belief that lies behind the problem of logical omniscience.

Rational creatures, or cognitive beings, are organisms or machines that are capable of making their behavior sensitive to facts about their environments. Our folk theory, as well as our attempts at more scientific theories of cognition and rationality, assume, in their explanations of this capacity, that cognitive beings have two independent but interacting components—one that is a representation of the way the world is—some kind of information storage device that tends to correlate in a systematic way with some features of the environment—and another that represents the goals, purposes, ends, desires that its actions are aiming to achieve or satisfy. What we believe—the way our information storage device represents the world to be—is supposed to be independent of what we want—our representation of an end state that we are disposed to attempt to reach. Our belief states are part of our capacity to achieve our ends, but they are supposed to be generalized capacities that would serve our ends whatever they happened to be. How we take the world to be may be influenced by the way we would like it to be, but such influences are regarded as distortions—wishful thinking or irrational pessimism. The problems about logical omniscience do not show that this conception of independent but interacting capacities is wrong—it just suggests that our ordinary attributions of knowledge, ignorance and belief may describe our representational states in a way that is more dependent on their relation to motivational states than we are inclined to suppose.

All of these problems we have been discussing arise because we are trying to give a characterization of available knowledge that is general enough to cover the role of knowledge in all kinds of cognitive situations. Perhaps the problems would look less daunting if we limited ourselves to purely intellectual cognitive problems; perhaps a linguistic solution to the problem—a solution that explained availability in terms of the structure of stored mental sentences or of the utterances used to express the agent's knowledge and beliefs—would be more plausible if we restricted our domain. Suppose we distinguish the computational problems that arise for robots trying to maneuver in their environments or athletes trying to catch fly balls or sink putts from more purely intellectual computational tasks and set aside problems of the former kind. If we focus on cognitive problems that abstract away from the physical skills necessary to carry out decisions, would a linguistic solution to the problem of logical omniscience then be more promising? I don't think so. Not all purely intellectual problems are problems about what to say. Consider a chess player, or a chess-playing machine. Set aside the hard problem of giving our chess-playing machine visual sensors and a robot arm so that it can move the pieces on an actual chess board. Concentrate only on the easier problem of designing a program that will make good decisions about what moves to make. In describing what such a machine knows as it plays a game, what we are interested in is the knowledge—about the game situation, and the other player's strategic dispositions—that the player has available to determine its moves in the game. Implicit knowledge is obviously not what we are interested in: the machine, in virtue of knowing the rules of the game, has implicit in it all the information it needs to choose a game-theoretically optimal strategy—to play logically perfect chess—but it obviously can't do this, since not all this information is available. But if we are not concerned with information that is merely implicit, neither are we concerned with the information that is available to the player for the purpose of giving descriptions of, or answering questions about the game situation or the other player's strategic dispositions. The strategic insights of a player, or a program, may be inarticulate—it or she or he may know what to do without being able to explain or justify the decisions—without being able to say what information about the particular game situation makes it effective strategy to choose the particular moves it chooses. To get at the notion of available knowledge that is appropriate for this kind of case, it is not clear that an appeal to the semantic structure of the form in which the information is stored, or in which it would be expressed, would be relevant.

The game situation is a central case where the problem of logical omniscience is particularly acute. Players of games of strategy, like participants in a distributed system, and like ourselves, have, and base their actions on, knowledge and beliefs about the knowledge and beliefs of other players and participants—this is the familiar distinctive feature of the game-theoretic situation. We need a concept of available knowledge not only for the theorist's attributions of knowledge to agents in such situations, but also to characterize the content of the agents' knowledge. It is the role of iterated knowledge and common knowledge that magnifies the problem of logical omniscience when different agents interact in cooperative and competitive situations. And when we are concerned about such iterated knowledge—when we ask whether he knows that she knows that he knows that if she takes his bishop he will take her knight—the relevant concept of knowledge, at each level, is the knowledge that is available, not for describing the situation, but for deciding what to do.[9]

Even if our main concern is with articulate knowledge, and the use of knowledge and belief to explain linguistic behavior, I think it helps to see

---

[9] There is a tendency to describe a situation of inarticulate knowledge as a case where a person knows something, but does not know that he knows it. But if knowledge can be inarticulate—available for guiding nonlinguistic action, but not for the expression of the knowledge in speech—then knowledge that one knows can be so also. One might not be able to say what one knows, even if one in some sense knows that one knows it.

the problem in a more general setting: to see linguistic action as a special case of action, and the use of knowledge to say how things are as a special case of the use of knowledge to make our actions depend, in ways appropriate to our ends, on the state of the world. The special case may have a particularly strong influence on the way we think about propositional knowledge and belief, and may help to hide some tensions and problems with those concepts—in particular, the way that what we know may be relative to what we do with what we know. But I think it is clear that there is a problem of logical omniscience that is broader than a problem about how we extract from the sentences we use to express our knowledge and beliefs information that is also expressed in such sentences. And I think if we get clear about the more general problem, it will help to solve more specific problems about computation and mathematical ignorance that do essentially concern linguistic representation. The problem of the mathematician or cryptographer trying to develop faster algorithms for factoring large integers, the problem of the chess player or programmer trying to develop strategies for deciding what moves to make in a game, and the problem of the baseball player trying to learn how to hit a curve ball, are problems that are similar at a certain level of abstraction, and I think we can get clearer about all these kinds of problems by seeing the way in which they are similar. All are problems of trying to develop ways of putting information we have into a form that is available to guide action. Any creature or machine with cognitive capacities complex enough to be interesting will face such problems, and any general account of cognition must give a prominent place to the means that creatures use to solve them.

REFERENCES

Anderson, A. (1951). A note on subjunctive and counterfactual conditionals, *Analysis* **12**: 35–8.

Aqvist, L. (1973). Modal logic with subjunctive conditionals and dispositional predicates, *Journal of Philosophical Logic* **2**: 1–76.

Barwise, J., and Perry, J. (1983). *Situations and Attitudes*, MIT Press, Cambridge, Mass.

Belnap, N. (1970). Conditional assertion and restricted quantification, *Noûs* **4**: 1–13.

Bigelow, J. (1978). Believing in semantics, *Linguistics and Philosophy* **2**: 101–44.

Boër, S., and Lycan, W. (1975). Knowing who, *Philosophical Studies* **28**: 299–344.

—— —— (1980). Who, me? *Philosophical Review* **89**: 427–66.

Burge, T. (1978). Belief and synonymy, *Journal of Philosophy* **75**: 119–38.

—— (1979). Individualism and the mental, in P. French *et al.* (eds.), *Midwest Studies in Philosophy, 4, Studies in Metaphysics*, University of Minnesota Press, Minneapolis, 73–122.

Carnap, R. (1939). *Foundations of Logic and Mathematics*, University of Chicago Press, Chicago.

—— (1947). *Meaning and Necessity*, University of Chicago Press, Chicago.

Castañeda, H. (1966). "He": A study in the logic of self-consciousness, *Ratio* **8**: 130–57.

—— (1967). Indicators and quasi-indicators, *American Philosophical Quarterly* **4**: 85–100.

Cherniak, C. (1986). *Minimal Rationality*, Bradford Books, MIT Press, Cambridge, Mass.

Church, A. (1954). Intensional isomorphism and identity of belief, *Philosophical Studies* **5**: 65–73.

Churchland, P. S., and Churchland, P. M. (1983). Stalking the wild epistemic engine, *Noûs* **17**: 5–18.

Cresswell, M. J. (1973). *Logics and Languages*, Methuen, London.

—— (1985). *Structured Meanings*, Bradford Books, MIT Press, Cambridge, Mass.

Cummins, R. (1986). Inexplicit information, in M. Brand and R. Harnish (eds.), *The Representation of Knowledge*, University of Arizona Press, Tucson, 116–26.

Davidson, D. (1984a). Belief and the basis of meaning, in D. Davidson (ed.), *Inquiries into Truth and Interpretation*, Clarendon Press, Oxford, 141–54.

—— (1984b). On saying that, in D. Davidson (ed.), *Inquiries into Truth and Interpretation*, Clarendon Press, Oxford, 93–108.

—— (1986). Thought and talk, in D. Davidson (ed.), *Inquiries into Truth and Interpretation*, Clarendon Press, Oxford, 155–70.

De Sousa, R. (1971). How to give a piece of your mind: or, the logic of belief and assent, *Review of Metaphysics* **25**: 52–79.

Dennett, D. (1978). *Brainstorms*, Bradford Books, Montgomery, Vt.

—— (1982). Beyond belief, in A. Woodfield (ed.), *Thought and Object: Essays on Intentionality*, Clarendon Press, Oxford, 1–95.

—— (ed.) (1987). *The Philosophical Lexicon*, American Philosophical Association.

Donnellan, K. (1966). Reference and definite descriptions, *Philosophical Review* **75**: 281–304.

—— (1971). Proper names and identifying descriptions, in D. Davidson and G. Harman (eds.), *Semantics of Natural Language*, D. Reidel Publishing Co., Dordrecht, 356–79.

—— (1974). Speaking of nothing, *Philosophical Review* **83**: 3–31.

Dretske, F. (1981). *Knowledge and the Flow of Information*, MIT Press, Cambridge, Mass.

—— (1988). *Explaining Behavior: Reasons in a World of Causes*, Bradford Books, MIT Press, Cambridge, Mass.

Dummett, M. (1964). Bringing about the past, *Philosophical Review* **73**: 338–9.

—— (1991). *The Logical Basis of Metaphysics*, Harvard University Press, Cambridge, Mass.

Evans, G. (1982). *Varieties of Reference*, Oxford University Press, Oxford and New York.

Fagin, R., and Halpern, J. Y. (1995). *Reasoning about Knowledge*, MIT Press, Cambridge, Mass.

Field, H. (1978). Mental representation, *Erkenntnis* **13**: 9–61.

Fodor, J. (1981*a*). Methodological solipsism as a research strategy in cognitive science, in J. Fodor (ed.), *RePresentations*, Bradford Books, MIT Press, Cambridge, Mass., 225–53.

—— (1981*b*). Propositional attitudes, in J. Fodor (ed.), *RePresentations*, Bradford Books, MIT Press, Cambridge, Mass., 177–203.

—— (1987). *Psychosemantics: The Problem of Meaning in the Philosophy of Mind*, Bradford Books, MIT Press, Cambridge, Mass.

Geach, P. (1967). Intentional identity, *Journal of Philosophy* **64**: 253–5.

Goldman, A. (1976). Discrimination and perceptual knowledge, *Journal of Philosophy* **73**: 771–91.

Grice, P. (1989). *Studies in the Way of Words*, Harvard University Press, Cambridge, Mass.

Groenendijk, J., and Stokhof, M. (1990). Dynamic montague grammar, in L. Kalman *et al.* (eds.), *Proceedings of the Second Symposium on Logic and Language*, Akademiai Kiado, Budapest, 3–48.

—— —— (1991). Dynamic predicate logic, *Linguistics and Philosophy* **14**: 39–100.

Harman, G. (1973). *Thought*, Princeton University Press, Princeton.

Harman, G. (1986). *Change in View: Principles of Reasoning*, Bradford Books, MIT Press, Cambridge, Mass.

Heim, I. (1982). *The Semantics for Definite and Indefinite Noun Phrases*, PhD thesis, University of Massachusetts.

—— (1992). Presupposition projection and the semantics of attitude verbs, *Journal of Semantics* **9**: 183–221.

Hill, C. (1976). Toward a theory of meaning for belief sentences, *Philosophical Studies* **30**: 206–26.

Hintikka, J. (1962). *Knowledge and Belief*, Ithaca, NY.

—— (1975). *The Intentions of Intentionality and other Modes of Modality*, Dordrecht.

Jeffrey, R. (1983). *The Logic of Decision*, 2nd edn., University of Chicago Press, Chicago.

Kamp, H. (1971). Formal properties of "now", *Theoria* **37**: 227–73.

—— (1988). Comments, in R. Grim and D. Merrill (eds.), *Contents of Thought*, University of Arizona Press, Tucson, 156–81.

——, and Reyle, U. (1993). *From Discourse to Logic*, Kluwer, Dordrecht.

Kaplan, D. (1969). Quantifying in, in D. Davison and J. Hintikka (eds.), *Words and Objections: Essays on the Work of W. V. Quine*, Reidel, Dordrecht, 178–214.

—— (1989). Demonstratives, in J. Almog *et al.* (eds.), *Themes From Kaplan*, Oxford University Press, Oxford, 481–563.

Karttunen, L. (1971). Some observations on factivity, *Papers in Linguistics* **4**: 55–69.

—— (1973). Presuppositions of compound sentences, *Linguistic Inquiry* **4**: 169–93.

Kripke, S. (1972). *Naming and Necessity*, Harvard University Press, Cambridge, Mass.

—— (1979). A puzzle about belief, in A. Margalit (ed.), *Meaning and Use*, Reidel, Dordrecht, 239–83.

Langendoen, D. T. (1971). Presupposition and assertion in the semantic analysis of nouns and verbs in English, in D. D. Steinberg and L. A. Jakobovits (eds.), *Semantics: An Interdisciplinary Reader in Philosophy, Linguistics and Psychology*, Cambridge University Press, Cambridge, 341–4.

Lau, J. (1994). *Belief in Semantics and Philosophy*, PhD thesis, MIT, Cambridge, Mass.

Lewis, D. (1969). *Convention*, Harvard University Press, Cambridge, Mass.

—— (1970). General semantics, *Synthese* **22**: 18–67.

—— (1973). *Counterfactuals*, Harvard University Press, Cambridge, Mass.

—— (1979*a*). Attitudes *de dicto* and *de se*, *Philosophical Review* **88**: 513–43.

—— (1979*b*). A problem about permission, in E. Saarinen *et al.* (eds.), *Essays in Honour of Jaakko Hintikka*, Reidel, Dordrecht, 163–75.

—— (1979*c*). Scorekeeping in a language game, *Journal of Philosophical Logic* **8**: 339–59.

—— (1981). Index, context and content, in S. Kanger and S. Öhman (eds.), *Philosophy and Grammar*, Reidel, Dordrecht, 79–100.

—— (1986). *On The Plurality of Worlds*, Basil Blackwell, Oxford.

Loar, B. (1987). Subjective intentionality, *Philosophical Topics* **15**: 89–124.

—— (1988). Social content and psychological content, in R. Grimm and D. Merrill (eds.), *Contents of Thought*, University of Arizona Press, Tucson, 99–110.

Loux, D. (ed.) (1979). *The Possible and the Actual*, Ithaca, NY.

Lycan, W. (1986). Tacit belief, in R. Bogdan (ed.), *Belief: Form, Content, Function*, Oxford University Press, Oxford, 61–82.

Montague, R. (1974). Pragmatics, in R. Thomason (ed.), *Formal Philosophy*, Yale University Press, New Haven, 95–118.

Moore, R. (1988). Is it rational to be logical?, in M. Y. Vardi (ed.), *Proceedings of the Second Conference on Theoretical Aspects of Reasoning about Knowledge*, Morgan Kaufman, Los Altos, Calif., 363.

—— and Hendrix, G. (1982). Computational models of belief and the semantics of belief sentences, in S. Peters and E. Saarinen (eds.), *Processes, Belief, and Questions: Essays on Formal Semantics of Natural Languages and Natural Language Processing*, Reidel, Dordrecht, 107–27.

Morris, C. W. (1938). *Foundations of the Theory of Signs*, University of Chicago Press, Chicago.

Perry, J. (1977). Frege on demonstratives, *Philosophical Review* **86**: 474–97.

—— (1979). The problem of the essential indexical, *Noûs* **13**: 3–21.

Powers, L. H. (1978). Knowledge by deduction, *Philosophical Review* **87**: 337–71.

Prior, A. (1960). Identifiable individuals, *Review on Metaphysics* **13**: 684–96.

Putnam, H. (1973). Meaning and reference, *Journal of Philosophy* **70**: 699–711.

—— (1975). The meaning of "meaning", in K. Gunderson (ed.), *Language, Mind, and Knowledge*, University of Minnesota Press, Minneapolis, 131–93.

Quine, W. V. (1966). Quantifiers and propositional attitudes, in W. V. Quine (ed.), *The Ways of Paradox and Other Essays*, New York, 183–94.

Salmon, N. (1986). *Frege's Puzzle*, Bradford Books, MIT Press, Cambridge, Mass.

Schiffer, S. (1972). *Meaning*, Clarendon Press, Oxford.

Scott, D. (1970). Advice on modal logic, in K. Lambert (ed.), *Philosophical Problems in Logic. Recent Developments*, Reidel, Dordrecht, 143–73.

Segerberg, K. (1973). Two-dimensional modal logic, *Journal of Philosophical Logic* **2**: 77–96.

Soames, S. (1985). Lost innocence, *Linguistics and Philosophy* **8**: 59–72.

Stalnaker, R. (1968). A theory of conditionals, in N. Recher (ed.), *Studies in Logical Theory*, Oxford, 98–112.

—— (1976a). Possible worlds, *Noûs* **10**: 65–75.

—— (1976b). Propositions, in A. MacKay and D. Merrill (eds.), *Issues in the Philosophy of Language*, Yale University Press, New Haven, 79–91.

—— (1977). Presuppositions, *Journal of Philosophical Logic*, 447–57.

—— (1984). *Inquiry*, Bradford Books, MIT Press, Cambridge, Mass.

—— (1986). Possible worlds and situations, *Journal of Philosophical Logic* **15**: 109–23.

Stalnaker, R. and Thomason, R. H. (1970). A semantic analysis of conditional logic, *Theoria* **36**: 23–42.

Stampe, D. (1977). Toward a casual theory of linguistic representation, in P. French, T. Uehling, and H. Wettstein (eds.), *Midwest Studies in Philosophy 2, Studies in the Philosophy of Language*, University of Minnesota Press, Minneapolis, 42–6.

Stich, S. (1983). *From Folk Psychology to Cognitive Science*, Bradford Books, MIT Press, Cambridge, Mass.

Strawson, P. F. (1952). *Introduction to Logical Theory*, Methuen, London.

Thomason, R. H. (1980). A model theory for propositional attitudes, *Linguistics and Philosophy* **4**: 47–70.

—— and Stalnaker, R. (1968a). Abstraction in first order modal logic, *Theoria* **34**: 203–7.

—— —— (1968b). Modality and reference, *Noûs* **2**: 359–72.

Urmson, J. O. (1952). Parenthetical verbs, *Mind* **61**: 192–212.

Van Fraassen, B. C. (1968a). Presupposition, implication, and self reference, *Journal of Philosophy* **65**: 136–51.

—— (1968b). Singular terms, truth value gaps, and free logic, *Journal of Philosophy* **63**: 481–95.

—— (1979). Propositional attitudes in weak pragmatics, *Studia Logica* **38**: 365–74.

Vlach, F. (1973). *"Now" and "Then". A formal study on the logic of tense anaphora*, PhD thesis, University of California, Los Angeles, Calif.

White, S. (1982). Partial character and the language of thought, *Pacific Philosophical Quarterly* **63**: 347–65.

Wilson, N. (1959). Substance without substrata, *Review of Metaphysics* **12**: 521–39.

Wittgenstein, L. (1961). *Tractatus Logico-Philosophicus*, Routledge & Kegan Paul, New York. Translation. Originally published in 1921.

INDEX